Swiss Bank Accounts

Michael Arthur Jones

LIBERTY HOUSE®

LIBERTY HALL PRESS books are published by LIBERTY HALL PRESS an imprint of McGraw-Hill, Inc. Its trademark, consisting of the words "LIBERTY HALL PRESS" and the portrayal of Benjamin Franklin, is registered in the United States Patent and Trademark Office.

FIRST EDITION
SECOND PRINTING

Library of Congress Cataloging-in-Publication Data

Jones, Michael Arthur.
Swiss bank accounts : a personal guide to ownership, benefits, and use / by Michael Arthur Jones.
p. cm.
ISBN 0-8306-4046-0
1. Bank accounts—Switzerland. 2. Confidential communications--Banking—Switzerland. 3. Banking law—Switzerland. I. Title.
HG1660.S9J66 1989   89-13022
332.1'09494—dc20   CIP

For information about other McGraw-Hill materials, call 1-800-2-MCGRAW in the U.S. In other countries call your nearest McGraw-Hill office.

Vice President and Editorial Director: David J. Conti
Book Editor: Lonnie W. Dalymple
Production: Katherine G. Brown
Book Design: Jaclyn J. Boone

Contents

Dedicated to the two women in my life:
my wife and my mother.

Acknowledgments

I would like to acknowledge the many people who have given so freely of their time, shared their experience and knowledge, provided advice and criticism, and in many other ways supported me in the writing of this book. In particular, I want to express my gratitude for the kindness shown me by Dr. Kurt Aeberhard, Jay Brandt, Barbara Büchler, Carol Gallagher, Hans Halbheer, Cassie Horning, Janelle Jones, Dr. Marx Kobler, Dr. Rudolph Lyner, Peter Rahn, Gus Meyer-Schurman, Lee Khoon Tan, A. Frank Winningham, Ron Woo, Mary Lynn Bird, and the many helpful employees of the Swiss National Bank and the Swiss Bankers Association. All provided assistance when it was needed, and to them I will be forever grateful. A special thanks is given to my wife, Shelley, whom I discovered to be a first-rate editor, and to my daughters, Jennifer and Katie, who have been my most loyal supporters.

Introduction

On December 2, 1986, Ronald Reagan assembled members of his staff, congressional leaders, and news reporters in the White House press room to make the first disclosures of impropriety in what has become known as the Iran-Contra affair. At that meeting, Attorney General Meese reported that certain members of the president's own staff had furtively channeled millions of dollars from illegal Iranian arms sales to Nicaraguan rebel leaders. In the days that followed, it was learned that the financial sleight-of-hand had been carried out through an elaborate arrangement of international arms dealers, U.S. government officials, foreign officials, and Swiss bank accounts.

It was not the first time that Swiss banks appeared in the forefront of world news. Sharing the headlines with the administration's arms imbroglio was the widening scandal of Wall Street's insider trading. The U.S. Securities and Exchange Commission was successfully extending its investigation of insider trading by following up on information originally obtained from *secret* Swiss bank accounts.

Also in 1986, the world watched as Ferdinand Marcos and *Baby Doc* Duvalier fled their countries amid stories of massive wealth (variously estimated in the billions of dollars) safely cached in Swiss bank accounts. Although the world was stunned by the amount of the fortunes involved, the fact that the patrimony had been stashed away in Switzerland prior to the dictators' departures was hardly news at all. In prior years the world had already heard of similar Swiss accounts owned by leaders of countries from Argentina to Zaire.

Switzerland, a pocketwatch-sized country tucked into the center of Europe, is celebrated as the home of fine timepieces, exquisite chocolates, and impregnable bank accounts. Other countries vie for supremacy in the watch and chocolate markets. But *bank accounts?* No other country, including those customarily thought of as havens for illicit funds and unreported revenues, can rightfully be said to be famous for its bank accounts.

But Swiss accounts are very well known, if only for the mysterious images suggested to us by the news media. Television, film, and novels have contributed to the mystery surrounding the bank accounts. And the images are indeed rich: unassailable secrecy; numbered accounts; persons moving incognito through the opaque bank doors along Zurich's famed Bahnhofstrasse; Nazi gold piled high in gleaming, underground vaults. Fortunes of staggering proportions are managed by financial geniuses in Geneva, Lugano, and Zurich in a dizzying world of high finance, swirling with political leaders, movie stars, and the ultra rich.

Many Americans are surprised to learn that Swiss banks serve other customers as well. The truth is that the vast majority of Swiss bank customers are ordinary savers and investors who use their accounts for ordinary purposes. As for the stories of international intrigue and covert payments, Swiss bankers are quick to point out that such stories unfairly represent the business affairs of the banks and their customers. In fact, the bankers have taken significant steps to rid themselves of what they believe to be unfair portrayals.

Yet the images endure as does a mythology which suggests that the accounts are illegal to own, difficult to open, and reserved for those with large amounts to deposit. Americans are often astonished to learn that it is perfectly legal for them to own a Swiss bank account. Not only are they extremely easy to open, it can frequently be done with a deposit no larger than that required to open an account in the United States.

There are many reasons why an American should consider opening an account in Switzerland. For thousands of Americans who already have accounts in Switzerland, the primary reason is the broad array of services available. Swiss banks offer services that are simply not available from American banks. But services represent only a part of what the Swiss have to offer. Americans look to the Swiss for:

- **S**ervices
- **W**ealth Preservation
- **I**ncome
- **S**afety
- **S**ecrecy

Those considering opening an account in Switzerland generally have many questions to be answered. Typical questions include

- Are all Swiss banks the same?
- Does deposit insurance exist in Switzerland?
- Are Swiss accounts really secret?
- What are private banks?

- What kinds of accounts are available?
- What are numbered accounts?
- How are deposits made?
- How can I get my money out?
- Do I have to pay taxes on my account earnings?
- Do I have to report the account to government authorities?
- What happens to my account when I die?
- What other services do Swiss banks offer?

The purpose of this book is to provide answers to all of these questions and many more that a potential customer might ask.

Part I (chapters 1-4) introduces the reader to the marvelous world of Swiss banks. Switzerland's unique position as a global finance center is described as the arena in which hundreds of banks offer their services to worldwide customers. A discussion of the legend and facts relating to Swiss banking secrecy is presented. Secrecy is shown to be an evolutionary concept that has undergone significant change in recent years. Intermittent battles and moments of cooperation between U.S. and Swiss officials are chronicled by looking at specific cases, including the Howard Hughes autobiography hoax, insider trading scandals, the largest tax evasion case in U.S. history, and the Iran-Contra affair.

Part II (chapters 6-14) describes the many types of accounts available to Americans and reasons why an American might choose to open an account. In addition, the reader is presented with factors to be considered in selecting a bank, opening an account, conducting transactions, and complying with both Swiss and American legal requirements.

This book was written with the conviction that Swiss bank accounts present extraordinarily useful vehicles for savings and investment. Though Swiss accounts are often appropriate for business entities, the book is intended as a guide for individuals who desire the unique combination of service, safety, and discretion that only banks in Switzerland can offer.

Part I
The Swiss and
Their Marvelous Banks

1

Switzerland
A Global
Financial Center

TO THE MOVERS AND SHAKERS IN THE WORLD OF FINANCE, IT IS WELL UNDERSTOOD THAT only three "global" financial centers exist: New York City, London, and Switzerland. The term *global* signifies a well-developed financial marketplace with the ability to conduct business and deliver wide-ranging financial services to customers around the world. Although differences exist among these centers, a number of common characteristics distinguish them from lesser financial marketplaces. A look at some of the common features will help you appreciate what a global financial center really is.

SIMILARITIES OF GLOBAL FINANCIAL CENTERS

The most apparent characteristic common to the world's three largest money centers is an enormous concentration of commercial banks. In addition to providing depositories for far-flung customers with excess cash, the banks serve the needs of customers with various borrowing needs. New York, London, and Switzerland each has an extremely dense concentration of banks—some controlled domestically, some by foreign owners. Furthermore, nearly every major bank headquartered in one of these centers has a branch office or subsidiary bank in each of the others.

However, concentration banking is not sufficient in explaining the global status of the world's geofinancial giants. Tokyo is home to six of the world's seven largest banks (measured in terms of total assets) with the seventh located in Osaka, less than an hour from Tokyo. Nevertheless, no one maintains that Tokyo has achieved world ranking as a center for financial activity. Conspicuously absent from the Japanese money circles is an international customer base, a feature enjoyed by New York, and Switzerland and envied by all other would-be money centers.

A proliferation of banks and a worldwide clientele are major factors in distinguishing the world's greatest financial centers from the others, but a number of other common features make London, New York, and Switzerland unique among the world's money centers:

- Large investment banking houses with the ability to assist customers in raising vast sums in capital markets, as well as provide expert guidance in mergers, acquisitions, and divestitures
- Security exchanges with the capability of trading stock and debt issues of worldwide corporations and governments
- Highly developed networks of security brokers and dealers
- Organized exchanges that allow for cash and futures trading in precious metals, foreign currencies, and commodities
- Facilities for trading in sophisticated and innovative financial instruments such as options, warrants, and investment trusts
- Highly respected and renowned portfolio managers for worldwide customers who wish to leave their financial matters in the hands of competent financial experts

Again, it is important to note that each of the three global centers offer *all* of these financial services to its customers, whether those customers are individuals, corporations, or governments.

DIFFERENCES AMONG GLOBAL FINANCIAL CENTERS

Despite the similarities among the three global financial centers it is important to note that two very large differences separate the Swiss financial markets from their largest competitors. Certainly, the most obvious difference is geography. London and New York are two of the world's largest cities, while the financial center known as Switzerland encompasses an entire country. Some might feel it inappropriate to compare cities and countries, but there is simply no more appropriate way to consider it. The financial services industry of Switzerland is not lodged in a single location. Instead, the industry is comprised of a complex network of institutions and people spread through the towns of Zurich, Geneva, Basle, Lugano, and others. The center is itself decentralized, which is not at all surprising for a country brimful of contradictions.

Switzerland—The Country

It has frequently been said that if the country of Switzerland did not exist, it would be hard to imagine that such a place would be possible. Located in the very center of the perennial battleground known as Western Europe, the country has successfully avoided the major economic and political turmoils that have persistently racked other European countries. Approximately 6.5 million Swiss inhabitants are crowded into a country less than one-half the size of South Carolina. Yet, 60% of the country is comprised of steep, uninhabitable Alps (Fig. 1-1a). With the exception of hydroelectric potential, there are no natural resources to speak of. Nonetheless, Switzerland is one of the most industrialized nations on earth, enjoying a worldwide reputation for precision machinery and chemical and dairy products.

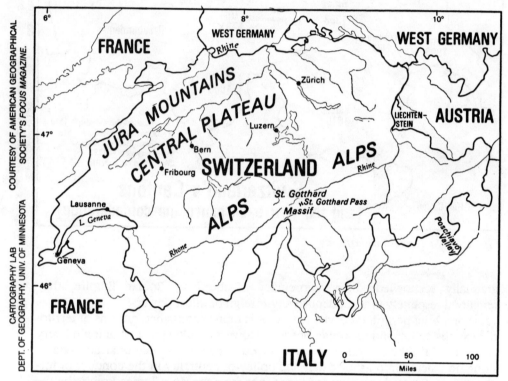

Fig. 1-1a. Switzerland: geopolitical divisions.

Millions of tourists each year enjoy the spectacular scenery of the Swiss Alps. Visitors are often surprised to learn that the official name of the country is the Helvetic Confederation. The country is actually a confederation of 23 statelike *cantons* (Fig. 1-1b). Each canton is vested with broad local authority to develop laws and enforce them within cantonal boundaries with only limited federal interference.

In Roman times, the area of today's Switzerland was known as *Helvetia*. A mountainous area, Helvetia was scattered with pockets of civilization that defied nearly every attempt to absorb them into other nations. In 1291, three cantons—Uri, Unterwalden, and Schwyz—formed a confederation for the purpose of providing a unified defense against foreign invaders. Through the centuries, other cantons were slowly added to the confederation. Although the Swiss cantons

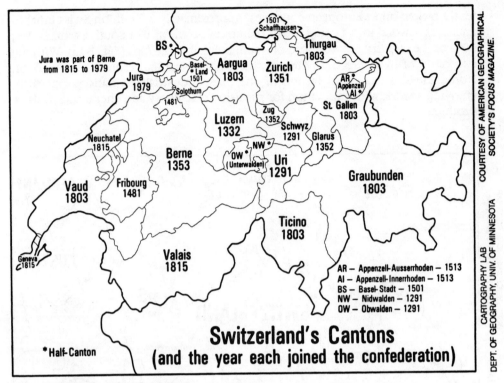

COURTESY OF AMERICAN GEOGRAPHICAL SOCIETY'S *FOCUS MAGAZINE.*

CARTOGRAPHY LAB
DEPT. OF GEOGRAPHY, UNIV. OF MINNESOTA

Fig. 1-1b. Switzerland: cantons.

gradually acknowledged the supremacy of the Holy Roman Empire, they remained resolutely independent of any foreign political powers.

For a brief period, the Swiss league of cantons entertained notions of territorial expansion beyond its Alpine borders. However, following a stunning military defeat in 1515, the confederation renounced forever the policy of armed aggression and entered into its long-standing policy of neutrality in the conduct of foreign affairs. Granted complete independence from the Holy Roman Empire by the Treaty of Westphalia in 1648, the cantons remained autonomous areas with a fiercely independent citizenry. Much of Switzerland was overrun by Napoleon's forces in 1798. It was Napoleon, however, who strengthened the federal government and further bound together the loose league of sometimes fractious cantons.

The present constitution of Switzerland dates from 1848 and is roughly based on the Constitution of the United States. Located in the capital city of Bern, the tripartite federal government is comprised of a seven-member executive body, a national legislature, and a judicial body. Ever careful to support the integrity of a decentralized rule-making system, the Swiss have granted to their federal government only limited powers. Its primary responsibilities extend only to matters of defense, foreign policy, railway and postal administration, and the national mint.

Non-Swiss are generally unaware of the distinct cantonal boundaries, even as they travel from one to the next. More striking to outsiders are the differences in language that one encounters (Fig. 1-1c). The Swiss observe no less than three official languages. In the northern and eastern cantons, a dialect of German (*Schwyzerdutsch*) is the primary spoken language, although the more formal High German is used for writing. French predominates in the western cantons, while Italian is the language in the south. In addition to these languages, a curious language known as *Romansch* is spoken in some of the eastern valleys of the canton of Graübunden. The language is a descendent of the provincial Latin spoken in the area in the days of the Roman empire.

The linguistic patchwork might appear cumbersome and unworkable to non-Swiss; but the Swiss people find the plurality of languages to be entirely natural and wouldn't dream of mandating a single national language. That the German, French, and Italian languages are official is attested to by the national currency, on which each of the languages can be found.

In spite of a diversity suggested by a backdrop of isolated valleys, high mountain passes, decentralized administration, and regional language differences, there exists a calm sense of unity among the Swiss people. Without a strong cohesiveness, it is unlikely that the country would have been able to weave the intricate pattern of financial institutions that so effectively serves a worldwide clientele.

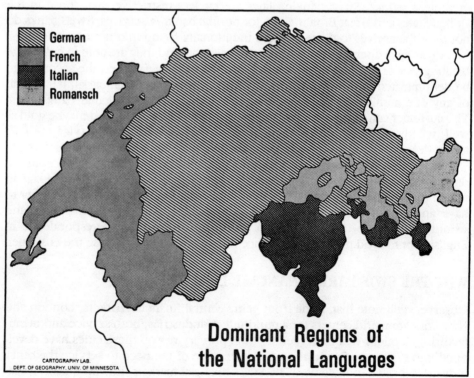

Fig. 1-1c. Switzerland: languages.

Universal Banking

Aside from matters of geography, institutional differences separate Switzerland from the other two major financial centers. Many banks in Switzerland are *universal banks*, a term generally unknown to both Americans and British. Universal banks do not restrict themselves to traditional saving and lending functions. Instead, they offer an astonishing array of financial services that make American "full-service banks" pale by comparison.

A customer in London or New York wishing to deposit funds or borrow money will customarily visit a bank. If that customer desires instead to raise a substantial sum of capital through issuance of securities, a visit to a prominent investment banker is in order. Should an investment or sale of precious metals, foreign currencies, or commodities be desired, the customer will need to seek out a broker capable of providing these specialized services. Additional brokers are available to assist in the purchase and sale of other financial interests, such as stocks, bonds, notes, and financial futures.

To obtain any of these financial services in Switzerland, one need merely visit a bank. A Swiss banker will be happy to open a checking or savings account; provide custodial protection of other valuables; and act as personal financial counselor, asset manager, and broker for almost any type of financial transaction.

How is this possible in Switzerland and not elsewhere? When it comes to permissible activities, Swiss banking laws are far less restrictive than those in the United States and Great Britain. Even for normal banking services, Swiss banks do not limit themselves to those services traditionally found in other countries.

Customers opening an account in Switzerland find they are able to customize banking services to fit their personal needs. If a customer wishes, the account can be denominated in U.S. dollars, Swiss francs, German deutschmarks, Italian lira, or any of a number of other possible currencies that the particular bank offers. The customer can choose to deposit securities as well as cash—and maybe gold as well, whether in the form of coins or bars. Whatever financial service the customer desires can probably be accommodated by an understanding Swiss banker.

Americans often marvel at the ends to which the Swiss will go to accommodate their customers' needs. Foreign customers normally specify the language in which to receive their account statements. Imagine asking an American banker to have an account statement prepared in French! Most bankers in Switzerland would not hesitate to comply with a request to send all correspondence in English—or to send no correspondence if that would better please the customer.

WHY THE SWISS ARE FINANCIAL LEADERS

Observers will note that, aside from being central financial markets, London and New York are world centers for a multitude of industries, both service and manufacturing. It might well be argued that the primary reason these cities have developed into such large financial centers is because of the need to service the other industries located in the cities. The Swiss financial markets, however, cannot reasonably be said to exist for the benefit of local industry. Although Switzerland also has achieved an advanced state of industrialization, the country is simply not large enough to require a massive financial center for its own purposes. The reason for the conversion of this minute country into a world-class financial center is that hundreds of thousands of non-Swiss have entrusted billions of dollars of their wealth to the management skills of Swiss bankers.

Why the Swiss? Why don't outsiders demonstrate a similar trust in their own financial people? What is it about the Swiss bankers that engenders such a feeling of trust? Part of the answer can be seen in looking at what the Swiss people have managed to accomplish for themselves. Along with its continuous federal budget surplus ($719 million in 1987), the Swiss have compiled an envious collection of superlative statistics, including

- The highest per capita income of any industrialized country
- The highest per capita savings of any industrialized country
- Highest annual per capita expenditure for insurance of any country in the world
- The world's lowest unemployment rate
- The lowest inflation in the industrialized west

Figure 1-2 provides further evidence of Switzerland's unique financial condition compared with other leading industrialized countries. All of these statistics may lead one to conclude that the Swiss people are deeply concerned about their own financial affairs. Let there be no doubt on that matter. They *are* concerned, but in a quiet, almost unnoticeable fashion. It is typically Swiss to save as much earnings as possible, not solely for the material rewards which can be bought, but for the security that wealth provides in a world of uncertainties.

It is fitting that Switzerland provided a cradle for the birth of the Protestant Reformation. From Zwingli's pulpit in 16th century Zurich, the world first began to hear of a revolutionary line of thinking. No longer was life on earth to be regarded only as a preparation for the hereafter. Protestantism placed at least equal importance on preparing for life on earth. Thus, it rejected the sinfulness of wealth and embraced the notion of commerce as a worthwhile activity. Men were not only free to save and invest, but could do so with the comfort that financial success was nothing less than a confirmation of God's everlasting grace.

Today the population of Switzerland is almost equally divided between Catholic and Protestant faiths. Nevertheless, the ethic of wise accumulation is permanently dyed in the fabric of the entire nation's morality. Unlike so many of their foreign neighbors, the Swiss steadfastly refuse to be ashamed or hypocritical in their attitude toward the acquisition of personal wealth.

Outsiders frequently marvel at the degree to which the Swiss have gone to assure their survival in a world of unending armed conflict. As mentioned previously, the country continues to maintain a policy of armed neutrality, and has not been involved in the export of military hostilities in 470 years. Most observers believe, however, that the Swiss are capable of defending themselves in the event that military aggression is brought to their borders.

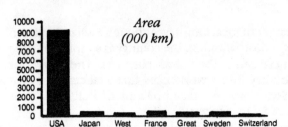

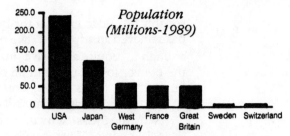

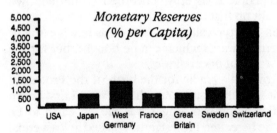

Fig. 1-2. Comparison of Swiss financial condition with other leading industrialized countries.

Certainly, no people are as well prepared as the Swiss to mount an immediate resistance to armed aggression. The Swiss army operates on a reserve system with just 2,000 full-time soldiers. Yet all capable male citizens between the ages of 20 and 50 are required to serve in the army for three weeks each year. These reserve soldiers keep their rifles and ammunition at home and are expected to annually prove their marksmanship abilities. Contingency plans to deal with invading armies have been developed, practiced, refined, repracticed and re-refined many times over. Non-Swiss military experts are in unanimous agreement that an attack on Switzerland by conventional forces would prove an insane adventure for the unlucky aggressor. The action would cost far more in human lives than could possibly be gained through military victory. Prince von Metternich's words of 150 years ago still ring true today: "Switzerland does not have an army—it is an army."

In addition to a strong commitment to military defense, the Swiss have an equally strong commitment to civil defense matters. And as one might expect, the Swiss civil defense system is second to none in terms of contingency planning and provisions. Men aged 20 to 60 who are not serving in the reserve army (because of age or medical disability) and women volunteers make up the country's civil defense service. A primary goal of the service is to set up and maintain public shelters to protect citizens from the effects of a nuclear war. In addition to stockpiling and maintaining the shelters, the civil defense members provide continuing education courses in nuclear survival for all citizens.

WHY SWITZERLAND IS A WORLD DEPOSITORY

The Swiss give ample evidence of thoughtful preparedness in meeting the contingencies of living in the modern world. They are obviously able to handle their personal financial matters and enjoy life with a limited threat of outside interference. Yet there are other important factors that explain why Switzerland has become the depository of massive amounts of foreign money.

Initially the Swiss were chosen as bankers for other Europeans because of the country's safe, central location and demonstrated ability to stay removed from the problems of other nations. While this might still influence individuals looking for safe havens for their money, there are even more compelling reasons why modern customers prefer the Swiss style of money management.

The Swiss Franc

In 1850 the federal government of Switzerland began issuing its first national currency. The Swiss adopted the name *Franc* for the currency, perhaps in hopes that it would acquire some of the reputation of the highly regarded French franc. From its beginnings, the Swiss franc has proven to be one of the most valued currencies in the world.

The value of a national currency is frequently judged by the currency's hardness. A *hard* (or strong) currency is one that tends to appreciate or, at minimum, hold its value in relation to other currencies. An investor holding a hard currency can generally expect to convert it into another currency in the future without bearing an unreasonable risk of loss during the holding period. Holders of *soft* (or weak) currencies bear a more sizeable risk of loss if that currency is converted at a future date. For these reasons, rational savers often seek the safety of hard currencies when their wealth is to be stored in a monetary form. They prefer to hold as small an investment as possible in soft currency.

The history of the franc shows that its value is ordinarily influenced by upward pressure against other major currencies. Its strength vis-a-vis the U.S. dollar is shown in Fig. 1-3. The strength of the Swiss franc is also illustrated by the fact that the franc, worth 23¢ in 1970, was worth 67¢ by the end of 1988.

Currencies are not only judged based on their hardness but also on their *convertibility*, a term that has undergone some change in meaning in recent years. At one time, the convertibility of a currency referred to the ability of its holder to exchange the notes into another commodity, such as gold or silver. The exchange was normally carried out through a national central bank that guaranteed the convertibility of its currency. As governments are no longer inclined to honor their guarantees (the United States halted the exchange of gold certificates in 1933 and silver certificates in 1963), convertibility has come to refer to the ability of foreigners to acquire and use another country's national currency. Thus, a freely convertible currency is now one that may be exchanged into other currencies with little or no governmental restrictions. All other factors being equal, savers would obviously be more inclined to hold convertible currencies than those which are not easily converted.

The Swiss government remains one of the minority of governments that places no restrictions whatsoever on the conversion of its currency. In fact, from the end of World War II to 1958, the Swiss franc was the *only* European currency that was allowed to be freely converted into U.S. dollars. Today, the U.S. dollar and the Swiss franc are the only fully convertible currencies in the world.

Considering both its hardness and convertibility, it is easy to understand why the Swiss franc is desired by savers throughout the world. The desirability of holding Swiss francs has resulted in massive inflows of foreign capital into the Swiss banking system by individuals, companies, and governments eager to buy and hold the coveted currency as a reserve against the future. In the early 1970s, the demand for Swiss francs by foreigners reached such proportions that the Swiss federal government became concerned about adverse economic effects.

The Swiss National Bank (the Swiss version of the U.S. Federal Reserve Bank) experimented with a radical form of intervention to ease the growing demand for its currency. The Swiss National Bank required all Swiss banks to pay *negative interest* on all new deposits from foreigners that were denominated in Swiss francs. In essence, the foreign depositors were charged a tax for the right to hold

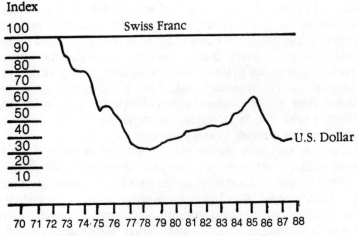

Fig. 1-3. The Swiss franc versus the U.S. dollar.

Swiss francs in their bank accounts. The Swiss later suspended the negative interest tax in favor of freer market equilibrium. Although the experiment has ended, the fact that the Swiss would be forced to go to such extreme measures confirms the worldwide respect for the Swiss national currency.

Unrestricted Capital Movement

Foreign customers of Swiss banks enjoy the ability to smoothly transfer funds. Switzerland guarantees the free and unrestricted movement of all incoming and outgoing funds. A review of the policies of other countries around the globe reveals that the freeflowing policy of the Swiss is not at all popular among the majority of governments.

Most countries, in fact, impose some form of monetary restriction. Common restrictions include quantity limitations (on incoming or outgoing funds), exchange through authorized dealers only, advanced governmental approval for certain types of transactions, restrictions based on the origin or destination of the funds, and taxes levied on funds crossing borders. Some countries, such as the United States, allow a generally free transfer of funds across borders but impose reporting requirements on those who want to do so.*

U.S. law currently requires that any person entering or leaving the country with more than $10,000 in domestic or foreign currency, traveler's checks, money orders, or bearer-form negotiable instruments must declare the amount to U.S. Customs officials. As explained more fully in chapter 4, additional reporting of money sent by mail or wire may be automatically triggered by money flowing into or out of American bank accounts.

Money movements across the Swiss border are not only unrestricted, they require no official notification. Should you wish to enter or leave Switzerland with a briefcase (or even a trunk) full of money, the Swiss customs official would show no concern whatsoever.

Broad Financial Services

Given a rock hard currency and an absence of any restriction on the flow of money, the Swiss have been able to develop other financial services that attract worldwide attention.

Securities trading facilities are spread across Switzerland. The country has no fewer than eight stock exchanges. The Zurich exchange is by far the largest and is planning to move to a new, modern facility in 1992. The second and third largest exchanges, in Geneva and Basle, have recently moved into new quarters. The Lausanne stock exchange is a distant fourth in size among the Swiss exchanges. But

---

*(Transfers to Cuba, Democratic Kampuchea, North Korea, Viet Nam, and Iran are either restricted by the U.S. or allowed only under special license.)

fourth among such company should not imply insignificance; Lausanne is still the 13th largest stock exchange in the world based on the number of shares traded.

The international character of the Swiss markets can be seen by looking at the securities traded on the exchanges. In 1988, 2,384 different bonds were quoted on the Zurich exchange. Of these, 880 were bonds of foreign issuers. An even greater degree of international trading is done in stocks. Of the 535 stocks listed on the Zurich exchange, 226 represented foreign companies. Almost half (110) of the foreign companies listed were American, with the remainder comprised of Canadian, West European, Asian, and South African stocks.

Switzerland's worldwide presence in the banking and securities trading industries is complemented by an equally global presence in the insurance industry. Since the mid-1800s, insurance companies located in Zurich and Winterthur have been growing solidly and are now among the largest in the world. The only financial center that generates a greater amount of annual insurance premiums is London.

That the insurance industry is an important international player is demonstrated by the fact that each year more than one half of all insurance and reinsurance premiums come from abroad. Much of the revenue is immediately reinvested in foreign securities.

Stable Political Climate

It is possible that no people on earth enjoy a more quiet functioning of their national government than do the Swiss. Political infighting at the federal level is almost nonexistent. The seven-member federal executive has been a four-party coalition since 1959, and it can be characterized as a body committed to tranquil political consensus. Presidency of the confederation passes in rotation to members of the federal executive, an annual event that receives little public notice. In fact, if you were to ask the average Swiss citizen the name of the person who currently sits in the president's chair, it is unlikely that that citizen would be able to answer.

The nation's bicameral parliament is equally lackluster in going about its assignments. Federal legislation is passed at an excruciatingly slow pace, which is fast enough for the Swiss. In the event that a real issue confronts parliament, the lawmakers are as likely as not to refer the issue to the people in a national referendum. Aside from an occasional national referendum, real political fireworks only occur at the cantonal level, and the issues are usually local ones.

All nations of the world are aware of Switzerland's unique dedication to peace. It is not surprising that when nations want to discuss peace, they frequently flock to Switzerland to do so. Geneva has been home to countless peace talks and summit meetings among heads of state. The city also serves as home to a number of United Nations agencies although, to preserve its neutrality, the country steadfastly refuses to join the United Nations.

Secrecy

If the foregoing is not sufficient to explain why customers prefer to conduct their financial affairs through Swiss banks, there remains an additional feature of the Swiss financial system that needs to be explored: the Swiss belief in the virtue of secrecy. Because of its importance in Swiss banking, the concept of secrecy will be explored in detail in following chapters.

2

Banks in Switzerland

CHAPTER 1 CHARACTERIZED SWITZERLAND AS A SMALL COUNTRY COVERED BY A DENSE network of banking institutions. Just how dense is the network? A few statistics will help provide a picture. Banking is Switzerland's largest industry. At present, 622 banks of various types operate in the country. Including bank branches, there are over 5,100 locations where banking can be performed. This number amounts to approximately one bank location for each 1,280 Swiss residents (compared with one per 3,600 residents in the United States). There are more bankers in the country than university students. Further, each of the three largest banks in the country has more employees than the combined number of Swiss physicians and dentists.

In Switzerland, as in most countries, banks differ widely in size and types of services offered. To describe the banking system, it first is necessary to categorize the banks. The Swiss National Bank provides the classification scheme shown in Fig. 2-1, and each category is explained in the following sections.

THE BIG THREE

Switzerland's three largest banks—Credit Suisse, Swiss Bank Corporation and Union Bank of Switzerland—are among the giants in the world's financial order. Just how large are they is a difficult question to answer. Banks are measured in a variety of ways, with each giving a different measurement of size. The British publication *Euromoney* ranks the largest banks in the world according to several

Large Banks		
Big 3	3	
Other	2	
Total Large Banks		5
Cantonal Banks		29
Regional and Savings Banks		214
Mutual Loan Associations		2
Other Banks		
Swiss Controlled	91	
Foreign Controlled	111	
Total Other Banks		202
Finance Companies		130
Branches of Foreign Banks		17
Private Banks		23
Total		622

Data per "Das Schweizerische Bankwesen im Jahre 1987," Nr. 72, Swiss National Bank.

Fig. 2-1. Swiss banks by type.

scales. The June 1988 survey revealed the statistics shown in Table 2-1 about Switzerland's Big Three.

Considering that there are tens of thousands of banks worldwide (over 15,000 in the United States alone), these statistics easily confirm that Switzerland's Big Three are members of a very select group. Yet, even the statistics cannot convey the true extent of the banks' size. A peculiar aspect of Swiss accounting practices is the deliberate understatement of a firm's assets, income, and equity position. The Swiss believe this practice to be a perfectly rational and conservative style of accounting, a uniquely Swiss measurement system that enables a firm to better endure difficult financial periods with little impact on the firm's reported financial health.

Many financial observers tend to compensate for the "hidden reserves" by making a *Swiss adjustment*. The usual adjustment is to multiply the reported earnings and equity figures by a factor of 2.00 to 2.25. If such an adjustment were made to their financial statements, the Big Three would find themselves at or near

Table 2-1. World Ranking of the Big Three.

1987 World Ranking in terms of

	Total Assets	Net Income	Equity
Union Bank of Switzerland	26	8	5
Swiss Bank Corporation	28	11	7
Credit Suisse	43	16	10

the top in all categories of measurement. Further, when one considers the size of the portfolios managed by the Big Three (variously estimated in the hundreds of billions of dollars), the institutions surely rank among the largest of any type of enterprise on the globe.

Without adjusting the reported numbers, however, the size of the banks is staggering. The assets of Credit Suisse, the smallest of the Big Three, far eclipses the combined assets of Nestlé, Ciba-Geigy, Sandoz and Hoffmann-La Roche, all immense Swiss industrial giants. The combined assets of the Big Three far surpass the Swiss gross domestic product. When measured in terms of shareholders' equity, only one U.S. bank, Citicorp of New York, is larger than Union Bank of Switzerland.

Because of their particular significance, each of the Big Three is explored in some detail.

Credit Suisse

Zurich's main train station (Bahnhof) pinpoints the very center of that city. Leading south from the station is a broad, tree-lined avenue named Bahnhofstrasse. Stretching ¾ mile to Lake Zurich, the street is intersected at its midway by two other streets, forming a square known to city residents as the Paradeplatz. The names are not unusual; a *Bahnhofstrasse* can be found in German-speaking cities and towns throughout Switzerland, Germany, and Austria; *Paradeplatz* is a common name for a town square. But only Zurich is home to *the* Bahnhofstrasse, known worldwide for the multitude of banks that flank the avenue.

Along the Bahnhofstrasse, beside and above shops laden with luxury merchandise, are offices and branches of scores of banks. Those windows that do not feature expensive gold watches, furs, and jet-set fashions display instead foreign exchange rates and stockmarket prices from around the world. The aura of immense wealth is heightened when one considers that beneath the street are immense stockpiles of gold, silver, and other treasures. The subterranean vaults run the full length of the street and cluster around the Paradeplatz. At the far end of the Bahnhofstrasse, standing sentinel over the legion of banks, is the Swiss National Bank, the Helvetic equivalent of the Federal Reserve Bank.

A visitor standing in the Paradeplatz for the first time cannot help but notice a very ornate four-story building. This exclusive piece of real estate occupies a full block and is the home of Credit Suisse, the oldest of Switzerland's Big Three.

Credit Suisse was founded in 1856 by businessman Alfred Escher. The primary purpose of establishing the bank was to provide a conduit for channeling local savings into construction of a major north-south railroad line. The financing of that railroad, which was to become the famed Gotthard Line, was originally planned by a group of German banks. Escher relied on Swiss nationalism to stir up interest in local financing for the project and cut the German financiers out of the action. The initial offering of stock to investors for the creation of the bank was certainly one of the most successful stock offerings in history. An initial public offering of 6,000 shares was met with a subscription demand for over 430,000 shares! Alfred Escher carefully patterned the new institution after Credit Mobilier, at that time an immensely successful French bank. As a result, Credit Suisse became the first universal bank in Switzerland. The provision of funds for 19th-century railroad development was followed by a heavy commitment to the construction of 20th-century hydroelectric projects.

By 1950, Credit Suisse's operations had spread worldwide. The bank has never been shy about joining forces with other institutions to gain entry into new business opportunities. The willingness to join forces is best illustrated by the bank's unique partnershp with the New York-based investment banking firm of First Boston Corporation. The two firms created Credit Suisse First Boston in the late 1970s to acquire a large portion of the emerging business in globally syndicated stocks. Sixty-percent owned by Credit Suisse, the London-based partnershp has proven extremely profitable, winning more international securities business than any other firm for the past several years.

Despite its seniority in terms of age, Credit Suisse remains the smallest of the Big Three. But don't let the relative standing among the banks fool you. The bank has over $70 billion in reported assets, 15,000 employees, and over 200 business locations. The only American bank with a greater net worth is Citicorp. Other American giants, such as J.P. Morgan, BankAmerica, and Chase Manhattan, are hundreds of millions of dollars behind.

Swiss Bank Corporation

The residents of Basle, Switzerland's second largest city, are referred to as Bâlois. The Bâlois are often characterized as well bred, disposed to snobbishness, and incurably wealthy. The characterization may not be fair, but the reasons for it are not hard to understand. Basle is the center of *old money* in Switzerland; for centuries the birthplace of the scions of banking and industrial families. Basler snobbishness is quite possibly an outsider's reaction to Basler pride. The Bâlois believe their hometown to be the geographical, cultural, industrial, and financial center of Europe. Indeed, there are convincing reasons why Basle might be considered the very center of Europe.

A veritable crossroads for European travelers, Basle straddles the Rhine river near the meeting point of the borders of France, Germany, and Switzerland. Visitors arriving at the large Basle-Mulhouse airport are sometimes surprised to find that the airport is actually situated in France. Despite the airport's location, the city of Basle is truly a transportation hub for the continent. Arguably located in the geographical center of the continent, the site has been a major crossing point of the Rhine river for millennia.

The Rhine divides Basle into two distinct parts. Kleinbasle, on the north bank, has become the industrial area for the city and is home to some of the largest chemical and pharmaceutical companies in the world. Grossbasle, on the steep south bank of the river, was the site of an old Roman fort and later the fortified town of medieval times. Today, Grossbasle is home to the financial and banking activity in the city, including the newly constructed premises of the Basle stock exchange, the headquarters of the Swiss Banking Association, and the Swiss Cantonal Bank Association. Here also is situated the Bank for International Settlements, the clearinghouse for many central banks of the world.

Despite a tradition of engaging in strong international commerce, Basle is home to few foreign-owned banks, perhaps owing to the relatively closed society of the Bâlois. But it is no surprise that a number of Swiss banks are located in the city, and the immense Swiss Bank Corporation is headquartered in the Grossbasle section. It was initially the result of six small banks joining forces in 1872 to provide a bank to handle large international business as well as local savings and credit. Through the years the bank has never stopped its steady growth. The bank attempts to be the leader in recognizing the need for new financial services and striving to be the first bank to offer them. Its image as an innovator has not slipped in recent years; in fact, it helped create the market for Euroequities and Euro-commercial paper markets in the early 1980s.

The bank's willingness to offer expanded services is further evidenced by its huge investment in electronic banking services. An international cash management service (SwisCash) enables multinational corporations around the world to instantly check their cash positions and obtain instantaneous transaction data.

Swiss Bank Corporation's tradition in international expansion began early, with a branch opening in London as early as 1898. The growth in the international sector has continued to current times. In an effort to gain an early toehold in the impending deregulation of the London securities markets (commonly referred to as the Big Bang), the bank purchased the London brokerage firm of Savory Miln. The bank recently extended its North American operations through the purchase of Continental Illinois Bank in Toronto. Further evidence of a commitment to international growth can be seen by the bank's decision to cooperate in the construction of a new office tower in New York. The New York headquarters is actually an extension of the Saks Fifth Avenue building, and the main entrance of the new building will be directly across from St. Patrick's Cathedral. When the building is completed in 1990, Saks will occupy the lower 10 floors while Swiss Bank Corporation will move into the upper 26 floors.

Union Bank of Switzerland

Less than an hour from Zurich, on the graceful shores of Lake Constance, lies a sprawling estate named Wolfsberg. The beauty of the grounds suggests that the estate is one of Switzerland's famed finishing schools. In part, that is exactly what the estate is: a training ground for a select few who will be returned to their homes with the expectation that they will act in a technically perfect and highly polished manner. Wolfsberg is owned by Union Bank of Switzerland (UBS) and serves as the location for the bank's extensive training programs, seminars, and councils for strategic planning. Aside from these sessions, the estate also serves as a kind of *boot camp* for the raw recruits of the bank, who receive their indoctrination on the Wolfsberg grounds.

Others would be less inclined to think of Wolfsberg as a finishing school and more disposed to refer to the estate as a kind of War College. This characterization is more apt than might first appear. Wolfsberg has a long standing tradition in military affairs. Built as a private estate in the early 1800s by an officer in Napoleon's army, the residence was designed to resemble a plush military camp in the hope that Napoleon would feel comfortable should he stop by during one of his forays across Europe.

It seems appropriate that UBS would desire just this type of property when it purchased the estate to house its training facility. For years UBS has been closely identified with the military. Most of the bank's senior management are also top ranking army officers as well. In fact, six members of the bank's executive committee hold the rank of colonel (with the bank's highest ranking military officer, a one-star general, in command of the training facility at Wolfsberg). When they are not taking part in military maneuvers, they are maneuvering to extend the bank's competitive position, an activity calling for equal nerve and the ability to work as members of a team. Some observers have suggested that the military training and approach to problem solving have had a large influence on the way that the bank is managed. This may well be true; but if so, it has certainly proven effective and may explain why the youngest of the Big Three is also the largest and fastest growing.

Union Bank's history began in 1912 with the merger of the Bank of Winterthur and the Toggenburger Bank. The union of these two country banks resulted in the largest retail bank in Switzerland, with more than 300 branches dotting the Swiss countryside. The bank's growth can only be characterized as aggressiveness in expansion. Having reached the status of the dominant retail bank in Switzerland, UBS has moved aggressively into more global activities.

In anticipation of Britain's deregulation of financial markets (the Big Bang), UBS purchased the huge London brokerage firm of Phillips & Drew in 1984. UBS subsequently moved its entire Eurobond operations to London and developed it into one of the largest Eurobond lead managers in the world. Although the firm had participated in offerings of corporate securities in the United States, in 1986 it became the first foreign bank to be the lead manager of a U.S. corporate bond issue. In 1987, UBS also became the first non-Japanese firm to manage a *Euroyen* issue on behalf of a Japanese corporation. Other recent tactics of the bank have included the acquisition of a seat on the New York Stock Exchange, the formation of UBS Futures Inc. to trade futures contracts in New York and Chicago, and the contribution of $1 million to sponsor the winning entrant in a round-the-world yacht race.

OTHER BIG BANKS

The Swiss National Bank's category of "other big banks" raises the question of why such a category even exists. Only two Swiss banks fall into this category, and it would seem more appropriate to simply have a *Big Five* category. The fact is that while these two banks are extremely large by world standards, they pale in comparison to the smallest of the Big Three. Nonetheless, they are universal banks that are widely regarded both at home and around the world.

Swiss Volksbank

With a staff of over 5,200 employees and 153 branches in Switzerland, Swiss Volksbank might be Switzerland's best kept secret. Founded in 1869 with the purpose of providing financial services for the *small saver*, the bank is quietly beginning to rival its larger competition in both domestic and international banking business. Ranked 102nd among the world's banks, the Berne-based bank has in recent years successfully courted foreign customers. Its publication *Investment Guide* has become popular among both customers and noncustomers, and is available in German, French, Italian, and English editions.

1985 was a bold year for the bank as it opened a branch office in London (with over 50 employees) and established a subsidiary company, Volksbank Finance Ltd., in the Cayman Islands for the purpose of raising funds in the international capital markets. Representative offices also exist in Sao Paulo, Singapore, and Tokyo.

Bank Leu

Considered to be the oldest bank in Switzerland, Bank Leu (pronounced Loy) has served its customers since 1755. Originally owned by the city of Zurich, the bank was named after the city treasurer. Because it handles a large volume of transactions for many of Switzerland's smaller banks, Bank Leu has sometimes been called the Swiss banks' bank. Relying less on commercial lending and more heavily on interbank lending, the bank has proven to be the epitome of a conservatively managed bank. An old joke among Swiss bankers is that Leu's familiar firm logo, a blue lion, has never been known to roar, only yawn.

Still, the bank has served generations of customers in foreign countries. Long considered a prime dealer in precious metals, the bank has one of the most respected numismatics departments in Europe. The bank suffered heavily from defaulted German and Balkan loans following World Wars I and II, but is rumored to have enjoyed the benefits of vast quantities of unclaimed Nazi gold.

Bank Leu is unique among the large banks of Switzerland. Unlike its competitors, Leu has not chosen to scatter branches throughout the country. It prefers to serve its customers from its ornate headquarters on Zurich's Bahnhofstrasse or from one of its 15 nearby branches. Also unique is Leu's travel agency, which is conveniently located in the Bahnhofstrasse premises.

CANTONAL BANKS

Similar to state-chartered banks in the United States, Switzerland's cantonal banks are authorized by the cantonal governments. There are 29 cantonal banks, with some cantons authorizing more than one bank. The existence of these banks reflects a strong desire to keep money invested locally, not a surprising attitude in a country characterized by strong regional loyalties.

To an American observer, cantonal banks may appear to be similar to savings banks. In fact, that is precisely what they consider themselves to be. The traditional business of the cantonal banks is to channel private savings into sources of mortgage lending. For most cantonal banks, private savings make up the majority of all liabilities, while mortgage loans represent the largest single type of asset. Although the domestic corporate sector provides some business for the banks, for most this is only a secondary, sometimes very minor, source of business.

Nevertheless, under the leadership of bankers with a flair for keeping customers happy, several of these so-called savings banks have managed to become among the largest banks in the world. Several of Switzerland's cantonal banks are among the world's 500 largest banks, and the largest of these, Zurich Kantonalbank, is actually larger than its neighborhood rival, Bank Leu.

To meet the competition of the other large banks, the cantonal banks have had to diversify their product lines, some to the point of actually becoming universal banks. Customers of cantonal banks frequently have all of the services available to them that the very largest banks have to offer. In addition, the customers of these banks enjoy a kind of security not available elsewhere in Switzerland: deposit insurance. As the federal government of Switzerland does not have an agency similar to the Federal Deposit Insurance Corporation (FDIC), the only governmental deposit insurance is that provided by the cantonal governments to customers of the cantonal banks.

The larger cantonal banks have long since established international banking departments, correspondent arrangements, and foreign offices to provide expanded services to an expanded customer base. In an effort to make these services available to customers of smaller banks as well, a group of cantonal banks was responsible for the takeover of Omnibank AG at the end of 1985. The takeover was designed to permit the banks to offer complete international services through their own facilities without relying on the facilities of the larger Swiss banks.

REGIONAL AND SAVINGS BANKS

Similar in business and operations to the cantonal banks, regional and savings banks also provide a source of mortgage loans. Characterized by a dense network of branch offices, the banks are still highly localized in the sense of customer base and closely resemble American savings and loan associations. Customers' savings accounts are the primary source of funds for these banks.

MUTUAL CREDIT ASSOCIATIONS

In Switzerland, there are currently two credit associations. Each is actually a federation of affiliated, but independent mutual credit associations, of which there are approximately 1,300 scattered throughout the country. Similar in nature to American credit unions, these agencies accept deposits from members and restrict lending to secured member loans. The Mutual Credit Associations are

- Swiss Federation of Raiffeisenkassen—with 1,228 affiliated agencies, the association's members are generally farmers and small business owners, each of whom owns a share of the local cooperative
- Fédération Vaudoise des Caisses de Crédit Mutual—with 14 affiliated agencies, smaller but similar in nature to the Raiffeisenkassen. All of the agencies are located in the western canton of Vaud

FINANCE COMPANIES

Classified as banks by the Swiss National Bank, this group of 130 institutions offers a limited scope of services. Generally foreign owned, the operations either provide credit to European customers of foreign companies, or assist in the place-ment of Swiss securities for foreign borrowers. The identities of the parent com-panies are often readily apparent, as the following names indicate:

- Greyhound Financial & Leasing Corporation AG
- Gulf and Occidental Investment Company SA
- Kidder, Peabody (Suisse) SA
- Sanyo Securities & Finance (Suisse) SA
- Volvo Finance SA

Normally, these institutions do not deal directly with individual customers, nor do they solicit publicly for deposits. Those few that do solicit deposits are subject to Switzerland's Federal Banking Law and must comply with all the provi-sions thereof. The remainder of the finance companies are regulated by only some of its provisions.

OTHER (NONPRIVATE) BANKS

This group of 202 banks represents a mixed collection of domestically and for-eign controlled institutions with varied business purposes and customer bases. Table 2-2 includes the Swiss National Bank statistics regarding these banks.

The reader should not be persuaded to believe that banks in this category are exclusively *smaller* banks. Included in the classification of Other Swiss-Con-trolled Banks is Trade Development Bank of Geneva, with a reported net worth of $566 million and Banca Della Svizzera, with a net worth in excess of $450 million. In the case of these *other* banks,the services offered are easily broad enough to classify the banks as large universal banks.

As indicated, the Swiss-controlled banks make up a heterogeneous collec-tion. Many actually specialize in more areas of banking than Table 2-2 might indi-cate. Were it not for their size and widespread services available, the Big Three and the Other Big Banks categories would be included in this classification.

The larger of the foreign-controlled banks qualify as universal banks, while the smaller of the foreign-owned institutions exist either to serve the Swiss subsid-

_____Table 2-2. Types of Other (Nonprivate) Banks._____

Type	Number
Swiss Controlled Banks, that provide	
1. Services to commercial customers	27
2. Securities trading and portfolio management	49
3. Consumer finance and installment credit	11
4. Other	4
Foreign Controlled Banks	111
Total *Other* Banks	202

iaries of foreign-owned corporations or to serve as a feeder to larger parent companies. Providing bank services to Swiss nationals is a very minor part of the business of these banks, although they are frequently used by nonresidents of Switzerland who feel more comfortable with a backhome bank. As detailed in chapter 6, there are important reasons why foreigners might consider using the services of this type of bank.

Not included in the above group are the branches and representative offices of foreign banks. Seventeen foreign banks maintain branch operations in Switzerland and generally operate in the same fashion as other foreign controlled banks. In addition, there are approximately 50 representative offices of foreign banks. The representative offices are not allowed to transact business in Switzerland but are engaged in the promotion of new business from Swiss subsidiaries of foreign companies as well as Swiss companies with subsidiaries abroad.

PRIVATE BANKS

Switzerland's private banks play an important and unique role in providing banking services. The 23 banks in this category include the oldest banks in the country and are unlike any banking institutions found in the United States. All private banks in Switzerland operate in the form of a partnership. A partnership in Switzerland, as in the United States, is a form of business with two or more owners who share unlimited liability for the obligations of the firm. The liability extends to the limit of their entire personal assets. Consequently, the deposits in private Swiss banks are backed by the personal fortunes of the owners. This collateral is no doubt very comforting to some; a type of deposit insurance with the backing of some of Switzerland's most wealthy families.

The banks are *private* in another sense as well. Providing that they do not publicly advertise for deposits, the private bankers are not required to publish their banks' financial statements. The operating statistics and balance sheets of private banks never leave the partners' meeting rooms. Thus, although one can state that there are large and small private banks in Switzerland, no one can say precisely how large or how small any particular bank is.

Pictet & Cie

In order for the reader to more fully appreciate the nature of private banks in general, one in particular will be examined. Founded in 1805 in French-occupied Geneva, Pictet & Cie is the third oldest of Geneva's nine private banks. Its offices are located in a nondescript building at 29, boulevard Georges-Favon. If passersby do not already know that the building lodges one of the world's most elite private banks, it would be difficult to deduce the fact from observation. The sign at the door does not shout the name of the bank, it merely whispers the letters:

P & Cie

Even though the firm's ancient symbol, a golden lion, emblazons the glass doors of the bank, it still refuses to proclaim the name of the bank. The banner portion of the symbol only indicates the founding date of the firm. The only clues as to the secret of the nameless, ordinary building are in the form of the people who arrive at the premises. A significant portion of the clientele appears to be very well heeled. Most appear to desire anonymity, quietly slipping in and out of the building, only to disappear into the quiet business of the city. Those unaware of the building's prestigious occupants are unlikely to be in need of the firm's services. Pictet's new clients rarely are walk-ins from the street. Acceptance at the exclusive offices of the bank normally requires a referral from another customer or, at minimum, referral by another financial institution.

Pictet & Cie is owned by eight general partners. It is the manner of all private banks to have at least one general partner whose name is the same as the bank's. In the case of Pictet & Cie, three of the partners bear the Pictet name. Although the French word "Cie" is the traditional abbreviation for *compagnie* (company), it is not unusual, in its English publications and correspondence, for the bank to refer to itself as Pictet & Co.

Possessing a banking license that enables it to operate as a full-service bank, Pictet prefers to continue its tradition of providing investment management services exclusively. The services are highly individualized and designed to meet the specific needs of the customers. This explains in part the unshakable customer loyalties that have developed. Loyalties are also the result of generations of trust with bankers of the Pictet name. It would be unusual for an American to be able to trace a banking relationship back to previous generations. Yet, the fathers, grandfathers, and great-grandfathers of some current clients of Pictet & Cie can point to a banking relationship that extend back to the fathers, grandfathers, and great-grandfathers or even earlier generations of Pictets. Furthermore, the progeny of current partners who are working in nonpartner, training positions at the bank suggests that personal, family relationships between the bankers and the customers will only endure.

Nonpartnered personnel are a large part of the formula that keeps professional service high and customer loyalties strong. The portfolio management department currently employs over 50 investment managers. Supporting the managers is a research department employing analysts who specialize in specific industry and geographical areas. Pictet's employees, who now number over 500, are handsomely paid and enjoy a lucrative profit-sharing plan. As a consequence, staff turnover is extremely low, and employees of the bank rarely choose to seek employment with competing firms.

Aside from managing other peoples' money, the bank has found it profitable to be active in the placement of securities. It is an active member of the ultra-elite *Groupement des Banquirs Privés Genevois* (Geneva Private Bankers Group), an organization of six banks that cooperate in domestic debt issues. The Group also acts as a member of underwriting syndicates of the large Swiss banks, allowing the bank to participate in floating large foreign issues in Switzerland.

For 150 years, the bank catered primarily to wealthy, European individuals. In the past 30 years, however, the customer list has been extended to include many non-Europeans. Having achieved economies of scale through computerization, the bank has shown a willingness to take on smaller customers. In addition, institutional money has been placed at the discretion of Pictet's portfolio managers in ever growing quantities. Although the bank is not refusing to open accounts for oil sheiks or the nouveau riche, it eagerly seeks greater infusion of the funds that institutions have to offer. Institutional money, from Swiss sources and worldwide clients, now accounts for about 30% of the total funds managed by the bank.

All of Pictet's clients are welcome in the elegant Geneva office. The exquisitely decorated offices have polished oak-paneled walls and cut flowers that are replaced daily. But behind the elegant surroundings are battalions of highly trained financial technicians, computer support personnel, and state-of-the-art communications systems, linked by satellite to London, New York, Tokyo, The Bahamas, and other financial nerve centers. Through its satellite network (GE Mark III system), the bank's computerized communications system is able to provide daily account balances and portfolio valuations together with performance measures. The information is available to customers via telephone 24 hours a day in two dozen countries around the globe.

Other Private Banks

As previously stated, private banks in Switzerland are not obligated to make public their financial statements, and none of them has yet elected to do so. Like all banks in Switzerland, however, they must have their accounts audited annually by independent auditors, and their certified financial statements must be available to the Federal Banking Commission. In addition, the banks are obligated to provide certain financial data to the Swiss National Bank.

Even if the financial statements of private banks were made public, they would not fully disclose the financial power of the banks. The assets that belong to the private banks are certainly miniscule in comparison with the funds that the banks manage for their customers. Estimates of Pictet & Cie's managed funds range from $10 to $15 *billion*. Geneva's Lombard, Odier & Cie, inconspicuously headquartered in a stone mansion on the Rue de la Corraterie, is reputed to rival Pictet in size of managed funds. But even Geneva's smallest private bank, Mirabeau & Cie, is the manager of customers' funds estimated to be in excess of $1 billion.

Although the largest concentration of private banks is in the city of Geneva, others are scattered about Switzerland, as can be seen in Fig. 2-2.

Private banking has undergone marked change in recent years. In 1900 there were 266 private banks operating in Switzerland. By the end of World War II that number had been trimmed to 50. With only 23 private banks operating today, the future of private banking has been subject to much speculation.

The reasons for the declining number of private banks are varied. Certainly, one danger to family-owned firms is dependency on continued offspring to sustain the family name. With the demise of the bloodline, some privately owned banks have been unable to continue operations. Most of these private banks were acquired by other banks, both public and private.

Some private banks have abandoned their partnership forms while seeking opportunities for expanded profits through mergers. The result has been the creation of new, publicly held banks. It is interesting to note that the huge Swiss Bank Corporation was initially created by the merger of six formerly private banks.

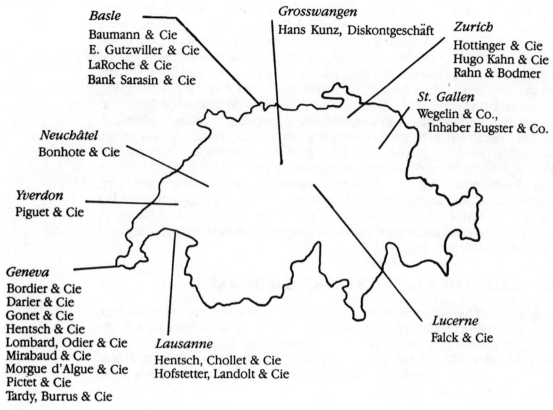

Fig. 2-2. Private banks of Switzerland.

Basle
Baumann & Cie
E. Gutzwiller & Cie
LaRoche & Cie
Bank Sarasin & Cie

Grosswangen
Hans Kunz, Diskontgeschäft

Zurich
Hottinger & Cie
Hugo Kahn & Cie
Rahn & Bodmer

St. Gallen
Wegelin & Co.,
   Inhaber Eugster & Co.

Neuchâtel
Bonhote & Cie

Yverdon
Piguet & Cie

Geneva
Bordier & Cie
Darier & Cie
Gonet & Cie
Hentsch & Cie
Lombard, Odier & Cie
Mirabaud & Cie
Morgue d'Algue & Cie
Pictet & Cie
Tardy, Burrus & Cie

Lausanne
Hentsch, Chollet & Cie
Hofstetter, Landolt & Cie

Lucerne
Falck & Cie

In recent years, three of the largest private banks have opted to incorporate, again for a variety of reasons. Bank Julius Bär went public in 1975 amid news reports that there were just too many Bärs in the family to effectively run the firm as a partnership any longer. The majority of the bank's shares are still held by the Bär family. Vontobel & Cie, long considered Zurich's most exclusive private bank changed its name to Bank J. Vontobel when it incorporated in 1984. The firm remains even more closely held than Julius Bär, 90 percent of the stock was retained by the Vontobel family while the remaining 10 percent was handed as gifts to bank employees. The stated purpose of incorporating was to enable the firm to increase its equity base and move into new forms of business, such as commercial lending. Others have suggested, however, that incorporation was less a matter of economics and more a matter of lack of heirs in the Vontobel family.

Desired economic expansion was also the reason expressed by Sarasin & Cie, which became Bank Sarasin & Cie, an incorporated private bank, in April, 1987. Although still technically a privately owned bank, the bank now is allowed to advertise for deposits from the public. Sarasin has gone to great efforts to convince its customers that they will always receive the same personal services that they previously enjoyed.

Other private banks remain resolutely opposed to any changes in their own-ership structure. An example is Zurich's Rahn & Bodmer, a successful private bank for over two centuries. According to Peter Rahn, heir apparent to leadership of the firm, the bank is committed to growth, but only to the extent that it can be financed internally. Evidence that the bank has been successful can be seen in the fact that the bank staff has been allowed to grow by over 40 percent since 1985.

Whether the number of private banks will continue to diminish is difficult to predict. One study of banking in Switzerland, performed by Arthur Andersen & Co., has suggested that the trend is unlikely to continue, at least in the near future. But even if there is no change in the *legal* form of private banks, changes in the kinds of services offered and types of customers serviced are expected to take place. Formal marketing plans have been established, and managers are being expected to achieve targets for growth. In addition, there is a continuing trend to accept smaller (albeit, well recommended) customers, as firms achieve the ability to cut portfolio costs and reduce individual portfolio oversight through the use of in-house investment pools.

REGULATION OF THE SWISS BANKING INDUSTRY

A discussion of Swiss banking would be incomplete without mentioning the regu-latory environment. Bankers in Switzerland, like their colleagues around the globe, are subject to strict controls for the protection of the customers and the implementation of monetary policy. Regulation is carried out through federal agencies as well as membership in private associations. A brief description of the regulatory environment follows.

Federal Banking Commission

Consisting of seven to nine members appointed by the Federal Council, this body is ultimately responsible for regulating banking activity in the country. The com-mission has the power to grant and suspend licenses, enforce statutes relating to banking activity, and review the audited statements of the banks.

Swiss National Bank

The Swiss National Bank is the central bank of Switzerland. In addition to provid-ing the confederation with a common currency, the bank is the governmental arm charged with carrying out the federal government's monetary policy. Similar to the Federal Reserve Bank in the United States, the Swiss National Bank issues directives concerning credit expansion, sets minimum reserve requirements for banks, and operates as a clearinghouse for interbank settlements.

Swiss Bankers Association

A trade organization open to all bank presidents, vice-presidents and directors, the Swiss Bankers Association (SBA) is quite possibly the most powerful nongov-ernmental body in the country. The SBA is devoted to looking after the interests of the Swiss banking establishment. Proclamations of the SBA (called Conventions) have always been viewed by the banking community as inviolable rules of conduct.

By convention, the organization sets a scale of charges in a cartel-like fashion, which members are obliged to follow and nonmembers invariably choose to adopt. That the organization has immense persuasive power over its members can be seen by the fact that the U.S. government has chosen to negotiate with SBA from time to time on matters concerning Americans with accounts in Switzerland.

Other banking associations exist in Switzerland for the purpose of supporting member interests. They include the Swiss Private Bankers Association, the Swiss Cantonal Bankers Association, and the Association of Foreign Banks in Switzerland. None of these other organizations, however, wields power over its members in the way that the SBA does.

3
Secrecy

No aspect of Swiss banking is as celebrated as the secrecy which surrounds customer deposits. To most Americans, the Swiss veil of secrecy is fascinating and exotic, a privilege not normally available to the common citizen. To the Swiss, secrecy is ordinary and commonplace, a fundamental right that logically extends to everyone and every aspect of living. The Swiss people view secrecy in banking as merely another example of the level of discretion to be expected in the conduct of one's private affairs.

Most societies place little premium on an individual's right to financial privacy. At the same time, government officials who steadfastly refuse to grant their own banks the right of privileged information occasionally find it necessary to rush to Switzerland when their own personal affairs require discretion. Past years have witnessed massive amounts of capital flight from Africa, Latin America, and western European countries with a simultaneous increase in foreign-owned deposits in Switzerland. Much of the wealth is alleged to have been deposited into the private accounts of governmental officials, including banking officials, military leaders, and heads of state. Even governments have availed themselves of the opportunities in Switzerland for shielding monetary transactions from public view.

The tradition of Swiss secrecy dates back to the time of the French Revolution and the need of the nobility to locate private depositories for their private wealth. The cidevants found that bankers in Geneva were not only tight lipped but willing to oversee the investment of their funds for the benefit of the owners. In the succeeding two centuries, the French have remained mindful of the secrecy, profitability, and close proximity of the Swiss vaults. They have continued to rely on the discretion of their bankers as the governments of their own republic rise and fall.

While secrecy in Swiss banking is a long-standing tradition, it has only recently been codified in the country's civil law. By the 1930s, the tradition was already legendary. But with the passage of the Swiss Bank Act of 1934, what had been custom became a legal requirement firmly rooted in federal law. The story of the enactment of secrecy provisions in the new federal statutes to thwart Nazi attempts to locate money stashed in Switzerland, has become a legend in itself.

SWISS BANKS VERSUS THE GESTAPO

Upon seizing power in Germany in 1933, Hitler was faced with monumental economic disorder. A series of laws designed to impose tight monetary control were enacted with the idea of regaining value and respectability for the German mark. The gradual return to economic stability was made more difficult by a massive flight of capital out of Germany. Thousands of Germans who had already lost substantial wealth were afraid of losing even more as the National Socialists extended their control over day-to-day affairs. They attempted to save what wealth remained by converting their savings into harder currencies on deposit in other countries. In addition to those merely uncertain about the economic future were farsighted Jewish families who began to sense larger confiscatory dangers.

Switzerland's vaults presented perfect depositories for worried Germans. Not only did Switzerland share a common border with Germany, but the banks had a well-known tradition of quietly accepting deposits of foreigners. Moreover, the majority of Swiss citizens speak German as their primary language.

Laws promulgated in Germany were intended not only to halt the outward flow of capital, but to reverse the flow as well. Germans were forbidden to send money abroad or to hold private funds in foreign accounts. Those who owned accounts abroad were required to disclose the accounts to authorities who would see to it that all amounts were immediately repatriated. The penalty for violation was death.

The law clearly put a halt to the overt transfer of funds to bank accounts abroad. However, it could not prevent covert transfers, nor was it successful in promoting full disclosure of all funds that had previously been spirited away. The German secret police (Gestapo) was charged with the responsibility for seeking out and gaining possession of the funds and punishing the transgressors.

Gestapo agents were dispatched to numerous countries, including Switzerland, with clear instructions to find German-owned bank accounts. The agents employed a variety of methods to extract information from bank employees, including bribes, threats, and even exploitation of romantic relationships with bank clerks. Gestapo agents would sometimes attempt to make deposits to the credit of a suspected account holder. In the event that the deposits were accepted by the bank, the existence of the account was considered confirmed. The success of the agents in obtaining account information through these means is well documented.

Once an account was discovered, the Gestapo would instruct the owner to request the immediate withdrawal of the assets, to be returned by mail or cable to Germany. Obviously, the bankers had no way to know if written withdrawal requests were being made freely or under duress. In typical Swiss fashion, the Swiss bankers announced that they would no longer accept withdrawal orders from German citizens unless the owner of the funds appeared in person. Furthermore, they made it known that they would only permit withdrawals in person if the owner appeared alone, unaccompanied by others unknown to the bank.

Initially, the German investigators had moderate success in gaining possession of fugitive capital. The difficulties posed by the Swiss did not entirely stop the flow of information out of the banks and into the hands of the investigators. In 1934, amid large public notice, the Nazis tried and executed three German citizens for the crime of owning foreign bank accounts. The Swiss, realizing that bank information leaks could result in further executions, moved quickly to plug any possibility of leaks with federal legislation. The result was Article 47 of the comprehensive Bank Act of 1934.

SECRECY LAW

As mentioned, the legislation merely provided the legal basis for what had formerly been general practice among Swiss banks. It was truly significant, however, in that the law provided severe criminal penalties for violators. The law stated that a violation of banking secrecy by anyone (including officers, employees or auditors) would be punishable by a prison term of up to six months and a fine of SFr. 50,000. Furthermore, the violation of professional secrecy would remain punishable even after termination of the official or employment relationship.

Also included in the legislation were similar penalties for those compromising secrecy by negligence as well as penalties for anyone attempting to induce others to break the confidentiality surrounding customers' deposits. Although these provisions were modified by later revisions of the law, the Swiss Penal Code provides for continuing assurance against all crimes of disclosure.

The penalties specified by the secrecy statutes might be considered by non-Swiss bankers as unreasonably harsh. The Swiss banking community, on the other hand, welcomed the law, believing it would heighten the profession of banking in the country. Essentially the law provided the bankers with a privileged relationship not unlike that enjoyed by physicians, lawyers, and clergy.

The bankers have not taken lightly the responsibility imposed on them by the privileged relationship. It is interesting to note that, since the passage of the law, not a single banker in Switzerland has been convicted of violating it. This is particularly surprising when one considers that even the slightest indiscretion (e.g., admitting that an individual is a customer) is considered a violation of the law. Bank secrecy is even more significant when one considers the true extent of the law. As previously mentioned, Swiss banks often provide services that are not considered to be within the domain of American banking activities. Thus, bank secrecy extends to matters of investments, portfolio management, custody of assets, counseling, and *normal* banking activities as well.

COMMON COURTESIES

In an effort to ensure the secrecy that its customers desire, the banks in Switzerland have adopted many practices that might appear peculiar to bank customers of other countries. The peculiarities are believed by the Swiss to be only common courtesies, services that all customers deserve. One such courtesy is the use of unmarked envelopes. New customers of Swiss banks are often surprised to find that all correspondence arrives from their banks in plain white or brown envelopes. A bank would never be so tactless as to include its name as part of the return address; in fact, rarely is a return address used by a bank.

Added discretion may include measures to give bank correspondence the appearance of *personal* mail. Typical measures include stamped (i.e., not metered) mail and handwritten envelopes. If a return address is used, it may contain the name and personal address of an officer of the bank. Customers may even have their mail disguised even more. It is not unheard of for a Swiss bank to correspond with its customers by using a bank agent in a foreign country to forward mail from that country. Thus, a customer in the United States may receive his Swiss bank statement in an ordinary envelope, hand addressed with return address in Frankfurt or Amsterdam.

Some bank customers prefer to receive no mail from the Swiss banks that hold their funds. Their bankers understand completely. Upon request, the bank simply holds all correspondence until further instructions are received.

NUMBERED ACCOUNTS

If normal Swiss bank accounts are not secret enough, the Swiss have allowed an added layer of secrecy with the so-called *numbered account*. No other element of Swiss banking has given rise to so much folklore. If the American public is confused about the true meaning of numbered accounts, it can no doubt be blamed on unscrupulous authors and screenwriters who have failed to do their homework. Let's be clear on the subject.

All bank accounts in Switzerland, like everywhere else, are assigned account numbers. By special request, some banks will agree to replace an account name on all bank records with a special code number. The number (or a series of letters and digits) is the only way a bank clerk can identify the account. The actual owner's name is known only to the bank manager and is recorded in a special ledger located in the manager's private safe.

Thus, the only real distinction between a numbered account and a regular account is that the ownership of a numbered account is known to fewer bank employees. The added secrecy consists merely of the reduced likelihood of an indiscretion on the part of a bank's clerical staff. From a legal perspective, a numbered account has no special significance; all bank accounts in Switzerland have equal status in the eyes of the law. Moreover, when one considers the criminal penalties associated with any breach of secrecy, it is easy to question the reason for existence of such an account. On the other hand, when one considers all that the Swiss have to be secret about, the numbered account may take on a special significance.

There is no doubt that customers do enjoy the added confidence that numbered accounts provide. It makes little difference whether the confidence stems from an actual improvement in secrecy or from meeting a customer's psychological need. The fact remains that a numbered Swiss account is considered the ultimate secret available to the owners of wealth. Even the Swiss themselves find the numbered account useful, as do an estimated 400,000 French with deposits in Switzerland.

Americans are not likely to be able to make use of such accounts, despite their popularity, without going to special efforts to own one. Bank accounts are easily opened by mail, but those banks that do offer numbered accounts will most likely require a personal visit by the prospective customer. The banker will want to discuss the reason for opening such an account and will comply only if the account is deemed appropriate.

All potential customers should be aware that Swiss bankers, according to their own code of conduct, will always require that a customer be identified before opening an account, numbered or otherwise. Notwithstanding the nonsense of novels and popular movies, it is impossible for funds to be deposited in a numbered account for the benefit of a customer that not even a Swiss banker can identify. There is simply no such thing as an anonymous account in Switzerland.

In the event that an American can convince a banker that a numbered account is warranted, there is a practical matter that should be considered. Because of the inability of bank clerks to establish proper ownership of the funds, withdrawals of cash, securities, or precious metals, without the assistance of the bank manager, may prove difficult if not impossible. Ownership of a numbered account may require personal appearance in order for such delivery to take place. In such a case, the withdrawal is made by the bank manager under his own signature while the customer waits in the manager's office. In special situations, an elaborate system of code words, through telephone or wire, may suffice for an authorization to transfer funds to or from a numbered account. Naturally, the code system can only be arranged in person at the bank.

Not all banks offer numbered accounts. In particular, small, private banks would find such accounts superfluous, even insulting, since their staffs are often quite small.

PIERCING THE VEIL OF SECRECY

Contrary to the belief of many, banking secrecy rules are not inviolable. There are conditions that may permit Swiss and non-Swiss government investigators to pierce the veil of secrecy. The conditions that allow for penetration are precisely defined in statute and require exact legal procedure. If it is not possible for bankers in Switzerland to provide absolute secrecy, it is at least possible for them to demand that every legal procedure has been followed before any account information is released to government officials.

Generally, Swiss courts have determined that secrecy may be breached in circumstances in which the public good is best served by disclosure of private information. Disclosure of account information may result from civil or criminal proceedings in Switzerland, requests from foreign governments, and as a result of certain bankruptcy and estate matters.

Swiss Legal Proceedings

A violation of either Swiss federal or cantonal laws may override the secrecy provisions of the 1934 banking law. With respect to civil (non-criminal) matters, the
laws of the federal government and most cantons leave it to the courts to determine whether a bank may be forced to disclose customer information. Swiss
courts reflect the attitudes of the Swiss people. The judges are fully aware of the
moral significance of a decision to require disclosure and use their powers spar-
ingly. Furthermore, the courts and the bankers are aware of the potential consequences of inadvertently releasing data concerning the financial affairs of third
parties. They take every conceivable precaution to protect uninvolved individuals
from any accidental disclosures.

Less protection is available to those charged with violations of the Swiss criminal code. Persons charged with crimes may not use bank secrecy laws to shield
their financial affairs from investigators. Again, the courts continue to be cautious
in the use of information obtained from banks, with everlasting care to avoid
injury to third parties.

Considering that most foreign customers of Swiss banks are unlikely to
become violators of Swiss laws or entangled in legal proceedings in Switzerland,
the ability of the Swiss domestic law to penetrate the veil of bank secrecy has little
real significance for foreign depositors. However, there are also conditions that
can result in the release of bank-held information to foreign officials.

Foreign Requests for Information

To understand the circumstances in which banking secrets may be made available
to foreign investigators, a distinction must again be made between civil and criminal proceedings. Swiss courts have consistently held that civil matters in foreign
countries are of no interest whatsoever to them. Thus, in the event of a suit in an
American court for breach of contract, divorce, or any other civil complaint, all
financial records maintained in Switzerland are closed.

An information request relating to criminal proceedings in a foreign country
is a far more complex issue. The Swiss might cooperate with foreign courts of law
in providing bank account information but only if the alleged criminal action
under investigation is also classified as a crime under Swiss law. In addition, specifically defined crimes agreed to in treaties between the Swiss and foreign governments might result in the transfer of otherwise secret information.

Foreign officials requesting the release of information cannot expect to sift
through mountains of bank data hoping to find incriminating evidence against
unknown parties. Before honoring a foreign request for bank records, Swiss
authorities require that evidence be presented showing that a specifically named
individual has likely used a specifically identified bank for transactions relating to
the crime. Even if banking records are turned over, the bankers are only obligated
to provide information about the transactions involved. Information concerning
unrelated transactions is customarily deleted, along with the identity of any third
parties.

Bankruptcy and Inheritance Matters

Further limits to the absoluteness of bank secrecy can be found in the statutes surrounding bankruptcy. As with civil proceedings, the limits of disclosure requirements are defined by national boundaries. Banks in Switzerland must declare all assets owned by a bankrupt individual to the official Swiss receivers in bankruptcy. In addition, the assets must be distributed by the bank when officially instructed to do so. Requests by foreign receivers in bankruptcy, however, carry no official sanction in Switzerland and are customarily ignored.

According to Swiss law, banks have the responsibility to their deceased customers to divulge bank holdings to the heirs or executors of the estate. In typical Swiss fashion, however, the banks are forbidden to give such information to government officials—domestic or foreign. As far as the bankers are concerned, the right of secrecy possessed by the deceased immediately passes to the heirs or the estate.

A VOTE OF CONFIDENCE

The majority of Swiss citizens are immensely proud of their marvelous banks. It is clear that the Swiss banking system is the centerpiece of the financial center. Not all Swiss, however, are pleased. Some would radically change the banking system by stripping it of many of its unique features (particularly the secrecy tradition) that account for the financial center's success.

In 1984, banking critics succeeded in placing before voters a proposed constitutional amendment that would have significantly modified bank practices. The proposal was sponsored by the Social Democratic Party of Switzerland, which collected the 100,000 signatures necessary to bring the referendum to a vote. In addition to making banking records more easily available to foreign governments, the referendum would have required banks to disclose their *own* hidden reserves, a practice wildly inconsistent with prudent Swiss accounting.

Proponents of the referendum, insisted that present banking laws prompted illegal activities in other countries by providing hidden accounts enabling criminals to *launder* their dirty money. Furthermore, they charged that secrecy statutes were draining many developing countries by allowing corrupt government officials to secretly pile up personal fortunes while plundering their countries' treasuries.

Opponents of the referendum stressed to voters the adverse economic impact that such a law would have on the Swiss economy. Admitting that secrecy is a major factor in attracting foreign deposits, bank supporters warned of the certain outflow of billions of dollars of deposits, with resulting economic recession and massive unemployment. Also, the opponents of the referendum asked voters to truly consider the moral issues associated with diminished personal privacy.

The outcome of the vote was a strong vote of confidence for Swiss banks and their practices. The referendum was defeated by a 3-to-1 margin in the largest voter turnout that Swiss voters could remember.

It is difficult to know whether the average Swiss citizen was more persuaded by the argument of national fiscal health or by the threat to individual privacy that a suspension of secrecy laws would have provided. Considering that the dismantling of the secrecy laws would have had little impact on the private lives of Swiss citizens, most observers have concluded that the economic realities of the situation were more persuasive in deciding voters' minds.

The Swiss are nothing if not realistic. They are fully aware that the secrecy provisions of their country's law have aided in making Switzerland a world financial center. Their bankers are also aware that, in the modern world, private individuals are no longer the largest holders of wealth. To remain viable institutions, banks now must compete for corporate assets and trust funds; customers with little need for the legendary Swiss secrecy. Furthermore, competition for large foreign funds requires that banks cooperate with foreign institutions and governments. And cooperation with governments must necessarily include an occasional prying of the lid of secrecy which has hermetically sealed private money in past years.

OF DICTATORS AND DEPOSED POLITICAL LEADERS

Perhaps nowhere is this new spirit of cooperation more evident than in Switzerland's apparent rethinking on the subject of personal fortunes owned by foreign government officials. In years past, the death or overthrow of a leader of an undeveloped country posed little financial threat to that leader's family, providing that the leader had been prudent enough to sock away money or gold in a Swiss account or two. Many third-world leaders are believed to have shown such prudence, as Fig. 3-1 indicates.

The exact amounts that these individuals have stashed away are, for obvious reasons, unknown. Haille Selassie was reported to have made an annual deposit of some 500 kilograms of gold, amounting to more than $15 billion by the time of his death. Others, such as Zaire's Mobutu, have never been able to match Selassie's sensational wealth. While the press usually estimates his personal fortune in the $4- to $5-billion range (roughly equivalent to Zaire's foreign debt), Mobutu has publicly stated that he has no more than a modest $50 million in personal funds on deposit in foreign banks. The exact amount would be impossible for even the banks to determine. Like so many other dictators, Mobutu has exclusive signature authority over all funds owned by his country's national bank. It is simply impossible for foreign banks to know whether funds being moved among bank accounts represent personal fortune or state resources.

Successor regimes have been known to appeal to the Swiss for aid in returning the stolen treasuries of their countries. For example, the government of Santo Domingo unsuccessfully tried for years to enlist the aid of the Swiss government in locating approximately $500 million surreptitiously removed from the public coffers by the Trujillo family and believed on deposit in Geneva. Similarly, the governments of Ethiopia and Iran were thwarted in their efforts to repatriate lost funds. But unsuccessful pleas by looted countries may well be a thing of the past. Swift action on the part of Swiss government officials have managed to block the withdrawal of funds from the accounts of two dictators who recently fled their countries.

Political Leader	Country
Arellano	Honduras
Batista	Cuba
Bokassa	Central African Republic
Duvalier	Haiti
Marcos	Phillipines
Mobutu	Zaire
Nol	Cambodia
Peron	Argentina
Pahlevi	Iran
Suarez	Bolivia
Selassie	Ethiopia
Somaza	Nicaragua
Theiu	South Vietnam
Trujillo	Dominican Republic
Zulfikar	Pakistan

Fig. 3-1. Political leaders widely believed to have established personal Swiss bank accounts.

Not long after Ferdinand Marcos fled the Philippines, the successor government dispatched Pedro Yap, a member of the Philippine Commission of Good Government, to Berne. His purpose was to open talks with the Swiss government concerning the billions of dollars of embezzled Philippine funds allegedly on deposit in personal accounts of Marcos. Upon arriving in Switzerland, Yap was informed that the Swiss government, on its own volition, had already ordered all banks to freeze any accounts believed owned by Marcos and his family. The action had been decided upon the previous day at a meeting of the Federal Council, which instructed the Swiss Banking Commission to carry out the action.

Bankers in Switzerland reacted to the freeze order with a surprise that was at least as great as Yap's. The Swiss federal government had never before ordered the freezing of foreign-owned bank funds in anticipation of receiving a request to do so from a foreign government. A Swiss official explained that the decision was made without a request for legal assistance in an effort to assure continuing good relations between Switzerland and The Philippines. Formal charges were soon forthcoming from Manila; in April 1986, Marcos, four family members, and 21 of the former dictator's cronies were charged with having embezzled as much as $5 billion from various governmental sources, including a tidy 15% cut from all Japanese war reparations.

Marcos challenged the Swiss government's right to freeze his accounts and indicated his intentions to travel to Switzerland to meet with his bankers on the issue. While the Swiss are obligated to accept appeals filed on Marcos' behalf, they have taken the unprecedented step of barring Marcos from entering the country while the legal system determines the rightful ownership of his bank accounts. By all indications, the legal proceedings are likely to drag on for years.

Watching the Marcos affair from his plush residence in France was exiled Haiti President-for-Life, Jean-Claude Duvalier. Duvalier had fled Haiti in February 1986 following violent demonstrations protesting gross maladministration. Also watching from Port-au-Prince were Haiti's new military rulers, who immediately scrambled to assemble a request for a Swiss freeze on Duvalier's assets. The petition charged Duvalier with embezzlement of approximately $800 million. Again, with uncharacteristic speed, banks in Switzerland were informed that any funds belonging to Duvalier were to be immediately frozen. Because of the two-week delay between the Marcos freeze and the delivery of the request from Haiti's new leaders, many believe that the freeze will prove to have been ineffective. It is likely that Duvalier foresaw the hazards of keeping his money in Switzerland and transferred at least some of his assets to a more secure depository.

It is hard for most people to imagine a more secure depository than a bank in Switzerland, but the Marcos and Duvalier cases have given the world notice that Switzerland is apparently no longer a secure home for dictatorial pension funds. More importantly, the cases have shown that the concept of secrecy in Swiss banking is subject to evolution. Since the Marcos and Duvalier freezes, other evidence of evolution has become apparent.

MORE EVIDENCE OF CHANGE

The Swiss Banker's Association first adopted rules governing the acceptance of new customers by *convention* in 1977. The purpose of the convention was to discourage the transfer of funds from countries placing restrictions on the export of money and to avoid developing business relationships with individuals suspected of involvement in illegal activities. The new rules required all banks to determine the identity of customers wishing to open accounts and ascertain the origin of large funds being deposited. Chapter 9 discusses how the convention is currently being implemented when new customers open accounts.

Exceptions to the customer identity rule were allowed under the terms of the convention. In particular, Swiss lawyers were permitted to establish special accounts (called Form B accounts) for unnamed clients. The only requirement for such an account was that a lawyer certify that he or she knew the identity of the account holder and that the money contained in the account was obtained by legal means.

Effective September 1987, the rules were modified. Although the use of lawyer-opened accounts was not banned, the rules governing such accounts became much stiffer. Lawyers opening accounts for their clients must now declare that withholding the account holder's identity is absolutely necessary in order to execute other, legal business for the client. Accounts may not be opened by lawyers merely to conceal the owner's identity from the bank.

No doubt influenced by worldwide headline news regarding the personal fortunes of Marcos and Duvalier, the Swiss bankers also agreed to observe new procedures when opening personal accounts for foreign leaders. The banks agreed that, in the future, all such accounts must be approved by top management, who will decline any business believed related to capital flight, tax fraud, or other illicit activities.

Many believe that secrecy rules in Switzerland have changed significantly. Certainly the Swiss have shown some willingness to cooperate with foreign officials tracking or halting illegal money movements. Swiss cooperation, however, is not automatic. As the next chapter demonstrates, American investigators have learned that inviolable limits still remain.

4

United States
vs. Swiss Secrecy

THE DEGREE OF BANKING SECRECY THAT AN INDIVIDUAL CAN EXPECT IN THE UNITED
States is not neatly defined. U.S. bankers are quick to point out that they are
bound by professional ethics to maintain the confidentiality of their customers'
affairs. In some states, courts have held that there exists an implied obligation to
customers to protect them from unreasonable disclosures of bank account information. However, not all states have such laws, and it is often because bank customers have no protection from *reasonable* disclosures that many Americans
become nervous and find more secure depositories overseas.

American banks are bombarded daily with requests from individuals, businesses, and law enforcement officials seeking information about customers. One
California bank told a U.S. House subcommittee in 1977 that it received about
1,000 inquiries each month from federal and local government investigators. To
make matters worse, private requests greatly exceed those from the government.

For nongovernmental inquiries, the release of information is usually considered to be a courtesy to a customer: the provision of corroborative information
that will allow the customer to write a check, rent a house, or borrow money from
another credit institution. Typical requests are to verify whether a person is a customer, the length of the banking relationship, whether loans are being repaid on
time, or if the account has sufficient funds to cover a check being tendered by the
customer. As one American banker has stated, "If the request sounds bona fide,
why not respond? We make the same requests of others."

Banks in the United States have little choice in the matter when the request for information comes from more official sources. Common law has consistently provided to federal and state investigators legal access to account information for bank customers. Also, grand juries and courts customarily subpoena records for their own purposes.

Congressional actions to protect the right of individual privacy have been feeble at best. For example, The Privacy Act of 1974 outlined the types of personal information in governmental files that may be publicly disclosed. It placed no restrictions, however, on the information that the government may gather, either from other government agencies or from nongovernmental sources. The much heralded Financial Privacy Act of 1978 was equally ineffectual in safeguarding personal confidentiality, especially relating to banking data. Instead of imposing limits on governmental investigators seeking information, the act merely established the procedures to be followed by investigators in obtaining confidential records.

BANK SECRECY ACT

Perhaps no congressional action has so pleased government investigators as much as Public Law 91-508, the so-called Bank Secrecy Act of 1970. In spite of its name, the federal law imposed vast record-keeping requirements on banks and mandated automatic reporting requirements on both banks and private citizens. Congress left no doubt about its intentions in passing the legislation. The stated purpose is "to require the maintenance of . . . records [which] have a high degree of usefulness in criminal, tax, or regulatory investigations or proceedings."

Record-keeping Requirements

The Secrecy Act's record-keeping requirements were designed to ensure that the details of every banking transaction would be preserved and remain forever available to aid in government probes. The wording of the law is explicit, requiring banks to make

1. "a microfilm or other reproduction of each check, draft, or similar instrument drawn upon it and presented to it for payment; and
2. a record of each check, draft, or similar instrument received by it for deposit or collection, together with an identification of the party for whose account it is to be deposited or collected. . . ."

Reporting Requirements—Banks

Under the provisions of the Secrecy Act, automatic reporting to the federal government is required of financial institutions for any transaction considered to have a high degree of usefulness to the government. At present, the threshold level for usefulness is $10,000, and banks (together with nonbank financial institutions, such as credit unions and savings and loan associations) are required to fill out a special report whenever a customer executes a transaction of that amount or more.* Although certain large commercial customers of banks have been granted exemptions from the reporting requirements based on the sheer volume of oversized transactions, no individual customer has been granted an exemption.

Bankers throughout the United States have become familiar with IRS Form 4789—Currency Transaction Report, the form on which unusual transactions are reported (see Fig. 4-1). The information remains available to a legion of government investigators, but the form does not lie idle in a government warehouse. All forms are forwarded to the Detroit IRS office, which has the task of entering the information into government data banks. Computers compare the information against other IRS records. Presumably, discrepancies can result in tax probes.

Reporting Requirements—Individuals

The Secrecy Act created further reporting requirements on anyone (individuals or businesses) transporting *monetary instruments* across U.S. boundaries. Monetary instruments were defined by the act to include U.S. and foreign coin and currency, traveler's checks, and any security or negotiable instrument in bearer form. The report is to be filed on Customs Form 4790 (see Fig. 4-2) and is presently required for all transactions involving $10,000 or more. Although the information is filed with the U.S. Customs Office, the information is available to other departments or agencies of the federal government upon request. An expanded discussion of customs reporting requirements is included in chapter 10.

Some have contended that the ability of investigators to obtain banking records constitutes an invasion of the right to privacy protected by the Fourth Amendment. Indeed, the U.S. Supreme Court has recognized that certain *private books and papers* may not be used in evidence against an individual for the same reasons that a person cannot be compelled to be a witness against himself. However, the court has also stated (*U.S.* v. *Miller*) that banking records of individual customers (which banks must maintain in compliance with the Bank Secrecy Act) are *not* to be considered private papers, but instead are the business records of the banks. In reaching its conclusion, the court went so far as to state that there is a "lack of any legitimate expectation of privacy concerning the information kept in bank records." With the weight of privacy acts, secrecy acts and Supreme Court decisions behind them, it is no surprise that the FBI, SEC, IRS and other governmental agencies remain undaunted in their efforts to seek whatever information they need from U.S.banks.

SWISS COOPERATION WITH U.S. INVESTIGATORS

The freewheeling approach of American investigators frequently works well when a monetary trail leads offshore. A high level of cooperation exists between the United States and the many countries that hold a similar regard for the finan-

---

*It is interesting to note that casinos are considered banks for the purposes of the act and must file a similar report whenever an individual buys or redeems chips in the amount of $10,000 or more.

Form **4789**	**Currency Transaction Report**	OMB No. 1545-0183

Form **4789**
(Rev. September 1988)

Department of the Treasury
Internal Revenue Service

Currency Transaction Report
▶ File a separate report for each transaction.   ▶ Please type or print.
▶ For Paperwork Reduction Act Notice, see page 3.
(Complete all applicable parts—See instructions)

OMB No. 1545-0183
Expires: 1-31-89

If amended report, see
instructions and check
here . . . . . ▶ ☐

Part I   Identity of individual who conducted this transaction with the financial institution

1 If multiple individuals involved, see instructions and check here . . . . ▶ ☐

2 Last name	3 First name	4 Middle initial	5 Social security number

6 Address (number and street)	7 Occupation, profession, or business

8 City	9 State	10 ZIP code	11 Country (if not U.S.)

12 Method used to verify identity: a Describe ▶ ....
   b Issued by ▶   c Number ▶ ....

13 Reason items 2-12 are not completed: a ☐ Armored car service (enter name) ▶ ....
   b ☐ Mail deposit/shipment   c ☐ Night deposit or ATM transaction   d ☐ Multiple transactions (see instructions)

Part II   Individual or organization for whom this transaction was completed

14 If multiple individuals or organizations are involved, see instructions and check here . . . . ▶ ☐

15 Individual's last name	16 First name	17 Middle initial	18 Social security number

19 a Name of organization	b Check if: (1) ☐ broker/dealer in securities, or (2) ☐ financial institution (see instructions)	20 Employer identification number

21 Address (number and street)	22 Occupation, profession, or business

23 City	24 State	25 ZIP code	26 Country (if not U.S.)

Part III   Customer's account number(s) affected by transaction

27 S ☐ Savings ▶ ....   T ☐ Securities ▶ ....   H ☐ CD/Money market ▶ ....
   C ☐ Checking ▶   L ☐ Loan ▶   O ☐ Other (specify) ▶

Part IV   Type of transaction. Check applicable boxes to describe transactions

28 ☐ Currency exchange (currency for currency)

29 CASH IN:		30 CASH OUT:	
D ☐ Deposit	F ☐ CD/Money market purchased	C ☐ Check cashed	R ☐ CD/Money market redeemed
G ☐ Security purchased	H ☐ For wire transfer	T ☐ Security redeemed	U ☐ From wire transfer
P ☐ Check purchased	A ☐ Receipt from abroad	W ☐ Withdrawal	B ☐ Shipment abroad
	K ☐ Other cash in (specify) ▶		Y ☐ Other cash out (specify) ▶ ....

31 Total amount of currency transaction (in U.S. dollars). ▶ $	32 Amount in Item 31 in $100 bills or higher $	33 Date of transaction (month, day, and year)

34 If other than U.S. currency is involved, please furnish the following information: a Exchange made ☐ for or ☐ from U.S. currency

b Currency name	c Country	d Total amount of each foreign currency (in U.S. dollars) . . ▶ $

35 If a check or wire transfer was involved in this transaction, please furnish the following information (see instructions):
   a If more than one check or wire transfer is involved, see instructions and check here . . . . ▶ ☐

b Date of check or wire transfer	c Amount of check or wire transfer (in U.S. dollars) $	d Payee

e Drawer of check	f Drawee bank and MICR number

Part V   Financial institution where currency transaction took place

36 Check applicable box to indicate type of financial institution   a ☐ Bank (enter code number from instructions here) ▶ ....
   b ☐ Savings and loan association   c ☐ Credit union   d ☐ Security broker/dealer   e ☐ Other

37 Name of financial institution	38 Employer identification number

39 Address (number and street)	40 Social security number

41 City	42 State	43 ZIP code	44 MICR number

Sign Here ▶	45 Signature (preparer)	46 Title	47 Date
	48 Type or print preparer's name	49 Approving official (signature)	50 Date

Fig. 4-1. IRS Form 4789—Currency Transaction Report.

Form 4789 (Rev. 9-88)   Page **2**

Multiple Transactions
(Complete applicable parts below if box 1, 14, or 35a on page 1 is checked)

Part I Continued—Complete if box 1 on page 1 is checked

2 Last name	3 First name	4 Middle initial	5 Social security number
6 Address (number and street)		7 Occupation, profession, or business	
8 City	9 State	10 ZIP code	11 Country (if not U.S.)

12 Method used to verify identity: **a** Describe ▶
b Issued by ▶ --   **c** Number ▶ -------------------

2 Last name	3 First name	4 Middle initial	5 Social security number
6 Address (number and street)		7 Occupation, profession, or business	
8 City	9 State	10 ZIP code	11 Country (if not U.S.)

12 Method used to verify identity: **a** Describe ▶
b Issued by ▶ --   **c** Number ▶ -------------------

Part II Continued—Complete if box 14 on page 1 is checked

15 Individual's last name	16 First name	17 Middle initial	18 Social security number
19 a Name of organization	b Check if: (1) ☐ broker/dealer in securities, or (2) ☐ financial institution (see instructions)	20 Employer identification number	
21 Address (number and street)		22 Occupation, profession, or business	
23 City	24 State	25 ZIP code	26 Country (if not U.S.)

15 Individual's last name	16 First name	17 Middle initial	18 Social security number
19 a Name of organization	b Check if: (1) ☐ broker/dealer in securities, or (2) ☐ financial institution (see instructions)	20 Employer identification number	
21 Address (number and street)		22 Occupation, profession, or business	
23 City	24 State	25 ZIP code	26 Country (if not U.S.)

Part IV Continued—Complete if box 35a on page 1 is checked

35 b Date of check or wire transfer	c Amount of check or wire transfer (in U.S. dollars) $	d Payee
e Drawer of check	f Drawee bank and MICR number	

35 b Date of check or wire transfer	c Amount of check or wire transfer (in U.S. dollars) $	d Payee
e Drawer of check	f Drawee bank and MICR number	

| Customs Use Only

Control No.
31 USC 5316; 31 CFR 103.23 and 103.25
Please Type or Print | DEPARTMENT OF THE TREASURY
UNITED STATES CUSTOMS SERVICE
**REPORT OF INTERNATIONAL
TRANSPORTATION OF CURRENCY
OR MONETARY INSTRUMENTS** | Form Approved
OMB No. 1515-0079
This form is to be filed with the
United States Customs Service

Privacy Act Notification
on reverse |

PART I FOR INDIVIDUAL DEPARTING FROM OR ENTERING THE UNITED STATES

1. NAME(Last or family, first and middle)	2. IDENTIFYING NO. (See instructions)	3. DATE OF BIRTH (Mo./Day/Yr.)
4. PERMANENT ADDRESS IN UNITED STATES OR ABROAD		5. OF WHAT COUNTRY ARE YOU A CITIZEN/SUBJECT?
6. ADDRESS WHILE IN THE UNITED STATES		7. PASSPORT NO. & COUNTRY
8. U.S. VISA DATE	9. PLACE UNITED STATES VISA WAS ISSUED	10. IMMIGRATION ALIEN NO. (If any)

11. CURRENCY OR MONETARY INSTRUMENT WAS: (Complete 11A or 11B)

A. EXPORTED		B. IMPORTED	
Departed From: (City in U.S.)	Arrived At:(Foreign City/Country)	From: (Foreign City/Country)	At: (City in U.S.)

PART II FOR PERSON SHIPPING MAILING OR RECEIVING CURRENCY OR MONETARY INSTRUMENTS

12. NAME (Last or family, first and middle)	13. IDENTIFYING NO. (See instructions)	14. DATE OF BIRTH (Mo./Da./Yr.)
15. PERMANENT ADDRESS IN UNITED STATES OR ABROAD		16. OF WHAT COUNTRY ARE YOU A CITIZEN/SUBJECT?
17. ADDRESS WHILE IN THE UNITED STATES		18. PASSPORT NO. & COUNTRY
19. U.S. VISA DATE	20. PLACE UNITED STATES VISA WAS ISSUED	21. IMMIGRATION ALIEN NO. (If any)

22. CURRENCY OR MONETARY INSTRUMENTS DATE SHIPPED DATE RECEIVED	23. CURRENCY OR MONETARY INSTRUMENTS ☐ Shipped To ☐ Received From	NAME AND ADDRESS	24. IF THE CURRENCY OR MONETARY INSTRUMENT WAS MAILED, SHIPPED, OR TRANSPORTED COMPLETE BLOCKS A AND B. A. Method of Shipment (Auto, U.S. Mail, Public Carrier, etc.) B. Name of Transporter/Carrier

PART III CURRENCY AND MONETARY INSTRUMENT INFORMATION (SEE INSTRUCTIONS ON REVERSE) (To be completed by everyone)

25. TYPE AND AMOUNT OF CURRENCY/MONETARY INSTRUMENTS	Value in U.S. Dollars	26. IF OTHER THAN U.S. CURRENCY IS INVOLVED, PLEASE COMPLETE BLOCKS A AND B. (SEE SPECIAL INSTRUCTIONS)
Coins .... ☐ A. ▶ $		A. Currency Name
Currency .... ☐ B. ▶		
Other instruments (Specify Type) .... ☐ C. ▶		B. Country
(Add lines A, B and C) .... TOTAL AMOUNT ▶ $		

PART IV GENERAL - TO BE COMPLETED BY ALL TRAVELERS, SHIPPERS AND RECIPIENTS

27. WERE YOU ACTING AS AN AGENT, ATTORNEY OR IN CAPACITY FOR ANYONE IN THIS CURRENCY OR MONETARY INSTRUMENT ACTIVITY? (If "Yes" complete A, B and C)   ☐ Yes   ☐ No

PERSON IN WHOSE BEHALF YOU ARE ACTING ▶	A. Name	B. Address	C. Business activity occupation or profession

Under penalties of perjury, I declare that I have examined this report, and to the best of my knowledge and belief it is true, correct and complete.

28. NAME AND TITLE	29. SIGNATURE	30. DATE

(Replaces IRS Form 4790 which is obsolete)   **Customs Form 4790 (120384)**

Fig. 4-2. U.S. Customs Form 4790—Report of International Transportation of Currency of Monetary Instruments.

cial privacy of their citizens. The processes for requesting and transmitting financial intelligence between cooperating governments are finely developed and
allow for rapid, almost automatic, execution.

Much to the chagrin of American investigators, the Swiss veil of secrecy does
not allow for easy penetration. As a result, U.S. and Swiss authorities are often at
odds, resulting in delicate diplomatic problems for the two countries.

In recent years, charges of complicity in criminal activity have been leveled at
the Swiss banking industry by frustrated U.S. law enforcement officials. Even
Congress has expressed its contempt for the Swiss banking system, charging that
it allows the stashing away and laundering of *dirty money* from organized crime,
illegal political contributions, gambling, securities law violations, and, in years
past, illegal gold ownership. The result has been considerable bad press in the
U.S. and indignation on the part of the Swiss, who maintain that their reputation
has been unfairly damaged by the accusations.

Worried about its image as a home for dirty money, the Swiss have slowly
implemented changes in banking procedures to alleviate the pressures of dealing
with deep-pocketed American customers. The first significant change was an
action taken by the Swiss Bankers' Association in 1968. In the wake of U.S. congressional hearings to determine the extent that Swiss banks were being used to
shield the flow of illegal funds, the association urged its members to use extreme
care in dealing with the new American customers, being especially careful to
avoid those clients who might be using their accounts to promote or hide illegal
activities.

After the considerable handiwork necessary to reconcile American common
law with continental law, the U.S. and Swiss governments in 1973 signed the
Treaty of Mutual Assistance in Criminal Matters, which became effective in 1977.
The treaty resulted in agreement to a restricted list of 35 offenses (see Appendix A)
which constitute the basis upon which the Swiss will *consider* an official U.S.
request for information. Naturally, the Swiss government reserves the right to
deny *any* request, and has frequently done so on the grounds that disclosure
would compromise Swiss sovereignty, security, or other essential interests.

Most observers would agree that the treaty has worked well for both sides.
Still, the headlong manner of U.S. investigators has often collided with the rigid
posture of Swiss officials when the investigations are for *crimes* not recognized as
such by the Swiss penal code and not included in the 1973 treaty. In some cases,
the investigators have enjoyed victory; in others, the bank customers emerged vic-
torious.

One of the first cracks in the granite wall of Swiss secrecy appeared in early
1972 when news stories revealed a marvelous hoax. Although many Americans
may recall the story of a fake Howard Hughes autobiography, they may not be
aware of the role that Swiss banks played in the financial side of the affair. The
degree to which one Swiss bank played a significant part in the uncovering of that
hoax provides fascinating reading as well as an ominous warning to those who
believe they may safely *fool the bank*.

FOOLING THE BANK—The Howard Hughes Hoax

In December 1971, McGraw-Hill Publishing Company announced that it intended to publish an autobiography of the famous billionaire Howard Hughes. The book was to be based on extensive interviews with the reclusive Hughes, the first given to anyone since 1958. Although McGraw-Hill was not aware of it at the time, there had been no interviews of Howard Hughes. The book was a complete fake, written by Clifford Irving and sold to McGraw-Hill as the biggest publishing coup of the year. Irving, a writer with a modicum of past success, had become a student of deceit while working on his previous book *Fake,* the story of art forger extraordinaire Elmyr de Hory.

The Hughes book was initially intended by Irving to be an *authorized biography,* carefully blended from previously published accounts and his own fertile imagination. But Irving was able to enrich his book and elevate it to autobiography status by the inclusion of stolen, unpublished material, including the reminiscences of Noah Dietrich, Hughes's former personal secretary. Aside from a convincing manuscript, Irving was able to dazzle McGraw-Hill editors with forged correspondence from Hughes (which somehow managed to pass a handwriting analyst's test) and proof of secret meetings with Hughes in the form of bona fide travel expense reports (which the unwitting publisher dutifully paid).

An agreement was reached between McGraw-Hill and Hughes (acting through Clifford Irving, of course) whereby $750,000 would be paid to Hughes for exclusive rights to the material. At the time of the press release, the publisher had already written checks amounting to $100,000 in advances to Irving and $650,000 to Howard Hughes. McGraw-Hill executives were expecting to reap an overall profit of two to three million dollars from the book.

At no time during Irving's planning was any thought given to Howard Hughes's personal reaction to the book. After all, Hughes had already been the topic of countless articles, biographies, and even motion pictures. Yet nine days after McGraw-Hill's proud announcement, a man claiming to be Howard Hughes telephoned the New York bureau chief for *Time* magazine and proclaimed the book to be a fraud. A few days later, Hughes arranged to be interviewed by seven journalists using an elaborate telephone hookup. Convincing all that he was the real Howard Hughes, the billionaire again reviled Clifford Irving and his counterfeit autobiography. In spite of enormous media attention, Irving stuck to his story of secret meetings with Hughes and McGraw-Hill continued to press forward with the publication of the autobiography.

News accounts of the controversial book included pictures of McGraw-Hill checks, which had been properly endorsed by H.R. Hughes. The checks also appeared to have been endorsed by the headquarters branch of Credit Suisse in Zurich. Time incorporated, fearful that it also had been subject to an elaborate ruse (its publication *Life* had purchased the condensation rights from McGraw-Hill for $.25 million), sent a representative to call on Credit Suisse. As expected, the *Time* representative only received a courteous lecture on the secrecy laws of Switzerland from one of the bank's directors. But in an unexpected move, the bank director contacted *Time* a few days later and gave information that hit like a bombshell: the bank indeed had an account in the name of H.R. Hughes, but the owner was definitely not Howard R. Hughes. The bank stated that it could elaborate no further on the matter without a court order issued by the appropriate Swiss authorities.

On the basis of a complaint immediately filed by McGraw-Hill, the Zurich cantonal police were able to launch an investigation as to the ownership of the account. The facts merely added another level of mystery to the case. According to the bank records, H.R. Hughes was a woman, Helga R. Hughes, and the $650,000 had been withdrawn from her account, which was now closed. While Zurich police were teletyping a physical description of Helga Hughes to Interpol, McGraw-Hill was hurriedly cancelling all plans to publish the autobiography.

McGraw-Hill executives began asking the question: "Why were the checks made out to H.R. Hughes instead of Howard R. Hughes?" Not only was it determined that Clifford Irving had specified this requirement, the accounting office at McGraw-Hill pointed out that once, when it had erroneously typed the name of Howard R. Hughes on a $275,000 check, Irving insisted that the check be reissued in the form that the eccentric Hughes wanted.

Under intense questioning from reporters, police, and an irate publisher, Irving eventually conceded that the autobiography was bogus and that his wife, Edith, was the mysterious Helga R. Hughes. As the Irvings laid out the entire story, it became clear that the slick movement of money into and out of bank accounts was aided, and eventually defeated, by Swiss banks.

In May 1971, Swiss-born Edith Irving had opened account No. 320496 at Credit Suisse. Disguised with a wig and eyeglasses, she offered a forged Swiss passport that showed her to be Helga R. Hughes. The account was to be a *current account* (noninterest-bearing account that allows withdrawls with no previous notice); therefore, the opening could be handled by a clerk in the bank's spacious lobby. After making an initial deposit of SFr.1,000 (approximately $229), Helga left the bank. She returned later that day to pick up her checkbook and make an additional deposit of $50,000, the first McGraw-Hill payment to H.R.Hughes.

Removing the wig and glasses, Edith Irving walked across the Paradeplatz and entered the Swiss Bank Corporation. Using an identity card showing her to be Hanne Rosencrantz, another account was opened. Hanne Rosencrantz was the name of the current wife of Edith's former husband, and Edith had stolen the identification during a recent visit to the Rosencrantzes to visit her children.

During the remaining months of 1971, Edith Irving, as Helga Hughes, deposited an additional $160,000 in checks from McGraw-Hill into the Credit Suisse account. At other times, she withdrew cash from the account, walked across the square to Swiss Bank Corporation, and redeposited the funds into the Rosencrantz account. In this manner, the entire $650,000 that McGraw-Hill had paid to Hughes eventually vanished from the banking system without a trace.

In a bizarre finale to the proceedings, *Helga* withdrew the last $325,000 from Credit Suisse on December 28, 1971. With the cash stuffed into a flight bag, Helga became Hanne once again and made her final walk across the Paradeplatz. Upon arriving at Swiss Bank Corporation, she was informed that there was now another account at the bank in the name of Hanne Rosencrantz, and that the bank was disturbed because of the identical names, addresses, and dates of birth of the two account owners. By a peculiar coincidence, the *real* Hanne Rosencrantz had selected the same bank to open a trust account for her son just a few weeks earlier. Edith was shaken by the information. The discrete bank manager suggested that all confusion could be resolved if Edith would merely transfer her account to another Swiss Bank Corporation branch. The manager helped her select the Bellvueplatz branch, and the account was quietly transferred. When Zurich police later impounded the account, most of the Hughes money was found intact.

Convicted in a Swiss court on charges of forgery and fraud in connection with the illicit bank accounts, Edith Irving served 14 months in a Swiss jail.*

The actions of the Swiss banks involved in this case are worth considering. No doubt, the swift uncovering of the scam was due in large part to a willingness by Credit Suisse to provide information. In fact, the initial disclosure by the bank was a voluntary action. While not identifying a customer, the bank aided confused publishers immeasurably by its willingness to state that a particular individual was *not* a customer. Armed with evidence of a likely fraud, the Zurich police were able to launch the investigation that resulted in more thorough disclosures.

Certainly, the bank foresaw the potential for a tremendous amount of adverse publicity. The amount of public interest in the Howard Hughes autobiography had already reached a high level before the Hughes payments had been traced to the bank. The bank perhaps saw a golden opportunity to convert certain adverse publicity into evidence that the bankers of Zurich were at least as interested as Americans in seeing that justice be served.

A further thought as to the motivation of Credit Suisse is that the bank had obviously been fooled in an amateur confidence scheme. Although the bank suffered no financial loss as a result of its gullibility, the managers at Credit Suisse certainly did not want to appear to have been easily used.

Swiss Bank Corporation, the final depository of the Hughes money in Irvings' scheme, reacted in a considerably different manner when it learned that it was the custodian of illicit funds. It must have been obvious to SBC managers that their bank held funds of questionable ownership. After all, the bank had pointed out to Edith Irving that the name on her account was of doubtful authenticity. But the bank's reaction (in suggesting that the money be transferred to another branch) was to ensure that the sizeable balance remain in the bank. Further, when the Irvings furnished the details as to the money's whereabouts and the funds were impounded by the cantonal police, SBC still refused to comment publicly as to the ownership, balance, or even the existence of an account that may have been involved.

TAX EVASION—The Marc Rich Case

In October 1984, the U.S. government concluded a prolonged and tiring prosecution of the Swiss-based commodity trading company Marc Rich AG and its American counterpart, Clarendon Ltd. With an ultimate settlement of almost $200 million, the case was easily the largest successful tax fraud case in U.S. history.

---

*(She also served two months in a U.S. prison for her part in the scam, and Clifford Irving served 17 months of 2 1/2-year sentence.

Although not a banking story, the facts of the case are convenient for gaining an understanding of the differing viewpoints of Swiss and American governments on the subject of tax evasion. In addition, the case makes it possible to observe the ends to which the Swiss government will go to assure the right to privacy.

Both companies were controlled by commodities broker Marc Rich, a Belgian-born immigrant whose family fled to America to avoid persecution by the Nazis. A dropout from New York University, young Rich found a position in the mail room of the commodities trading firm of Philipp Brothers. In a modern version of an Horatio Alger success story, Rich took advantage of his endless energy and financial savvy to quickly skip his way up the ranks of the organization. As a trader with an astounding sense of timing, Rich is credited with playing a significant part in the rise of that company (now known as Philbro-Salomon) to the largest commodities trading firm in the world. Named the manager of the firm's Madrid office in 1973, Rich was considered by most insiders to be the heir apparent to the chief executive's position. But Rich, together with colleague Pincus "Pinky," Green, left the firm in 1974 to start their own firm, March Rich AG. The new company was based in Zug, Switzerland, in a canton known for favorable tax treatment for locally based but foreign-owned companies. Trading in gold, silver, strategic metals, arms, chemicals, grains, sugar, and oil, the firm was a phenomenal success. By 1982, it employed over 1,400 people in 30 countries. Much of the $10 billion in annual trading was carried out through Marc Rich International, the U.S. subsidiary located in New York.

Troubles began in 1981 with allegations that Marc Rich had violated federal price controls on crude oil. From 1973 to 1981, federal controls fixed artificially low prices on *old* oil (oil produced from older, existing wells) with higher price limits on *new oil* (oil produced from new discoveries). According to government investigators, Marc Rich had purchased, sold, repurchased, pooled, and pumped both old and new oil through a bewildering array of transactions (called daisy chains) that made it difficult, and in some cases, impossible, to determine the true origin of the crude. As a result, Marc Rich was able to market old oil as new oil, and pocket $100 million in illegal profits. Through a Panamanian subsidiary, the illegal profits were silently siphoned out of the United States to Switzerland.

The initial grand jury investigation into price-control violations found evidence of an entirely different criminal activity as well. In late 1977, at the height of the Iran hostage crisis, American firms were barred from trading with Iran. Evidence uncovered by the investigators indicated that Marc Rich's American operations had purchased 6.2 million barrels (with a $200 million price tag) from the National Iranian Oil Company in direct violation of the ban.

A singular aspect of American tax law is the definition given to income. Aside from specifically excluded sources, income taxes apply to "income from whatever source derived. . . ." The broad definition can easily be construed to include income from illegal activities, and the IRS has never been reluctant to press for collection of taxes on illegal profits. Consequently, not only was Marc Rich charged by the Justice Department with price violations, the company became the object of an IRS claim of evasion of taxes on the illegal profits. In addition, charges of trading with the enemy were brought against the company.

To cement their case, investigators subpoenaed a multitude of documents located at the parent company headquarters in Zug. As might be expected, the firm refused to comply with the subpoena, arguing that, as a Swiss firm, it was not subject to the jurisdiction of American courts. Investigators then appealed to government officials in Berne, who displayed a notably Swiss attitude to the whole affair. The officials pointed out that such crimes as the violation of price controls and trading with an enemy were totally foreign to them and they saw nothing in any treaties between the United States and Switzerland that obliged them to cooperate in the case.

As for the charges of tax evasion, the Swiss officials also refused to intervene, explaining (as they have so often in the past) that although they recognize tax evasion as an illegal action, it is not considered by them to be a *criminal* activity. Accordingly, the action did not warrant an invasion of the company's privacy.

To better understand the Swiss posture on this issue, it is necessary to look more closely at the difference in American and Swiss attitudes on the subject of tax evasion.

Tax Evasion—The United States and Switzerland

Individuals and companies that are required to pay taxes on income have available to them a variety of methods to minimize or eliminate entirely the amount of taxes paid. Some of the methods are legal, others not. The minimization of taxes through *legal* methods is customarily referred to as **tax avoidance.** Americans who avoid taxes through legal planning are protected from prosecution by tax authorities. The often quoted words of Judge Learned Hand (*Commissioner v. Newman*) emphasize this notion:

> Over and over again the courts have said that there is nothing sinister in
> so arranging one's affairs as to keep taxes as low as possible. Everybody
> does so, rich or poor, and all do right, for nobody owes any public duty
> to pay more than the law demands: taxes are enforced extractions, not
> voluntary contributions.

American tax authorities and courts take an entirely different approach on **tax evasion.** Defined as the use of *illegal* methods to reduce or eliminate tax liabilities, American law has long regarded tax evasion as a criminal activity. American taxpayers might also commit *tax fraud,* whereby they attempt to cover their illegal (evasive) activities by making false statements or filing false tax returns. In the United States, the distinction between tax evasion and tax fraud is not a significant one, as it is difficult to conceive of a tax-evasion scheme that would be conducted without a commission of tax fraud as well. Further, it is generally impossible to show that fraud has taken place until evasion has been proven. For that reason, the IRS generally pursues a course of charging tax evasion, and if successful in achieving a conviction against a taxpayer, then manages to collect a fraud penalty along with the disputed tax, other penalties, and interest. In addition, the hapless taxpayer can also receive a jail sentence.

Tax offenses in Switzerland can also be categorized as either evasion or fraud; but contrary to American law, the legal distinction between the two acts is very sharp. It is that distinction that has caused distress for American tax-enforcement officials.

The Swiss regard tax evasion as the underpayment of taxes that results from a failure to report income. Since the tax collection system in Switzerland is very efficient at collecting the proper amount of taxes at the source, tax evasion is difficult at best and certainly not regarded as an important problem. Consequently, tax evasion is *not* considered by the Swiss to be a crime. Resolution of tax-evasion cases is handled administratively and not in a court of law. Because of the insignificant nature of the offense, the secrecy of one's private affairs (including bank account records) cannot be breached because of a mere charge of tax evasion.

The act of deliberately deceiving the government through false and inaccurate statements is considered by the Swiss to be a commission of fraud, and the legal system of the country deals with the offense in a much harsher fashion. Unlike a tax-evasion case, where the extent of the punishment is simply a penal fine, a tax-fraud case may result in both fine and imprisonment. Moreover, because of the criminal nature of fraud, Swiss courts have been persuaded in some cases to order the release of otherwise secret information to aid in legal investigations.

As stated previously, Swiss government officials are adamant in their refusal to order the handing over of any documents to foreign-government investigators in absence of a specific agreement to do so. Even then, the crime being investigated must also be considered a crime on Swiss soil. Because substantially all of the charges brought against suspected tax cheaters in the United States are for tax evasion, appeals for help from Berne officials are routinely ignored. The Swiss have remained resolute on this point in spite of constant criticism by foreign law enforcement authorities. Even when world attention is on a battle to obtain documents held in their country, as happened in the Marc Rich case, the Swiss continue to exhibit the same fierce territorial ethic that characterized their ancestors in the mountainous stronghold.

The Battle for the Marc Rich Papers

In April 1982, the Justice Department found itself up against the stone wall of Swiss secrecy in the Marc Rich affair. The Swiss refusal to accept as legitimate any charges of price-control violations or trading with an enemy precluded any assistance on the basis of treaties between the governments. In addition, the ability to obtain the documents through charges of tax evasion appeared equally hopeless. To obtain any needed documents, the U.S. court would have to deal directly with Marc Rich. Following many months of requests and appeals, the patience of the court was exhausted. Judge Leonard Sand met the stout refusal of Marc Rich to deliver documents with a contempt of court fine of $50,000 per day against its American subsidiary.

The stalemate, and fines, dragged on for months. Each week a representative of the company appeared at the courthouse in New York to respectfully pay the fine. In an apparent effort to escape the contempt fine, the parent company in Zug managed to transfer the ownership of the American subsidiary by selling it to Alexander Hackel, a minor shareholder of the large company. Marc Rich International became Clarendon Ltd. The action did nothing to stop the ever-accruing fine, but it did succeed in infuriating Judge Sand. As a result, Sand ordered an immediate freeze on all of Clarendon's assets in the United States.

Eventually, even Marc Rich was unable to withstand the hemorrhaging caused by the heavy fines. The firm announced that it intended to comply with the U.S. government's demands and deliver the contested documents. In a surprise move, the Swiss government, which had been closely watching the affair, warned Marc Rich that it would be in violation of the secrecy laws of Switzerland if it acquiesced to the American demands. The specific law cited by the Swiss authorities related to the divulging of business secrets. The Swiss expressed concern that third parties could suffer from the information contained in the Marc Rich documents and that the disclosures of the proprietary information would constitute *economic espionage.*

Adding action to their words, Swiss government officials swooped in on the Marc Rich offices in Zug and hauled off truckloads of the documents desired by the Americans. The action resulted in sharp diplomatic exchanges between the two countries that added yet another skirmish to the battle.

And the $50,000 per-day fines continued. A new tactic on the American side was the filing of extradition papers on both Marc Rich and Pincus Green, under a 1900 treaty between the two countries. The Swiss refused to accept the extradition papers, pointing out that they were not prepared in one of the official·Swiss languages. They further noted that the U.S. government refuses to accept any papers that are not prepared in English. The U.S. promptly trotted out an interpreter who prepared the extradition papers in German. The Swiss, after a careful study of the papers, announced that the allegations cited in the extradition request were not covered in the 1900 treaty, and that extradition of both Rich and Green was simply not possible.

Settlement

Unable to withstand the constant drain on its resources because of the fines and the loss of business caused by the din of battle, Clarendon and Marc Rich agreed to plead guilty to the criminal tax charges. The nearly $200 million dollar settlement included back taxes, interest, penalties, and the $21 million already paid in contempt-of-court fines. The settlement also unfroze the assets of Clarendon Ltd. and permitted both companies to resume operations in the United States.

Lessons of the Battle

Despite the achievement of some success in the U.S. tax case against Marc Rich, the truth remains that the outcome was really a negotiated truce. The American government investigators were unable to prevail in their charges of illegal profiteering and trading with an enemy nation. Marc Rich paid tax evasion penalties without actually admitting a crime. That the government was unable to prevail can be blamed on its inability to force the government of Switzerland to cooperate in the case. Having achieved some degree of success in recent years in penetrating the veil of secrecy in Switzerland, the government learned a very hard lesson: penetration can only be achieved if there exists a specific agreement to aid in very specific crimes; otherwise, the expectation of help can only be considered foolhardy.

It is also clear from the case that tax evasion is one area in which the Swiss remain resolutely firm. They simply refuse to recognize the act as a criminal one and remain totally unsympathetic with the plight of American tax officials who must enforce laws that say otherwise. However, the refusal of the Swiss to recognize tax evasion as a crime does not imply that Americans can count on Swiss banks to easily hide unreported revenues. Other weapons in the arsenal of the IRS make it difficult for Americans to use foreign bank accounts to hide funds, whether they be honest earnings or ill-gotten gains. As more thoroughly explained in chapter 10, American taxpayers are required to disclose the existence of funds on deposit in other countries, and this provision in the law causes a tax evader to commit an additional act of fraud if the evader fails to report the funds.

A final note is necessary concerning a new tactic that emerged in the height of the Marc Rich battle: the use of a pecuniary fine against a domestic subsidiary to force its Swiss parent to act in violation of Swiss laws. While the tactic was not successful in forcing the parent company to violate the law, the bloodletting served well to eventually weaken and defeat the company. As more and more Swiss banks seek to expand their operations through branches and subsidiaries in the United States, there becomes a very real probability that the tactic may again be used by eager, but frustrated, American investigators.

5

Emerging Change

As we have seen, relations between U.S. investigators and Swiss government officials over financial records domiciled in Switzerland have sometimes been less than cordial. Disagreements have even resulted in sharp exchanges between diplomats of the two countries.

But there are signs of an end to diplomatic conflict and an emerging spirit of cooperation between the countries. The change stems in part from new legislation in Switzerland, making it possible for the U.S. to obtain greater amounts of information under the terms of the 1973 treaty. Switzerland's adoption of insider trading laws and the country's consideration of a money-laundering bill are the best examples of the spirit of cooperation on the part of the Swiss.

But the change is also the result of a new willingness on the part of the United States to observe all procedures when the information is legally available and show restraint when the desire for information runs counter to Swiss law.

INSIDER TRADING

In the United States, it has long been illegal for an investor to take advantage of *inside* information to earn profits in the securities markets.

Insider information may be defined as privileged information concerning future events or other disclosures likely to affect a company's stock price. The prohibition against using insider information not only applies to corporate insiders but extends to anyone who might have received an insider's tip. The Securities and Exchange Commission (SEC) is charged with the responsibility for investigating suspected insider trades and prosecuting offenders. Convicted violators of the trading statutes face prison terms, forfeiture of profits, and fines.

U.S. officials are all too aware of the possibility of illegal trades being executed on behalf of anonymous insiders by silent, foreign brokers residing beyond the jurisdiction of the SEC. To the extent that foreign brokers can be compelled to disclose the affairs of their customers, insiders have only limited security. On the other hand, offshore brokers who cannot be compelled to respond to SEC inquiries are in a unique position to conceal the complete security trading records of their clients.

Few countries have laws against insider trading. Prior to 1987, France, Great Britain, and Denmark were the only European countries to have enacted legislation forbidding the practice. Insider trading laws are even more rare outside of Europe. Even so, most countries are undesireable from the perspective of a would-be insider trader. The degree of confidentiality available in most trading centers is simply insufficient to provide any degree of comfort to surreptitious investors. It is for this reason that Switzerland became a popular place for illegal traders. As we have seen, not only are the ledgers of Swiss bankers closed to outsiders, but the bankers of Geneva, Lugano, and Zurich have the capability to act as securities brokers.

Historically, SEC investigators attempting to prove suspicions of insider trading have met with the familiar rebuffs of Swiss bankers. Nevertheless, increasing evidence of insider trading, persistent SEC requests for the delivery of bank records, fear of stiff penalties against Swiss banking subsidiaries in the United States, and concern for Switzerland's growing reputation as a haven for dirty money has led to a gradual change in thinking on the part of the Swiss.

The Swiss Banking Commission in January 1982 asked the federal government in Berne to consider making insider trading on stock exchanges a criminal offense. Knowing the legislative process in Switzerland moves, at best, with glacial speed, Swiss and U.S. officials set about reaching an interim solution that would allow Swiss cooperation in tracing insider trades. The result was a 1982 bilateral accord named Convention XVI. A complicated document, Convention XVI required Swiss banks to ask foreign customers wishing to trade in American stocks to sign a waiver allowing the banks to reveal the names of the traders should they subsequently become suspects in an SEC investigation. The accord required U.S. investigators to make formal requests for information through the U.S. Justice Department. An independent Swiss panel was given the power to review the evidence supplied by the U.S. officials and to approve or disapprove the request.

For obvious reasons, the extent to which Convention XVI was able to impede insider trading activities is unknown. No doubt the waiver scared off some would-be traders. Even more terrifying to the potential traders were the subsequent stories of successful SEC penetration of formerly secret accounts. Headline news stories told of government investigators, armed with detailed banking records, scoring with arrests, convictions, fines, and jail terms for formerly successful insider traders.

For example, in May 1984, the Swiss Federal Tribunal ordered five banks (Credit Suisse, Swiss Bank Corporation, Citibank, Chase Manhattan Bank, and Lombard, Odier & Cie) to make known the identities of traders who made massive purchases of Santa Fe International stock and stock options just prior to a $2.5 billion takeover by Kuwait Petroleum. A quick appeal made by the *unidentified customers* of the banks was rejected by the Swiss Federal Council and the SEC was handed all they requested. Felony charges were soon brought against several individuals, including a former director of Santa Fe and the Interior Minister of Qatar. The Santa Fe case represented the first time ever that the SEC managed to acquire bank information on suspected insider trading.

In spite of Convention XVI, the SEC did not score an uninterrupted series of successes in gaining access to Swiss ledgers. On a number of occasions, the Swiss government flatly refused to submit to SEC requests to help prosecute suspected insider trading cases. In refusing the requests, the Swiss insisted that SEC officials were merely on fishing expeditions and that the banks' records were unavailable in such circumstances.

Frustrated by what it felt was an unreasonable lack of cooperation, the SEC asked Congress to consider adopting *waiver-by-conduct* law. Under such a law, any act of engaging in a securities transaction in the U.S. securities markets would constitute an automatic waiver of any secrecy provision that a foreign financial institution or customer might claim. Thus, by the mere act of executing a trade on the New York Stock Exchange, a Swiss bank would automatically waive its right to secrecy regarding the trade. The proposed law found scant sympathy from U.S. congressional leaders who feared a massive exodus of foreign trading from American shores as well as depressed market prices for American securities. But the reaction from the Swiss government and the banking community of that country was nothing less than vitriolic. The Swiss charged that the imposition of SEC jurisdiction through a waiver-by-conduct law was an unwarranted attempt to spread the *lex Americana*. They warned that future cooperation with the U.S. authorities would become impossible if the United States continued on a course designed to encroach the sovereignty of foreign nations. The Swiss were especially indignant in view of their own public efforts to declare insider trading a criminal offense in Switzerland.

Incidents of insider trading exploded into major headline stories in late 1986 and throughout 1987. Certainly the most far reaching case was that of Dennis Levine. Acting on an anonymous tip, SEC enforcement officials compiled evidence of highly suspect trades being executed through the Caracas office of Merrill Lynch for the benefit of a bank account in the Bahamas. The bank, a subsidiary of Zurich's own Bank Leu, was forced by Swiss and Bahamian authorities to divulge the name of the account owner. The trader, Dennis Levine, subsequently pleaded quilty to making more than $12 million in profits on stocks of companies he knew to be takeover targets. Aside from giving up his profits, Levine was fined $362,000 and sentenced to two years in prison. But Levine also agreed to cooperate with SEC officials in providing further information of vast insider trading activities. That evidence has resulted in numerous convictions, including that of the infamous Ivan Boesky and several top-level managers of leading brokerage firms.

As the prosecution of insiders dominated news headlines in the United States in the mid-1980s, the Swiss government continued laboring to enact laws forbidding the practice. By October 1986, the upper house of the Swiss parliament finally agreed to a bill outlawing insider trading. One year later, the lower house voted overwhelmingly to approve the legislation and the law went into effect on July 1, 1988.

Unlike U.S. law, the bill was not aimed at every possible insider. Instead, the law took direct aim at insider trading in conjunction with large corporate events, such as mergers, takeovers, and new security issues. The language of the statute provides for penalties of prison terms or fines for convicted violators. A translation of the law appears in Appendix B.

The Swiss legislation was unquestionably welcome news to American investigators. Convention XVI, although moderately useful in the past, was superseded by a more effective and familiar investigative tool. With insider trading a crime under Swiss laws, SEC officials can now request inspection of Swiss bank account records of suspected insider trading under the terms of the 1973 Treaty of Mutual Assistance in Criminal Matters.

MONEY LAUNDERING

The signifigance of the insider trading law to American investigators was not lost on the Swiss. One month after the passing of the legislation, Switzerland's Minister of Justice Elisabeth Kopp, traveled to Washington to sign a Memorandum of Understanding with Attorney General Edwin Meese. The memorandum underscored the need for close cooperation between Switzerland and the United States in future criminal investigations. It sought to reaffirm a peaceful understanding between the two countries in the wake of vigorous diplomatic tugs-of-war. The Attorney General agreed to observe legal precedent and punctilio in all future petitions for legal assistance, and to display moderation and restraint whenever legal assistance is not possible. In a sense, the Americans agreed to avoid imposing their own regulatory views and philosophies on the Swiss and to abstain from threatening the Swiss with retaliatory legislation such as the waiver-by-conduct-rule.

The Swiss Minister, in return, granted to the Americans a splendid quid pro quo. In the memorandum, the Swiss agreed to recognize that money laundering is, in many cases, an undertaking of organized crime, and therefore a criminal act covered by the 1973 treaty. As such, legal assistance in tracing widespread money laundering became a new possibility for American investigators.

Structuring and Smurfing

As chapter 4 pointed out, the Bank Secrecy Act of 1970 imposed on American financial institutions a requirement that all transactions of $10,000 or more be reported to the federal government. Those criminals who routinely generated large amounts of cash from their ventures had much to fear from the new law. Obviously, automatic reporting of large cash movements would immediately fix a spotlight on illegal activities. Further, those individuals wishing to avoid the reporting of funds earned through *legal* means, and thus evade taxes on that income, were also at risk of attracting attention to their efforts.

Tax evaders and other criminals had immediate incentives to come up with new ways to avoid spotlighting their profits. Money laundering schemes were developed to aid in disguising the money. Money laundering is any process that gives money from illegal activities (dirty money) the appearance of respectability from honest labors (clean money).

It takes little imagination for a bank customer to get around the spontaneous reporting of banking transactions. One need merely structure all transactions so that banking credits and debits amount to less than $10,000 each. A depositor wishing to deposit, say, $15,000 of dirty money need only to make two deposits of $7,500 each to completely avoid bank reporting. Thus, with the advent of the Secrecy Act of 1970 came the birth of a new activity known as *structuring* or *smurfing* in which bank customers structure transactions in such a manner as to avoid focusing a federal spotlight on large currency movements.

The explosive growth in drug trafficking in the 1970s and 1980s gave a whole new dimension to money-laundering activities in the United States. Organized crime syndicates hire expert *smurfs* to convert dirty money to untraceable funds through legally unreportable methods. Often, teams of smurfs arrive in a city with millions of dollars of dirty cash, visit numerous banks and their branches, and quickly convert the cash into money orders, cashiers' checks, and bank drafts in amounts of $9,999 or less. Many of the instruments are redeposited through a system of bank accounts or transported overseas, to be later repatriated as clean money.

Money Laundering Control Act

Included as part of the widesweeping drug control legislation signed by President Reagan in late 1986 were provisions of the Money Laundering Control Act. The law was designed to directly combat money laundering schemes of drug traffickers, tax evaders, and other lawbreakers.

The new statutes made it a crime to structure any banking transaction to avoid reporting requirements under the Bank Secrecy Act. Further, banks were instructed to be on the alert for suspicious transactions that have the appearances of a laundering scheme. As protection for reporting dubious transacitons, the law absolved all financial institutions and their employees from any legal actions by customers as a result of disclosures pursuant to the new law.

A law that protects bankers from the wrath of customers whose account records have been divulged to authorities would be unthinkable in Switzerland. Yet it was against the backdrop of the American legislation that the Swiss Justice Minister Kopp signed the Memorandum of Understanding in November 1987. That memorandum, which held possibilities for American inspection of bank account records of suspected money launderers, is not the only sign of Swiss willingness to deal with the money laundering problem.

Prior to her meeting with the Attorney General, Kopp's own ministry issued a report to the Swiss parliament recommending that it declare money laundering a crime, carrying a mandatory prison sentence.

Given the extraordinarily slow pace of the Swiss legislative process, it is very unlikely that such a law could be enacted before the mid 1990s. Critics of the proposed legislation argue that the proposal appears to have a made-in-the-USA label. There is a strong feeling that, coming on the coattails of the insider trading laws, the money laundering law only confirms that Swiss statutes are now being determined by American economic and moral woes. Some bankers in Switzerland have taken a firm stand against the legislation and argue that their *code of due diligence* is sufficient to weed out occasional bad customers.

Whether Switzerland ever adopts an antimoney-laundering bill may be irrelevant. Given the gradually changing posture of the Swiss in matters relating to foreign investigation, those with large amounts of money to launder will not be hanging around the Bahnhofstrasse to discover whether money laundering becomes a crime in Switzerland. They have no doubt already begun their search for other, more secure havens for their dirty money.

IRAN-CONTRA AFFAIR

One of the more publicly visible attempts by U.S. investigators to gain access to *secret* Swiss bank account records was the successful effort in 1987 of the special prosecutor in the Iran-Contra scandal. The case provides a good final example for this chapter for several reasons. Certainly, the case is the most recent of the U.S.'s highly publicized attempts to obtain such data. As of this writing, the final outcome of the special prosecutor's investigation remains unclear. Aside from its timeliness, the case provides a revealing look at how the U.S. has learned to effectively use the 1973 treaty that makes disclosures of secret records possible. Absent from the proceedings are any of the inept maneuvers and retaliatory actions that characterized the Marc Rich investigation. Even more significant, however, are the reactions of the Swiss in the case. A number of steps taken by the Swiss authorities and the individual bank involved were clearly beyond normal expectations. Because of the importance of the case, the chain of events that culminated in the release of the bank records will be examined in some detail.

Following the December 2, 1986, press conference in which President Reagan announced evidence of money flowing from illegal Iranian arms sales to the coffers of Nicaraguan rebel (Contra) leaders, government investigators began searching for documents that could shed additional light on the matter. Some of the earliest information gathered included evidence that a Swiss bank account had been used to conceal the flow of the illicit funds. In particular, the evidence indicated that Marine Lt. Col. Oliver North, a member of the National Security Council, controlled an account at the Geneva branch of Credit Suisse. Realizing that the bank records could provide information on the total amount of arms sales, the disposition of the proceeds from the sales, and the principal participants involved, investigators were eager to get their hands on the information as quickly as possible.

Just four days after the initial disclosures of the Iran-Contra connection, the Justice Department publicly announced that it would request the legal assistance of the Swiss government in freezing the account (thus preventing any further movement of funds) and gaining access to its records under the provisions of the

1973 treaty. Two days later, in a note to Berne, the United States also notified the Swiss government that it would soon be seeking assistance with respect to the account at Credit Suisse and any other bank accounts that might come to light in the course of the investigation. The note was not an official request for aid but merely an indication that assistance from the Swiss would be sought. The reason for the informal notification is unclear, but the U.S. officials presumably wanted additional time to prepare a precisely worded request. The officials had obviously learned from past action that haste and imprecision would hinder the prompt peeking into Swiss ledgers.

Not having received an official request to provide aid to the investigation, the Swiss Foreign Ministry nonetheless notified Credit Suisse, and the other two large banks, that it had received notification of the intent of the U.S. to seek legal assistance from the Swiss. The Swiss officials requested the banks to determine if they possessed accounts that might be of interest to the U.S. officials and, if so, to put the accounts under close scrutiny. It should be emphasized that the actions by the Justice Department (in making known their intentions) and by the Foreign Ministry (in advising the banks of the U.S. intentions), were unusual in nature. But Credit Suisse added an additional, unexpected dimension to the preliminary proceedings. Acting on its own accord, the Geneva branch went beyond providing close scrutiny and took the precautionary measure of immediately freezing North's account and an additional account that it believed would become the target of American inquiry. Further, the bank publicly acknowledged that it had taken such action. A spokesman for the bank announced that the action was taken to allow the U.S. sufficient time to lodge a formal request. He emphasized, however, the temporary nature of the freeze and mentioned that without formal notification from the Swiss government within two weeks the blockage would automatically be lifted.

Within two weeks, however, the American officials delivered their formal request, in French, to the Swiss officials in Berne. The Swiss began the task of testing the request for its propriety under the provisions of the 1973 treaty. Accepting it as valid, the government ordered an immediate freezing of the suspected accounts. At the time of the official freeze, the accounts contained a combined balance of nearly $8 million.

The Swiss order also set into motion the remaining steps necessary to discard the shroud of secrecy surrounding the account records and deliver that information to U.S. investigators. Swiss law provides that any interested party may appeal the decision requiring the banks to divulge the information. The parties may be the individuals or companies owning the accounts or any third party that has been involved in a transaction with the account but would suffer unnecessary embarrassment from the release of that information. Appellants have 10 days from the announcement of the freezing of the account to file an appeal with the Swiss Ministry of Justice and Police.

At the end of the appeal period, the Ministry reported that eight appeals had been filed with its office, but, as a matter of policy, refused to disclose the identity of those seeking appeal. Press reports in the United States indicated that Oliver North was not among those appealing the U.S. request. But reports did indicate that three of North's associates were asking for protection under secrecy laws: Albert Hakim, an Iranian-born American businessman; M. Ghorbanifar, an Iranian businessman and arms dealer; and Richard V. Secord, a retired U.S. Air Force general. Each asked the ministry to reject the American petition on the grounds that the U.S. investigation was for political rather that criminal offenses.

By mid-February 1987, the Swiss Ministry of Justice and Police had denied the appeals of all parties. The appellants had available to them one remaining avenue of escape from the American investigators: appeal to the Swiss Federal Tribunal. Located in Lausanne, the three-member Federal Tribunal is the supreme court of Switzerland. Appellants to the Federal Tribunal are entitled a full hearing, and an appeal before the court can often take years before a decision is handed down. As expected, each party in this case filed an appeal with the high court, building their cases around the argument that they were being persecuted by U.S. officials for political activities. The U.S. special prosecutor, Lawrence Walsh, expressed discouragement at the prospect of a superannuated legal process that could only delay his efforts.

With surprising alacrity, the Federal Tribunal rejected all appeals by August 1987, paving the way for the bank documents to be turned over to the special prosecutor's office. In rejecting the appeals, the court noted that neither selling arms nor giving money to political groups can be considered a criminal act under Swiss law. However, the court decided that secrecy could be lifted because the participants in the affair were under investigation for fraudulently deceiving the U.S. government in the conduct of their covert operations.

Following the court's decision, Credit Suisse began the process of inventorying each document and determining whether the material should be turned over. Also, a final review by a Swiss magistrate was made to determine whether the release of any of the material would violate national security or cause harm to the banking system. A first installment of copies of the bank records was delivered to members of Walsh's staff in mid-September. The final installment, consisting of copies of thousands of documents weighing 60 pounds, was delivered to the investigators in early November.

Certain conclusions, significant for our purposes, can be drawn from the events described. Not the least significant is that the U.S. Justice Department, acting on behalf of the special prosecutor's office, has shown that it has finally mastered the process necessary to effectively cooperate with the Swiss government in extracting desired records. Fortunately for the special prosecutor's office, the dialogue between the two countries remained constructive and was not reduced to a state of ineffective diplomatic dialectics. The investigators achieved their objectives through systematic and timely actions, without resorting to threats or fines.

Also noteworthy in the case was the apparent willingness of a bank in Switzerland to voluntarily block accounts which it believed would become the target of a U.S. investigation. Without compulsory notification from government authorities, Credit Suisse took this action at the first hint of legal improprieties by the account owners. The action is somewhat reminiscent of the Swiss decision to voluntarily freeze various accounts owned by Ferdinand Marcos when it appeared that a formal request to do so was forthcoming.

Finally, the speed in which the matter was ultimately settled is truly significant. From the first hint that a scandal might exist to the date of the release of Swiss bank-account data relating to the scandal took exactly 11 months and one day. Not only did U.S. officials move quickly in preparing a properly executed request for legal assistance, but the court abandoned the plodding pace that characterizes most Swiss legal proceedings.

Both the judicial and the legislative branches of the U.S. government have sought to balance the right of privacy for citizens with the needs of government to probe. In recent years, however, the balance seems to have tipped in favor of the IRS, the SEC, and other investigative agencies. Additional weight has been provided by actions of the Swiss government. In particular, the signing of the 1973 Treaty of Mutual Assistance in Criminal Matters, the enactment of anti-insider trading laws, and the proposed ban on money laundering schemes have proven to be invaluable aids in tracking foreign criminal activity.

In fairness to the Swiss banking system, it should be said that there has never been a single instance of a foreign authority penetrating the veil of secrecy without due appeal to the Swiss government. And appeals have only been decided in favor of foreign investigators when ample evidence suggests that the criminal activity has in fact occurred. Regulatory fishing expeditions have never been successfully mounted by foreign examiners and are unlikely to ever occur.

Thus, in the absence of criminal behavior, Swiss banking secrecy remains as airtight as ever for foreign customers, and privacy for law-abiding Americans remains a principal advantage for owning such an account. In part II of this book, a variety of other reasons to have an account in a Swiss bank will be examined, and some reasons for which a Swiss account would *not* be appropriate will be suggested. In addition, for those who find they desire the Swiss touch in their personal financial affairs, a complete description of the process of opening and maintaining an account is outlined.

Part II
How to Open and Maintain a Swiss Bank Account

6

Why Should You Have
a Swiss Bank Account?

SOME AMERICANS REACT TO THE SUBJECT OF SWISS BANK ACCOUNTS BY IMMEDIATELY questioning the legality of owning such accounts. Although an impression of illegality may exist in the minds of many, bank accounts in Switzerland are perfectly legal for Americans to own. For that matter, American citizens may legally own accounts in any country as long as balances exceeding $10,000 are reported annually to the IRS.

Perhaps the impression of unlawful ownership exists because of sensational news stories implicating Swiss banks in illegal transfers of money. As we have seen, some Swiss banks have found themselves to be unwitting partners in a number of highly publicized scandals. No doubt the legendary secrecy of Switzerland is also cause for suspicion of account owners. Complete financial privacy that is guaranteed by federal statutes is uncommon in our modern world.

But it is unfair to assume that a foreign-owned Swiss account signals probable immoral activities or evidence of ill-gotten gains. Those who react to Swiss bank accounts with righteous disdain are simply unaware of the many reasons why a person might find one useful. Hundreds of thousands of foreigners, including a good many Americans, have discovered that Swiss banks provide assurances and services that cannot be matched in their own countries.

What are the reasons for maintaining a bank account in Switzerland? To give as complete an answer to this question as possible, it is necessary to address two corollary questions:

1. Why would anyone want an American bank account?
2. Why have others opened Swiss bank accounts?

71

WHY WOULD ANYONE WANT AN AMERICAN BANK ACCOUNT?

Recent years have shown American bankers to be feeble guardians of customers' deposits and stockholders' investments. Although bankers are in the business of earning profits by taking risks, an abundance of evidence indicates that bankers are ignoring the limits of normal risktaking and granting an increasing number of loans to unqualified borrowers possessing little or no chance of repaying the debts.

When an occasional bad loan occurs, the bank is forced to write it off the books. Nearly every bank possesses resources sufficient to allow recovery from an occasional bad loan. In fact, bankers actually expect to write off a number of bad loans each year. However, if a bank makes bad loans on a massive scale, it may not be possible to simply write them off and continue operations. Further, large loan losses not only deplete a bank's resources but make headline news and can scare away customers desiring more safety for their savings. The result can be insolvency, forcing a bank to close its doors and its owners to suffer write-offs of their own. This is known as a bank failure.

Bank Failures

Once rare in the United States, bank failures have become commonplace in the 1980s. From the end of World War II to 1981, an average of only six banks failed in the United States each year. But in 1982 the financial news stunned many Americans by reporting an incredible 42 failures. Bankers today are already referring to 1982 as *the good old days*. The data portrayed in Fig. 6-1 explains why.

Not shown in the graph are the 4,000 banks that failed in 1933, at the depths of the Great Depression. The relatively high numbers between 1934 through 1945 represent the final casualties of the depression era. As we will see, the much greater numbers of the 1980s are the result of an entirely different set of problems.

Perhaps more startling than the number of bank failures is the Federal Deposit Insurance Corporation's (FDIC) official list of *problem banks*. The FDIC rates banks based on a variety of factors included in its so-called CAMEL formula (capital, assets management, earnings, and liquidity). A problem bank is one whose overall health has deteriorated to an unstable and life-threatening condition. The FDIC carefully monitors the vital signs of all problem banks since they are prime candidates for future failures. As Fig. 6-2 indicates, the number of problem banks, like the number of bank failures, has achieved unprecedented heights in recent years.

As for nonfailing, nonproblem banks, the level of profits in recent years hardly presents a picture of health. In 1987, profits for all commercial banks, when measured as an overall return on assets, amounted to a hideously low .13%, the worst performance level since the depression.

While a good many of the institutions failing in recent years are smaller banks, the very large are by no means immune to bad fortune. In May 1984, one of the nation's largest banks, Continental Illinois National Bank & Trust Co. of Chicago, secretly announced to federal regulators that it was unable to meet its

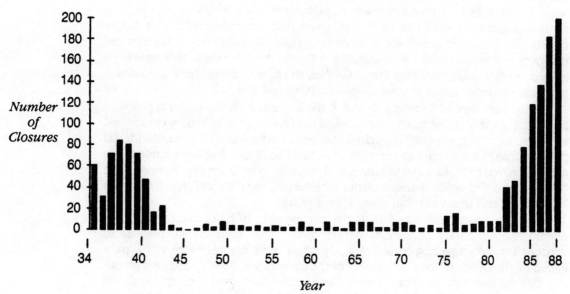

Fig. 6-1. Graph of bank failures—1934-1988.

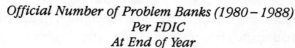

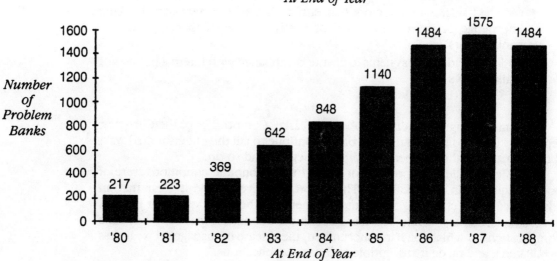

Fig. 6-2. Graph of problem banks—1980-1988.

depositors' claims. In quickly arranged emergency meetings with the FDIC, the Federal Reserve, and representatives of several major banks, a bailout plan was worked out. The FDIC agreed to contribute $1.5 billion to Continental Illinois with the other major banks kicking in an additional half a billion dollars to prop up the collapsing bank. The bank was saved, but the catastrophe that failure would have caused is almost too terrible to imagine. At minimum, it is estimated that over 100 smaller banks with deposits at Continental Illinois would have been ruined along with the banking giant. Further, the failure would have placed several hundred more banks in immediate danger of collapse.

Some have argued that bank failure in the United States is a regional problem and point to the fact that nearly one-third of the failed banks in 1987 were located in Texas. Certainly, unusual drought conditions and a slump in worldwide oil prices contributed in part to the rash of failures in Texas. But the problem has already proven to be national in scope, and virtually every state experienced bank failure during the 1980s. Bankers currently joke that the only difference between Texas banks and those in other states is four years.

Why do American banks fail? Is the current rash of bank failures merely a reaction to temporary conditions or are there more fundamental reasons to account for the staggering losses? A study of all bank failures since 1979, published by the Office of the Comptroller of the Currency in 1988, presented revealing data on this subject. The Comptroller's report indicated that, in nearly all cases, the cause could be considered *internal* rather than the result of broader, economic conditions. The report disclosed that of all banks studied,

- 89% had poor policies and planning
- 81% had nonexistent or poorly followed loan policies
- 63% maintained inadequate controls or supervision of key bank officers
- 59% had inadequate problem loan identification systems
- 60% had boards of directors that either "lacked the necessary banking knowledge or were uninformed or passive in their supervision of the banks' affairs"
- 69% had inadequate systems to ensure compliance with internal policies or banking laws

In summarizing the findings, Robert L. Clarke, Comptroller of the Currency, reported, "Our findings suggest that banks continue to fail the old-fashioned way: through managerial incompetence, director neglect and so on."

The Comptroller's report did not suggest that economic conditions were of no consequence in bank failures. The report, however, made it clear that an adverse economic climate is contributory rather than the prime cause for failures. According to Clarke, "While depressed economic conditions may have been the complications to which the bank succumbed, the disease of managerial weakness debilitated it and made it susceptible to those complications."

Lesser Developed Country Loans

To date, very few failures have been associated in any way with bad loans made to foreign governments. Although bankers may be reluctant to admit it, loans outstanding to lesser developed countries represent the greatest danger to American banking that the industry has had to face in modern times. Lesser Developed Country (LDC) loans represent a powder keg that, if allowed to explode, could bring the American banking industry to an all time low in terms of profits and public trust and an all time high in terms of loan write-offs and banking failures.

While American bankers have long made their resources available to help finance foreign governments and their modernization projects, the amount of foreign borrowing reached record highs in the 1970s. The massive borrowing by developing countries, particularly in Central and South America, was deemed prudent by American bankers because of the modest level of interest rates and encouraging forecasts of economic growth in many third-world countries. U.S. banks eagerly loaned hundreds of billions of dollars to finance development efforts.

But during the late 1970s and the first half of the 1980s, the world witnessed an unanticipated downturn in worldwide economic growth together with unprecedented heights for interest rates. The economic state for many LDCs was exacerbated by huge increases in populations and unemployment.

A danger flag for American bankers was raised in August 1982, as Mexico announced that it was incapable of repaying currently maturing debt. American bankers agreed to *reschedule* the loans, allowing the Mexican government to put off repayment until a later date. But the Mexican problem proved to be only the first signal of a much larger regional problem. Other danger flags were hoisted to fly in the face of American bankers, who dutifully scurried to reschedule more and more Latin American debt. To bankers, the term *rescheduled loan* has a softer sound than *defaulted loan* and by delaying the payment of the debt, the banks were able to avoid the embarrassing write-off of billions of dollars. In the meantime, the lenders were able to accrue additional interest, albeit at often lowered rates.

The first real shock to the American banking community came in February 1987, when Brazil's President José Sarney announced that his country was not only incapable of repaying $68 billion of currently maturing debt, but was suspending all future interest payments as well. The announcement caused many banks in the United States to establish reserves to help absorb possible future write-offs. Citibank led the way by adding $3 billion to its reserves.

Establishing loan-loss reserves is a proper course of action for banks facing probable write-offs. But with $400 billion of LDC loans at the end of 1987, the loan-loss reserves of American banks remained at a meager 25 percent of the LDC debt on their books. The unwillingness to admit larger future losses reflects perhaps a hopeful rather than realistic view of future events.

A number of smaller U.S. banks have agreed to *swap* the balances of their maturing LDC loans for interest-bearing *exit bonds* issued by the debtor governments. The banks, however, are not escaping entirely from loss. In the negotiated swaps, the banks have been receiving about half of the original amount of the debt, forcing write-offs for the remainder. Larger banks have generally avoided the swaps, preferring to live with the illusion of eventual collectibility.

American bankers are not the only lenders to be caught in the death grip of LDC loans. Japan and a number of European countries have also provided development loans to third-world countries, but American banks are by far the largest lenders. American banks also have a unique problem not faced by other lenders: loans to LDCs are almost always denominated in dollars. In recent years, foreign lenders have watched their risk of loss be cut by as much as 50 percent as the dollar has sharply fallen against other major currencies. Thus, losses from default experienced by the foreign lenders are made up by favorable swings in the foreign exchange rates. American banks, on the other hand, are not similarly affected by changes in the value of the dollar, and must recover the full amount of their debt in order to keep from suffering losses.

Federal Deposit Insurance Corporation

Customers of American banks are repeatedly told that their deposits will not be lost because of bank failure. The Federal Deposit Insurance Corporation (FDIC) provides the protection at most banks in the United States. As long as the FDIC itself avoids bankruptcy, depositors can count on a relatively quick recovery of the deposits squandered by their friendly neighborhood bankers. But ironically, the safety provided to depositors through deposit insurance may well prove to be the downfall of FDIC

Congress created the FDIC in 1934 to ease the fears of depositors who had witnessed the closure of thousands of banks during the first few years of the Great Depression. Originally providing deposit insurance on all balances up to $2,500, the limit has been gradually raised through the years to present $100,000 level.

The FDIC does not provide protection to all banking deposits in the United States. Because of the $100,000 maximum, deposits at many insured banks are not fully covered. Further, approximately 2 percent of the nation's banks have chosen not to become members of the FDIC, leaving their depositors' accounts entirely uninsured. For these reasons, only two-thirds of the total dollars on deposit in U.S. banks are covered by deposit insurance.

FDIC officials never pass up the opportunity to repeat the statement that "no depositor has ever lost a penny of an FDIC-insured deposit." However, it is costing the FDIC more and more each year to continue making the claim. Payouts to depositors in 1987 amounted to $4.6 billion, of which $2.5 billion was hoped to be recovered from sales of assets of defunct banks. The net losses must be made up from insurance premiums collected from member banks as well as investments in the Deposit Insurance Fund. At the end of 1987, the Deposit Insurance Fund amounted to $18.3 billion, or when stated in terms of 1987 payout multiples, four remaining years.

While everyone agrees that the FDIC has eased depositors' concerns for the safety of their money, many economists charge that the insurance is actually detrimental to the health of the banking system and accounts for a good many of the high number of failed banks. The critics argue that the very existence of deposit insurance encourages banks to take unreasonable risks in the pursuit of profits. If a bank succeeds in high-risk ventures, the rewards are higher reported profits and increased managerial compensation. If a bank experiences unrecoverable losses, the management will never have depositors' losses on their consciences, for the depositors will always be protected by the FDIC, and only the bank's shareholders can be the losers.

History clearly suggests that the criticism is valid. From 1908 to 1917, seven states experimented with deposit insurance for their own state-chartered banks. The experience was the same in all states: insured banks failed at a significantly higher rate than similar, uninsured banks. With the exception of a deposit insurance program in Mississippi, all deposit insurance funds met an early death by bankruptcy. Mississippi's fund managed to last until 1930, when it met a similar fate.

While deposit insurance may have freed bank managers from the discipline of making rational decisions about the creditworthiness of borrowers, it has also freed bank customers from worry about the safety of their deposits. But most critics argue that if deposit insurance did not exist, customers would be forced to make rational decisions about the creditworthiness of the banks. The institutions would then need to attract customers based on financial strength rather than the number of drive-up windows or the color of checks available.

The FDICs Deposit Insurance Fund is not limitless. As of the end of 1987, resources amounted to approximately 1% of the total of insured deposits. An economic collapse of even mild proportions could instantly deplete the fund.

Finding a worthwhile alternative to bank accounts presents a challenge. The normal alternative is to open an account at a savings and loan association. But if the banking industry has proven to be less than stellar, the savings and loan industry can only be termed a black hole.

Savings and Loan Failures

Savings and loan associations (S&Ls) have always been popular savings alternatives to commercial banks. At present, an estimated 100 million Americans hold over $1 trillion in various accounts at S&Ls. But Americans are just beginning to realize that the S&L industry is an advanced state of crisis.

Of the nation's 3,000 S&Ls at the end of 1988, no less than 350 were insolvent, with assets (consisting principally of uncollected loans) amounting to less than debts. Another 500 were barely solvent and sliding toward the edge of insolvency. While one half of the remaining S&Ls are continuing to show profits, the remainder are generating losses to erode what remains of the capital they still possess. Overall, the industry's operating losses in 1987 and 1988 averaged $1 billion a month.

Many blame the S&L problem on deregulation of the industry in the early 1980s. With the blessing of Congress, the industry was allowed to expand its conservative home-loan business into new and unfamiliar business opportunities with potentially superior financial returns. While many S&Ls took chances on high-rise office buildings and speculative industrial parks, others completely abandoned real estate activities in favor of financing car dealerships, fast food chains, and other novel lines of business. To say that sailing into the uncharted waters of commercial lending was a mistake for the S&L industry would be a gross understatement. Many experts believe that the industry's abandonment of real estate-based lending is the largest single reason why the industry is now awash in a sea of red ink.

There is also evidence that a significant portion of the failures was the direct result of fraud in the industry. Official estimates are that as much as one half of the S&Ls closed in recent years were victims of fraudulent schemes by S&L management, their customers, or both.

The Federal Savings & Loan Insurance Corporation (FSLIC) has managed to pay off all depositors to date, but it has refrained from shutting down large numbers of insolvent S&Ls because it simply does not have the funds to pay off the depositors. Even if it had abundant funds to pay off depositors, it is unlikely that the FSLIC could close all insolvent S&Ls, as the FSLIC simply does not have the personnel to do so. The staff was hard pressed to come to the rescue of the 205 institutions that were forced to close in 1988. Thus, financially distressed S&Ls continue to keep their doors open and continue taking new deposits, which will most likely require FSLIC repayment in the future.

Paying off depositors of failed S&Ls has long ago depleted the insurance fund, and the FSLIC is now forced to borrow money to shut down defunct institutions. In the summer of 1987, Congress approved a plan allowing the fund to borrow up to $10.8 billion to pay off customers of hundreds of S&Ls. The amount, however, only served to prime the federal pump. Additional borrowings in 1988 were followed by a $50 billion bailout plan proposed by President Bush three weeks after his inauguration. In the proposal, the largest government bailout in history, bonds would be sold to help finance the closing of the nation's thrift institutions. The price tag represents $200 dollars for each American citizen.

Others have proposed a merger of the FSLIC and FDIC in an effort to provide additional reserves for the ailing S&L industry. Critics point out that while the plan may succeed in speeding up the closing of already bankrupt thrifts, it would also accelerate the depletion of the FDIC's reserves, which are hardly sufficient to keep up with the failing-bank problem.

Both the FDIC and FSLIC were created by Congress to provide protection to the customers of banks and S&Ls. It is ironic that the two insurance funds must look to Congress to provide them with protection from depositors wanting their money back. The federal government has the monumental task of bailing out the insurance funds as it considers how to craft an Endangered Species Act to preserve banks and thrift institutions.

Given the infirm state of the American savings industry, it is indeed a pertinent question to ask why anyone would want an American bank account. In the author's opinion, domestic banks are still the best institutions available to Americans for handling routine transfer payments through demand deposits (checking accounts). Checking accounts provide temporary lodging for funds that will soon become expenditures. The convenience of such accounts far outweigh the risk of loss or annoyance of waiting for a governmental insurance fund to restore the balance if the institution becomes insolvent.

However, checking accounts with balances normally in excess of insured levels pose a very real problem for the account holders. Because *each* account in an

FDIC or FSLIC insured institution is covered up to a $100,000 maximum, it is possible to obtain coverage on amounts in excess of the maximum by spreading the balance among multiple accounts. Customers holding excessively large balances need to weigh the risk of a single checking account with the cost and bother of maintaining multiple accounts. For those customers who find multiple accounts too burdensome, a rigid analysis of bank solvency should be performed before allowing uninsured excesses to reside in a single account.

For customers with savings to deposit, American banks and thrift institutions may have outlasted their purpose. Statistics show that it is increasingly harder to find a reputable savings institution with a balance sheet portraying a solvent financial position. A customer with funds exceeding the insured level in an open savings account, passbook account, or certificate of deposit is playing a fool's game. For those with balances less than the insured level, the danger is not negligible. Anyone who has lived through the ordeal of awaiting repayment of an account balance while the FDIC personnel check records behind the locked bank doors will attest to the wisdom of seeking a healthy financial institution. The wait is not only nerve racking, it is noninterest bearing.

Still, statistics show that most Americans are not worried about their savings balances, as long as the *Insured FDIC* or *Insured FSLIC* decal adorns their savings institution's doors. Presumably, the customers rely on the FDIC or the FSLIC to bail them out and the U.S. Congress (and ultimately the U.S. taxpayer) to bail out the insurance funds.

Other Americans feel that the peace of mind from FDIC insured savings is no more comforting than that achieved from inhabiting a condemned building that is insured against fire by a bankrupt casualty insurance company seeking a taxpayer bailout. Accordingly, they have abandoned their insured accounts in favor of safer, overseas accounts.

WHY HAVE OTHERS OPENED SWISS BANK ACCOUNTS?

Long before American savings institutions became unsafe depositories for customers' savings, many Americans opened bank accounts in Switzerland. And even if banks and other thrift institutions in the United States were safe havens for those wanting to protect their earnings, Americans would no doubt continue to seek the services and expertise offered by Swiss bankers. Americans would not be alone in this practice, as savers from nearly every country in the world also avail themselves of the banking services offered by the Swiss.

Why have people around the globe abandoned their countries' own banks in favor of those in Switzerland? There are two broad reasons:

1. Switzerland provides a haven for *frightened money*. Money is said to become frightened when it is exposed to the threat of confiscation, unreasonable taxes, and erosion of value. Switzerland has proven to be a place to calm depositors' fears of governmental policies and world events that erode or wipe out savings and rob depositors of financial security.

2. Switzerland allows an unusually broad array of financial services to be offered to bank customers. Although not all services are unique to Switzerland, in no other place are they so concentrated in single institutions, administered by bankers who are considered by other bankers to be paragons of knowledge, understanding, and discretion.

A Haven for Frightened Money

Those interested in preserving a portion of their earnings have found a variety of means to accomplish that objective. Some prefer to store their wealth in *hard* or tangible form, such as art, jewelry, bullion, etc. Others prefer to hold indirect claims on assets in the form of stocks or bonds. Most individuals prefer to maintain some portion of their savings in the form of money. As with all investments, some forms have proven to be better stores of value than others.

When savings take the form of tangible assets or paper securities, U.S. banks play only a minor role in the savings process by making safe deposit boxes available. Banks play a more important role for savers of money by providing accounts to store the funds and compensating savers with interest on the balances.

Americans are well aware of the general tendency for prices to rise (inflation). Everyone has heard commentary on how little a dollar will buy compared with an earlier time. Because changes in price levels cause the purchasing power (or *real value* of money) to decline, it can be said that inflation erodes the value of money on deposit. Savers have found that, even allowing for interest, they frequently suffer a loss of purchasing power by holding their savings in the form of dollars in bank accounts.

Even if price levels did not change, it is still possible for currencies to lose value vis-à-vis other currencies. A decrease in a currency's value against other currencies is referred to as a *weakening* of that currency, or in more direct terms, a foreign exchange loss. Gains are also possible in the event that a currency of a country *strengthens* against those of other countries. Foreign exchange losses are of little concern to those who do not spend their savings on foreign goods. But for those who do purchase foreign goods or services, exchange losses result in serious declines in the purchasing power of savings.

In the worst possible scenario, a combination of high rates of inflation and foreign exchange losses can result in a considerable loss in savings. This has been particularly true in recent years for those unlucky enough to hold dollars in their bank accounts. And since banks in the United States only allow dollars to be held on deposit in their accounts, customers have experienced the double-whammy of having inflation and the weakening U.S. dollar conspire to erode whatever wealth may be stored in the banks.

Like nonmonetary investments, some currencies have proven to be better stores of value than others. Although it is possible for Americans to obtain and hold *hard* currencies, the difficulties of the exchange process and foregone interest on the savings generally discourage savers from implementing such a savings strategy.

Unlike American banks, those in Switzerland are able to offer bank accounts that may hold U.S. dollars, Swiss francs, French francs, English pounds, Japanese yen, and other currencies as well. Not only may a savings account balance be denominated in each of these currencies, it may be comprised of a combination as well.

Interest-bearing savings accounts are most often denominated in Swiss francs. Because of the proven hardness of the franc, foreigners have found it possible to escape from declining world values for their domestic currencies and avoid inflation losses as well. Americans who have chosen to hold savings balances in Swiss francs rather than dollars have greatly benefited in recent years. Figure 6-3 points out the dramatic effect of choosing an alternative savings currency.

The graph compares the effect of a 30 percent tax-bracket American depositing $10,000 into a 3.5% yield Swiss savings account or in a typical 5.0% American savings account. U.S. taxes are assumed to have been paid out of the American savings account. Both Swiss and U.S. taxes are assumed paid out of the Swiss franc account (adjusted for permissible refunds and tax credits) at current exchange rates for each year.

The superior returns from the Swiss account are clearly due to the strength of the Swiss franc in world markets vis-à-vis the U.S. dollar. Further proof of the franc's strength is evidenced by the fact that in 1970 one Swiss franc could be exchanged for 23¢, while today it is worth 67¢.

Although some might scoff at a savings account that only pays 3.50% interest, the truth is that the interest is merely icing on the cake. When adjusted for foreign exchange swings, even a 0% interest rate in the Swiss franc account has generally proven superior to a 5.00% U.S. dollar account. Figure 6-4 shows the same analysis except that the Swiss-franc account is now assumed to earn 0% interest.

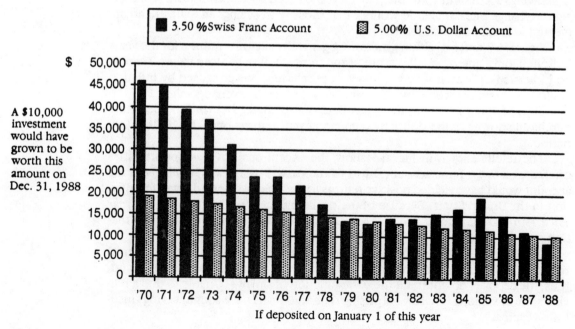

Fig. 6-3. A 3.5 % Swiss franc account versus a 5.5 % American dollar account.

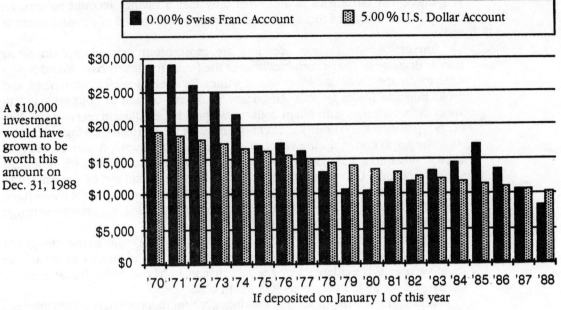

A $10,000 investment would have grown to be worth this amount on Dec. 31, 1988

Fig. 6-4. A 0 % Swiss franc account versus a 5.5 % American dollar account.

It is clear from the chart that a Swiss franc account earning a 0% return (such as a checking account) would have produced a higher return than a traditional U.S. savings account in 13 of the past 19 years. Faced with such returns from foreign exchange rates, it is little wonder that those with savings in Switzerland are pleased to accept a 3.50% return.

Figures 6-3 and 6-4, although showing generally superior returns for the years indicated, only give a partial picture of the franc's ability to store value. There is no indication, however, whether losses in purchasing power caused by inflation could have been overcome by offsetting gains in foreign exchange rates.

Figure 6-5 demonstrates the total effect of exchange rates *and* the declining purchasing power of the dollar by comparing *real* returns over the 1970 – 1988 period.

The results shown in Fig. 6-5 show the exceptional savings opportunities offered by a Swiss franc account. In 15 of the past 19 years, a 3.50% Swiss franc account would have yielded positive returns to the holder when adjusted for inflation in the United States. Because of the declining value of the dollar, *in no year since 1970 has a 5.00% U.S. dollar account yielded a positive return on an inflation-adjusted basis.*

The record of American banks in constantly providing inferior (negative) returns clearly shows that the accounts are not providing a store of value and, thus, the deposits do not fulfill the basic function of savings. Unable to find a reliable store of value, it is hardly surprising that Americans have sought savings institutions abroad.

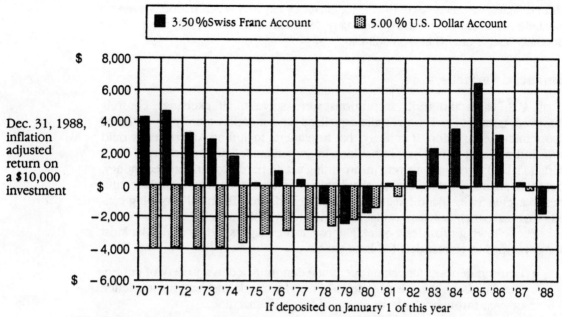

Fig. 6-5. *Real Returns in Swiss franc and dollar accounts.*

There are often other, more compelling fears that motivate non-American savers to search for safe havens. Most center around governmental policies that impose severe financial penalties on those who wish to save a portion of their earnings. Some countries mandate artificially determined rates of interest that result in domestic yields significantly below those paid in other countries. Others have instituted highly progressive taxation policies, which deviate significantly from world levels. As inflation pushes earnings into ever higher tax brackets, the taxes become confiscatory penalties. Once again, the only course of action for rational savers is to seek havens in which to escape financial repression.

Economic laws do not discriminate between savers in developed and third-world countries. The motivation for sending the savings abroad is frequently the same: to place personal savings in a form that will ensure that it is saved and can be used in the future.

Money fleeing from abnormal risks at home is frequently referred to as *capital flight.* Economists tend to agree that capital flight can be harmful if the depleted country is a third-world nation attempting to advance its stage of industrialization. Not only are needed funds lost, but the drain exerts a downward pressure on the home country's currency in the foreign exchange markets. The effect is the same, if less acute, for major industrialized nations. Repatriated funds, on the other hand, provide money for development and bolster local currencies.

It is not surprising that governments have reacted strongly to resident savings being sent abroad to foreign bank accounts. Nearly every country has enacted restrictions aimed at either limiting or banning such outflows.

Those few that generally allow free monetary transfers could easily change their regulations. History has shown that nearly every country (including the

United States) moves quickly to restrict currency exports when national interests are believed to be in jeopardy. For many savers around the world, the rule has become "Get it out while you still can."

Financial Services

If all U.S. bank and thrift institutions were solvent, all exchange controls removed, taxation levels universally equalized, and inflation merely an outdated economic phenomenon, it is likely that foreigners, including Americans, would *still* find practical advantages in banking in Switzerland. The reputation of Switzerland's banks goes a long way in providing a safe haven for frightened money, but there are many other services that banks provide as well. Through the centuries, banks in Switzerland have developed into one-stop financial shopping centers that make their services available to customers worldwide.

The following provides a quick glimpse at the major services available. Most are developed in greater detail in later chapters.

- Demand deposits (checking accounts) denominated in a variety of currencies. Funds on deposit may be disbursed by check, instructions in a letter, or even through telephone, wire, or facsimile machine.
- Savings accounts with a variety of rates and withdrawal restrictions to suit the individual customer. Depending on the bank, a variety of currencies may be available to allow the customer both hedging and speculative possibilities.
- Alternative savings vehicles that allow customers to acquire and deposit into their accounts a variety of short-, medium-, and long-term instruments denominated in most freely convertible currencies. The instruments may be issued by the banks themselves, other banks in Switzerland and abroad, or various local and national government units around the globe.
- Safe custody accounts for the deposit of stocks, bonds, investment fund shares, and precious metals. The bank, for a fee, collects interest, dividends, and principal repayments and assumes all other administrative responsibilities.
- Facilities for conducting foreign exchange transactions in one of the world's few absolutely free markets. Various accounts may be used to collect funds from sources around the world and to quickly transfer funds to worldwide destinations. The banks stand ready to help customers seeking advice or needing assistance in executing international transfers.
- Highly developed networks of branches, offices, and correspondent banks to assist customers vacationing, living or conducting business abroad.
- Credit cards that are well recognized in the international financial community and widely accepted throughout the world.
- Ability to internationalize investment portfolios by making available securities of major worldwide issuers. The variety of types of securities and issuers makes available a degree of diversification unknown to the majority of American investors.

- Precious metal investments of various species (gold, silver, platinum, or palladium) and form (bars and coin). Holdings may be simply credited to a bank account, held in separate custody by bank officials in the bank's vault, or placed by the customer in a safe deposit box.
- Financial counseling to assist customers in designing and executing a custom financial plan. Bankers have long been viewed by the Swiss people as private counselors whose job is to provide advice and carry out the customers' wishes.
- Portfolio management services that relieve the customer of much of the responsibility for savings and investment management. Depending on the customer's desires, portfolio management may range from simple notification services to full discretionary control.
- Absolutely confidential lending on a fully collateralized basis for customers with temporary or long-term financial needs.
- Complete trust services for the benefit of individuals or other entities specified by the account holder.
- Estate settlement planning. Distribution of assets in Switzerland can be made without long probate delays and at minimum expense. Switzerland does not levy an inheritance tax on foreign residents with assets in Switzerland.

The services offered by Swiss banks are indeed vast when compared with those available through U.S. banks. But Swiss banking becomes all the more remarkable when one considers that the legendary Swiss secrecy covers all of the relations between bank and customer.

For many Americans, secrecy is still the main attraction. American law carefully guards privacy in the conduct of personal affairs except, of course, those involving money. As chapter 4 pointed out, a legal basis for safeguarding financial affairs is practically nonexistent in the United States.

There are as many reasons for desiring secrecy in financial affairs as there are person seeking it. Familial relationships often provide the motivation. Privacy is frequently desired between individuals and heirs, spouses, exspouses, and soon-to-be exspouses. Others may want to hold no secrets from their families but may still prefer to play their financial cards close to their vests. Few individuals make public displays of their personal balance sheets; accounts in Switzerland assure that private financial information will never inadvertently become community-wide knowledge.

WHY YOU WOULDN'T WANT A SWISS BANK ACCOUNT

It was stated above that an account at a U.S. bank is not objectionable as long it is a checking account used for payments only and holds a balance not exceeding the insured level. In fact, a properly managed checking account is the most appropriate type of account for accepting deposits and making routine disbursements.

The same cannot be said of an American-owned checking account in Switzerland. Despite the international stature of Swiss banks, it is most unlikely that a check drawn on a Swiss bank would be accepted by a supermarket, service station, or store at the local shopping mall. Out-of-town checks are suspicious enough; out-of-country checks are simply not acceptable. Further, most banks will not credit a foreign check as a deposit to an account until the funds are actually collected from the foreign bank. Foreign checking accounts should be used by Americans only to transfer amounts between banks, countries, and investments.

Even the Swiss rarely use a checking account for paying bills and depositing paychecks. The Swiss postal authorities operate a postal check system, which serves as the chief bill-paying mechanism in the country. When Swiss citizens receive bills, they also receive *postal payment forms*. The forms are given to the post office, together with cash, to make payment. The postal service transfers the payments to the appropriate bank account. Bank accounts, for the Swiss, are *savings* accounts, and routine payments are almost always made in cash or through the postal system.

For those Americans with illegal funds to hide, it is again emphasized that no account in Switzerland is covered with an impermeable veil of secrecy. As we have seen, U.S. investigators armed with evidence of illegal money transfers are increasingly able to obtain the assistance of Swiss authorities in freezing an account and examining its records.

For those seeking *absolute* bank secrecy, there are other countries (such as Austria and Hungary) where it might be attained. Bank accounts in these countries are frequently conducted entirely on the basis of a passbook and a password. Bank officials are happy to open an account without establishing the owner's identity. Thus, it is entirely possible to walk into a bank in Vienna and open an account in the name of John D. Rockefeller, with a password of *Megabucks*. Future withdrawals are dependent upon *Rockefeller* producing a passbook and remembering the password.

For those who decide that an account in Switzerland is the right move for them, one of the first decisions will be to select the type of account or accounts to open. The next chapter describes those accounts ordinarily available to Americans.

7

Types of Accounts

WITHIN THE ARRAY OF SERVICES THAT SWISS BANKS OFFER IS A BROAD SELECTION OF BANK accounts. In fact, the variety of bank accounts is so broad that it poses a challenge to adequately describe them in a single chapter. Some types of accounts are very similar to those customarily offered by American banks; other types are nonexistent in the American banking system. Some Swiss account features are very much like those found in American accounts; others would be considered highly unsual, or possibly outrageous, to American bankers and their customers. But even among banks in Switzerland there is a variety of features and options available. Because of a variety of banking objectives and the types of accounts available, the Swiss people, like Americans, typically maintain more than one bank account.

The purpose of this chapter is to generalize about the common types of accounts available to American customers of Swiss banks. It is important to remember that banks in Switzerland, like some banks in the United States, often create special names to advertise the unique aspects of their specially created accounts. Thus, the Swiss have their own equivalents of *Christmas Club, Buck-Saver*, and *Rainy Day* accounts. In addition, Swiss banks use a variety of names to describe what are essentially identical accounts and then print the account names in the three official languages! For these reasons, the account descriptions in this chapter are often the descriptions of a group of very similar accounts. To the extent possible, English names, as well as the common German, French, and Italian equivalent, are shown.

DEMAND DEPOSITS

Americans traditionally own and make heavy use of checking accounts. Checks have become the most common medium of payment for both commercial and personal transactions. Formally speaking, checking accounts are considered to be a form of demand deposits—money on deposit at a bank or other thrift institution that may be freely withdrawn on customer demand. To withdraw the money from a checking account, a customer need merely write a check, payable to cash or another party, and the bank is obligated to honor the request.

As we have seen, checks are not widely used in the Swiss banking system. Nonetheless, demand deposits in the form of *current accounts* are extremely common and are used by both Swiss citizens and foreign customers.

Current Account

German: *Konntokorrent*
French: *Compte courant*
Italian: *Conto corrente*

Definition and Purpose. Current accounts are designed to hold funds that are always freely available to the account holder. Unlike other accounts, advance notice is unnecessary prior to making withdrawals. Customers may make withdrawals by check or other written notice, telex, telegram, telephone, or personal appearance. Also, automatic payments from a current account to other accounts or other parties may be arranged. Current accounts are also frequently used as temporary holding accounts for funds to be transferred to other designated accounts. As more thoroughly explained in chapter 11, customers who effect securities transactions through their Swiss banks are usually required to maintain a current account in order to facilitate the conversion of securities into cash balances and vice versa.

Denominations. A unique feature of current accounts is that the balance may be denominated in a variety of currencies. Some Swiss banks require that separate accounts be opened for each type of currency to be held. Thus, three separate accounts would be necessary if a customer desired to hold Swiss francs, U.S. dollars, and French francs. Most banks, however, allow multiple currencies in a single account and offer a variety of currencies to their customers. Bank statements issued to multiple-currency holders list the types and amounts of each currency held.

Generally, the smaller the bank, the smaller the variety of currencies that may be held in a current account. Large banks make many convertible currencies available. Common denominations at most of the larger banks include U.S. dollars, Canadian dollars, British pounds, Deutsch marks, Dutch gilders, French francs, and Italian lira. In addition, other currencies may be held by special arrangement.

It is not necessary that deposits be made in a specific currency in order to hold that currency in the account. Upon instruction from the account owner, the bank will convert the customer's deposit to the currency desired by the customer before posting a credit to the account. Thus, a check from an American customer, denominated in dollars, may be deposited to a current account after being converted by the bank into Swiss francs. For the Swiss banker, the exchange is a typical, everyday transaction. The banker makes the exchange at the prevailing rate of exchange and earns a fee for the service.

Checkbooks may be issued in connection with current accounts. It is common, however, for bankers to require a permanent minimum balance (e.g., SFr 25,000) before multicurrency check privileges are allowed. Assuming that such privileges have been granted, an account owner is free to write checks in any of the currencies that are on deposit. It is not necessary that there be a sufficient balance of a specific currency in order to write a check denominated in that currency, provided, of course, that there are sufficient *other funds* to cover the check. The Swiss banker will obligingly convert other currencies held (at the prevailing exchange rate and, again, for a fee) in order to cover the check written.

Interest. Swiss laws restrict the payment of interest on current accounts. Only residents of Switzerland may receive interest on current account balances and then only for balances denominated in Swiss francs. Banks are forbidden to pay interest on current account balances owned by foreigners. Even so, Americans are not losing a great amount compared with the Swiss who happen to hold Swiss francs in their current accounts: the amount of interest paid on current account balances usually ranges from 1/4% to 1/2%.

Withdrawals. Unlimited, with no prior notice.

Withholding Taxes. None for foreigners.

Statements. In the United States, bank customers expect to receive their statements promptly at the end of each monthly period. By custom, Swiss banks send out current account statements to their customers on a less frequent basis. Normally, statements are prepared on a quarterly or semiannual basis. However, those customers desiring to receive more frequent statements (and willing to pay the fee for a such special service) may obtain monthly, weekly, or even daily tallies of their current account balance.

Fees and Commissions. The fee structure charged by banks in Switzerland is set by the Swiss Bankers Association. Banks are free, however, to charge fees outside the standard fee structure for unique services that they make available. Standard fees for current accounts include:

- Semiannual maintenance fee   SFr.10
- Quarterly statement fee   SFr.20

In addition, banks customarily charge customers' accounts for incidental costs such as statement preparation and postage expense.

SAVINGS-TYPE ACCOUNTS

Savings-type accounts comprise the second most commonly used by both Swiss citizens and foreign customers.

Deposit, Private, or Personal Account

German: *Privatkonto, Gehaltskonto, Depositenkonto, Einlagekonto*
French: *Compte privé, Compte salaire, Compte de dépôt, Livret dé dépôt*
Italian: *Conto di deposito*

Definition and Purpose. They are designed for savers who desire to earn interest and still have the ability to withdraw modest amounts with little or no advance notification. The accounts are also ideal for effecting short-term investments in securities and metals while allowing interest to be earned on uninvested cash. In addition, the accounts enable interest to accrue on funds that may be used for a limited number of payments to third parties.

Denominations. Generally, deposit accounts are available in Swiss francs only. Cambio + Valorenbank, a Zurich bank, is one of the few institutions that offers a deposit account denominated in dollars. Foreign Commerce Bank, also in Zurich, allows deposit accounts with a variety of currencies.

Interest. The rates of interest paid on savings accounts vary by type of account and terms. As of January 1989, most savings accounts were paying 2% to 2 1/2% per annum. Generally, the more liberal the withdrawal privileges, the smaller the rate of interest.

Banks generally place a limit on the balance of a savings account that can earn interest. Account balances subject to a bank's quoted interest rate usually have maximums set at SFr 250,000, SFr 500,000, or SFr 1,000,000. Balances above the maximums earn interest at a reduced rate, often at 1%. Again the liberality of the bank's maximum balance is reflected in the interest rate paid. Thus, an account with a SFr 250,000 may earn at a 2 1/2% rate of interest, while a bank with a SFr 1,000,000 maximum will likely pay at a 2% rate.

Those banks that allow deposit account balances in currencies other than Swiss francs pay interest rates customarily associated with the respective currencies. As in the broad world markets, customers holding currencies most affected by inflation and subject to unstable exchange rates are compensated for such risks by higher interest yields. Conversely, customers holding those currencies less susceptible to the effects of inflation and more stable in terms of foreign exchange rates receive somewhat lower rates of interest. In January 1989, several banks quoted the annual rates for deposit accounts shown in Table 7-1.

Table 7-1. Interest Rates for Savings Accounts in Various Currencies.

SFr.	(Swiss francs)	2.00%
DM	(German marks)	2.75%
HFL	(Dutch gilders)	3.00%
Can$	(Canadian dollars)	7.50%
US$	(U.S. dollars)	5.00%
£	(Pounds sterling)	7.50%
¥	(Japanese yen)	2.75%

It is worth noting that such concepts as daily compounding and quarterly payment of interest is common to American bank accounts but remain unheard of in Switzerland. Interest is invariably compounded and paid at December 31.

Withdrawals. All banks place restrictions on the amount and timing of withdrawals from savings-type accounts. Common privileges allow the withdrawal of SFr 20,000 to SFr 25,000 per month with no advance notification. Larger amounts may be withdrawn but usually require a 30-day notice. Some banks may require a three-month notification period.

Special withdrawal privileges are allowed for special purposes. Almost every bank will permit a withdrawal of any size if the funds are to be used to purchase securities through the bank's securities department. Also, special withdrawal privileges are sometimes allowed for gold and silver purchases.

Withholding Taxes. Swiss federal law requires that banks withhold taxes on all interest paid to customer accounts. For many years the withholding rate has been a flat 35%. Americans are able to recover a substantial portion ($6/7$) of the amount withheld due to a tax treaty between the United States and Switzerland. In addition, the remaining $1/7$ may be used to offset U.S. taxes. The process for receiving a rebate on withheld Swiss taxes is detailed in chapter 13.

Statements. Bank statements are typically prepared on an annual basis, although customers may request more frequent statements. As with current accounts, specially prepared interim statements may be received for a special fee.

Fees and Commissions. Normal charges include a general maintenance fee of about one franc per month plus an annual statement fee of 2 to 5 francs.

Savings (Passbook) Account

German: *Sparkonto, Sparheft*
French: *Compte d'épargne*
Italian: *Conto di risparmio*

Definition and Purpose. Similar in nature to the private or deposit account, the savings account offers a higher rate of interest in exchange for more restrictive withdrawal privileges. Because of the restrictive terms, the account can accommodate a limited volume of personal payments and is not useful for the execution of frequent transactions (some banks allow for no payments to third parties). Instead, a savings account is designed to be used for the accumulation of intermediate term savings.

Denominations. Similar in nature to deposit accounts, the primary currency available to savings accounts holders is the Swiss franc. As with deposit accounts, a few banks offer the account in alternative currencies.

Interest. Increased restrictions on withdrawals from savings accounts are compensated for by an increase in interest paid. Banks offer an additional $1/4$ to $1/2$% interest above the rates paid on deposit accounts. As of January 1989, most banks were offering rates of 3%. Maximum balances subject to interest at quoted rates are similar to deposit accounts, although interest earned on excess balances may be as low ¹/2% or, in some cases, none at all.

Withdrawals. The most distinguishing feature of the savings account is the limited privilege of withdrawal. All of the large banks offer the same limitations on withdrawals: a maximum of SFr 10,000 per month, with a six-month notice required for larger withdrawals. Other banks establish notification periods based on the size of the withdrawals. A typical withdrawal schedule is that of Banque de l'Etat de Fribourg (Table 7-2).

__Table 7-2. Withdrawal Notification Requirements.__

Withdrawals (in SFr)	*Notification Required*
up to 10,000 per mo.	None
10,000 to 20,000	One-month notice
20,001 to 30,000	Two-month notice
30,001 to 40,000	Three-month notice
over 40,000	Six-month notice

Additional withdrawal privileges are permitted for securities or metal purchases through the bank's investment department. Bank Leu allows its customers to make payments to its travel agency from deposits in savings accounts without restriction.

Withholding Taxes. They are the standard 35%, subject to partial refund for Americans.

Statements. They are issued annually and more frequently at customer request.

Fees and Commissions. They are the same as for Deposit Accounts.

Investment Savings Account

German: *Anlagekonto, Anlageheft*
French: *Compte de placement*
Italian: *Conto di risparmio investimento*

Definition and Purpose. Similar to other saving-type accounts, the investment savings account is the most restrictive in terms of withdrawal privileges and allows no payments to third parties. The account is intended to be used by customers with medium- to long-term savings objectives.

Denominations. They are normally in Swiss Francs and occasionally are offered in other currencies.

Interest. Banks pay a premium of ¹/2 to ³/4% above savings account rates. As of January 1989, most banks were paying 3¹/4 to 3¹/2 %.

Withdrawals. Normally limited to SFr 10,000 per year without notification, a six-month notice is required for larger withdrawals. No restrictions exist for the purchase of securities or metals.

Withholding Taxes. They are the standard 35%, subject to partial refund for Americans.

Statements. Issued annually, more frequently at customer request.

Fees and Commissions. They are the same as for other savings-type accounts.

A comparative summary of the major features of demand and savings-type accounts is presented in Table 7-3.

Table 7-3. Demand and Savings-type Accounts Summary of Features.

	Demand Deposits	*Savings-Type Accounts*		
Type	Current Account	Deposit Account	Savings Account	Investment Savings Account
Currency	All widely traded currencies	Swiss francs	Swiss francs	Swiss francs
Interest (Jan. 1989)	None	2% 1% on balances exceeding SFr 100,000	3% 1% on balances exceeding SFr 250,000	$3^{1}/_{4}$% 0 - 1% on balances exceeding SFr 500,000
Withdrawals	Unlimited, No advance notification	SFr 25,000/mo. Larger amounts: 90-day notice	SFr 10,000/mo. Larger amounts: 6-month notice	SFr 10,000/year Larger amounts: 6-month notice
Withholding Taxes	None	35% (6/7 refundable to Americans)	35% (6/7 refundable to Americans)	35% (6/7 refundable to Americans)

SPECIAL SAVINGS ACCOUNTS

In addition to the traditional savings accounts, a growing number of banks are offering accounts to special types of savers.

Youth (Student) Savings Accounts

German: *Jugendsparkonto, Jugendsparheft*
French: *Compte juenesse, Livret juenesse*

Senior Accounts

German: *Alterssparkonto, Alterssparheft*
French: *Compte et livret aînés*

Most Swiss banks make available savings accounts with special terms for students (generally under 20 years of age) and senior citizens (over 60 years of age). The interest rates paid on the account balances are normally the same as those paid on investment savings accounts, although all other account provisions closely parallel those of normal savings accounts. The senior accounts are particularly popular. Migros Bank has indicated that over 70% of the savings deposits in its bank are owned by seniors.

Bonus Home Savings Account

Swiss Bank Corporation offers a Bonus Home Savings Account for those persons desiring to accumulate savings to finance the construction or purchase of a new home. The home may be a single family home, duplex, condominium, or vacation home, but must be located in Switzerland. SBC's Home Bonus Account has terms similar to an investment savings account; however, a 1-percent interest bonus is credited to the account balance if the eventual financing of the home is handled through SBC. Similar savings plans are offered through several of the cantonal banks.

FIXED TERM DEPOSITS

German: *Festgeld*
French: *Compte a terme fixe*
Italian: *Conto vincolato*

Definition and Purpose. The savings-type accounts just discussed are *open accounts* in the sense that deposits may be made at any time and withdrawals may be made as long as they do not violate the restrictions on amount and notification period. Swiss banks, like their American counterparts, also accept deposits at fixed interest rates for fixed periods of time. In the United States, such deposits are frequently referred to as time accounts. In Switzerland, the deposits are known as fixed term deposits.

Not technically an *account*, a fixed term deposit represents a money-market investment. A customer's money is loaned to a bank, which returns the principal and interest at the maturity of the loan. Fixed term deposits are included in this chapter because of their similarity to other bank deposits and the fact that they represent a popular alternative to open savings accounts.

The deposits are short term in nature and are especially useful for savers setting aside funds for anticipated future outlays. They also serve customers who desire to lock-in short-term interest rates. Time periods are usually fixed in accordance with the customer's desire, with a three-month minimum holding period and a 12-month maximum period.

Denominations. Most banks make available fixed term deposits in Swiss francs and U.S. dollars. In addition, a few banks also accept fixed deposits in a limited number of foreign currencies. For example, both Union Bank of Switzerland and Migros Bank accept fixed term deposits in U.S. dollars, Swiss francs, German marks, and pounds sterling.

Interest. Rates are available according to market conditions, varying according to the currency involved and the time period to maturity. Typical January 1989 interest rates are shown in Table 7-4.

___Table 7-4. Interest Rates on Fixed Term Deposits.___

	% 3 Months	% 6 Months	% 12 Months
Swiss francs	$2^{1}/_{2}$	$2^{2}/_{4}$	3
U.S. dollars	$6^{5}/_{8}$	$6^{3}/_{4}$	7

Withdrawals. None is permitted until the end of the fixed time period (at maturity).

Withholding Taxes. They are the standard 35 percent, subject to partial refund for Americans.

Statements. No statements are issued. As stated above, fixed time deposits are not accounts per se. Bank customers investing in fixed time deposits must have a current or deposit account at the bank to facilitate the transfer of funds. All fixed time deposits are charged to a customer's account and the maturity value of the investment is credited back to the account. Advice of the transactions is included in the customer's bank statement. For an additional fee, of course, the bank would be pleased to send an additional advice of charge and credit.

Minimums. As will be seen in chapter 9, required minimum balances for bank accounts vary widely among banks. This is not true of minimums required for fixed time deposits. As of January 1989, most Swiss banks required a minimum of SFr 100,000 to make a fixed time deposit denominated in Swiss francs and $50,000 for a U.S. dollar-denominated deposit.

FIDUCIARY TIME DEPOSITS

Swiss banks provide a unique alternative to short-term savers who feel that the savings accounts described above do not exactly meet their needs. At customer request, most Swiss banks will be happy to place client funds in interest-bearing money market instruments of foreign (non-Swiss) issuers. The Swiss bank acts in a fiduciary capacity, purchasing the instruments on behalf of a client, holding the instruments until maturity, and redepositing the maturity value of the investment into the client's account. Because the bank acts as a trustee for its client, the securities are actually purchased in the bank's name. No one except the Swiss banker is aware that there is another owner of the investment.

Because the financial instruments are the obligations of issuers other than the bank, the customer is said to be *at risk* for any losses suffered as a result of the investment. Losses could result from default by issuer or foreign exchange fluctuations during the holding period.

Investors do not appear to worry excessively about the at-risk label. While there is no way a bank could protect its customers from interest rate fluctuations and the vagaries of the foreign exchange market, it would feel honor bound to minimize any risk of default. After all, a default of money market instruments purchased by a Swiss bank on behalf of clients would probably cast a negative shadow on the Swiss bank's ability to judge the safety of investments. Investors can be assured that every precaution is taken to select only premium-grade investments for fiduciary deposits.

There are a number of reasons why a customer should consider a fiduciary time deposit in lieu of a routine fixed time deposit or a traditional savings account. A primary reason is that money market investments held outside Switzerland earn somewhat higher returns than those in Switzerland. Further, because foreign time deposits earn their interest outside Switzerland, they are not subject to Swiss income taxes and no taxes are withheld from the earnings of these investments.

If the combination of higher returns and lower taxes is not sufficient to attract savers to fiduciary-type deposits, there is still another advantage to these at-risk investments: the diversification that comes with holding a combination of foreign securities. The variety of short-term investments available allows for a diversification broad enough to take the worry out of money being placed *at risk*. As pointed out in chapter 6, the ability to diversify holdings is one of the primary reasons to own a Swiss bank account in the first place.

Although there are a number of instruments available, it is useful to divide them into two major categories: Euromarket deposits and U.S. money market instruments.

Euromarket Deposits

With the exception of Switzerland, the postwar economy of Western Europe was a wasteland of valueless currencies, ravaged financial institutions, and bankrupt national treasuries. Nonetheless, a number of countries, including most communist governments, chose to preserve their foreign exchange in the form of dollars on deposit in Western European banks. Thus were created large deposits of dollars in Western Europe that became known as Eurodollars. Eurodollar deposits were eagerly sought by European bankers since dollars could be profitably loaned out at a time when most European governments forbade the lending of their own national currencies. As postwar financial markets developed, the prefix *Euro-* was attached to a number of other non-European currencies (such as the Euroyen and the Europeso) and eventually spread to include European currencies on deposit in other European countries.

Thus, we find today Euromarks in Belgium, Eurodollars in Japan, and Euroyen in London, together with other Eurodeposits. In the modern world of international finance, all currencies on deposit outside their issuing countries are known as Eurocurrencies. They are often used to purchase Eurobonds (debt denominated in a foreign currency) or, perhaps, to acquire Euro-CDs (fixed term deposits denominated in foreign currencies) from large Eurobanks (those that seek deposits denominated in foreign currencies). All of the action takes place in the Euromarket, a broad term that has come to describe the supply and demand for deposits and loans denominated in foreign currencies.

Definition and Purpose. While the term *Euromarket deposit* could technically include certain noninterest bearing current accounts, the term is most generally used in Switzerland to describe fiduciary time deposits available by banks in currencies other than Swiss francs. The time deposits are purchased by the Swiss banks from other European banks in trust for clients who are technically at risk for the duration of the investment period. Investors generally refer to all investments of this type as a Euro-CDs, while the Swiss bankers prefer to distinguish between true certificates of deposit issued by foreign banks and other fiduciary time deposits in foreign banks. Whatever the name,the purpose remains the same: to provide an alternative to traditional savings accounts and time deposits, with higher returns and no withholding tax. Fixed terms range from one to 12 months.

Denominations. They are available in all widely traded currencies; banks will often quote rates available for U.S. dollars, Canadian dollars, Deutsche marks, and pounds sterling, Dutch guilder and Japanese yen, however a much greater variety is available.

Interest. Returns available reflect current interest-rate levels and duration of the investment period. Euromarket deposits earn one to two percentage points above fixed term deposits offered by the bank itself. The difference between the bank's rate of interest and that offered by non-Swiss banks represents the return associated with the money being placed at the customer's risk. Swiss banks with branches outside Switzerland often make available their own fiduciary time deposits. Because the bank is technically the borrower in such an arrangement, the customer is no longer at risk, and the yield from such investments is correspondingly lower.

Withdrawals. They are not possible until end of investment term. Understanding that unforeseen circumstances may cause a depositor to need funds prior to maturity, a Swiss banker is normally able to make a loan to the customer for 70 to 80 percent of the amount of the time deposit. The bank, of course, continues to hold the deposit in its own name as collateral for the loan.

Withholding Taxes. None are withheld.

Statements. None are issued as Euromarket deposits are not accounts. Advice of the purchase and settlement of a Euromarket deposit is included in the bank statement of a customer's current or deposit account.

Minimums. Like fixed time deposits in Swiss banks, standardized minimums have developed for fiduciary time deposits in the Euromarket. Most banks require a minimum of SFr 100,000 or the equivalent in another currency. However, there is not complete standardization in the required size of investments. Uebersee Bank, for example, requires only a SFr 50,000 minimum, with additional investments available in multiples of SFr 10,000. Bank Leu, on the other hand, accepts transactions in multiples of SFr 100,000 only.

Renewal. Banks offer a variety of automatic renewal (rollover) plans, including renewal of principal only, renewal of principal and interest, or renewal of principal, interest, and any idle cash that may be in a customer's bank account.

U.S. Money Market Deposits

Definition and Purpose. U.S. money market instruments provide an additional alternative to savings-type accounts and the fixed time deposits in Swiss banks. Similar in nature to other fiduciary deposits, the U.S. instruments are purchased from U.S. banks in the name of a Swiss bank but for the account of the Swiss bank's customer. As with other fiduciary deposits, the identity of the actual investor is known only to the Swiss bank. The deposits provide short-term, dollar-denominated investments backed by the U.S. government or creditworthy U.S. firms. The money market instruments normally available are: bankers' acceptances, certificates of deposit, commercial paper, and U.S. Treasury bills (Table 7-5).

___Table 7-5. Normal Terms for U.S. Money Market Instruments.___

	Bankers' Acceptances	Certificates of Deposit	Commercial Paper	U.S. Treasury Bills
Term (days)	30-180	30-365	30-270	30-180
Minimum Deposit	$10,000	$100,000	$25,000	$10,000

Because the above instruments are widely known and traded in the United States, the reader is urged to consult other sources for general descriptions and analysis. A comparative summary of the major features of fixed time deposits and fiduciary time deposits is presented in Table 7-6.

Once a potential customer is aware of the types of accounts and services available from Swiss banks, the next steps are to select a bank and initiate the opening process. Chapter 8 provides guidance with the selection process, and chapter 9 describes the opening process.

Table 7-6. Fixed Term and Fiduciary Time Accounts— Summary of Features.

	Fixed Time Deposits	Fiduciary Time Deposits Euromarket Deposits	U.S. Money Market Deposits
Denominations	Swiss francs & U.S. dollars	All widely traded currencies	U.S. dollars
Interest (%) (Jan. 89)	SFr 3 mo 12 mo SFr 3 3½ $ 8⅝ 8¾	Variable based on general interest rate levels	
Term	30-365 days	30-365 days	30-365 days
Withholding Taxes	35% (6/7 refundable to Americans)	None	None
Minimum	SFr 100,000	SFr 100,00	$10,000 - $100,000

8

Selecting a Swiss Bank

SWITZERLAND IS THE MOST DENSELY BANKED COUNTRY ON EARTH. THE COUNTRY NOT only is home to a large number of banks, it has many good ones. How does a potential customer from America go about the seemingly impossible task of selecting the right bank? Is location of any consequence? How might one judge the financial health of a foreign bank? Are there reasons why a particular bank would be a good choice or why it should be ignored? What are the factors that a new customer should consider when choosing a bank?

Selecting a bank is largely a matter of personal preference. There are banks that are perfectly acceptable to some Americans but, because of particular characteristics, are not preferred by others. The purpose of this chapter is to explore a number of factors useful in selecting the right bank and discuss the manner in which a bank may be contacted. In addition, addresses and selected financial information are presented in Figs. 8-1 through 8-11 for over 100 likely banks that might be of interest to Americans.

LOCATION

Studies consistently show that customers of American banks choose their banks primarily on the basis of convenience. Convenience in banking usually translates into location, drive-in facilities, and waiting time to conduct simple transactions. Obviously, the existence of drive-in teller windows and long waiting lines on payday have little bearing on the selection of an overseas bank for an American cus-

101

tomer. Nevertheless, location might still be a factor for many Americans contemplating a Swiss account.

Some of the estimated 150,000 Americans who own Swiss bank accounts have made the choice largely according to location. Famous resort towns, such as Davos, St. Moritz and Zermatt, are saturated with both local banking establishments and branches of many larger, nonlocal banks. Visitors to these banks can often spot American tourists, many of whom exhibit an "it's wonderful to be back" attitude upon entering *their* banks.

Locations might also be a consideration for customers who are not perennial tourists in the alpine landscape. Banks could be selected based on proximity to other firms in Switzerland with whom regular business affairs are conducted. In addition, selection could be based on the customer's language ability. While nearly every bank in Switzerland employs personnel able to communicate in English, French-speaking Americans might want to bank in Geneva or Montreaux, or other towns where French is the predominant language. Similarly, customers wishing to communicate in Italian might desire one of the Lugano banks, while German-speaking Americans might seek a bank in northern or eastern Switzerland.

Those Americans who occasionally visit Switzerland in connection with their banking or investing activities might want to consider a banking location that is convenient for that purpose. Each of the big three Swiss banks maintains a large banking facility at or near all major airports and train stations. Again, an observer in one of these banks can easily detect that the clientele is composed largely of foreign travelers.

FINANCIAL STRENGTH

While location appears to be very important to Americans in choosing their neighborhood banks, there is little evidence to suggest that the customers are concerned with the financial condition of the banks they choose to hold their funds. When concern is shown, it is often too late. It is the late concern that can result in a run on a bank by its depositors, causing the institution to become another statistic in the lists of "troubled and failed" banks.

Unfortunately, it is difficult for most Americans to assess the financial health of their hometown banks. Although banks can call a credit bureau to obtain information about its customers, there exists no credit bureau that can supply equally useful information about a bank's financial health. Although some brokerage houses perform financial analyses on banks, the information is more appropriate for investors and of lesser value for depositors. As a result, most customers are left alone to assess the creditworthiness of their banks. No doubt, most merely accept the Federal Deposit Insurance Corporation decal on the door as assurance that the deposits are safe.

For Americans contemplating the opening of an account in Switzerland, where deposit insurance is not generally available, the task of ascertaining a bank's financial health is equally challenging. Like American banks, all Swiss banks (except private banks) publish annual reports. Also like American banks, the financial statements included in annual reports are prepared with a nearly incomprehensible technical jargon designed more to satisfy the requirements of regulators than to provide intelligible reading for customers and shareholders. To make matters worse, Swiss accounting rules are sufficiently different from American accounting rules to confound most American financial analysts.

The fact is, no simple formula exists to determine if a bank is financially robust or moribund. Rules of thumb for evaluating solvency have been suggested by some bank analysts. Most tend to rely on measures of liquidity, as determined from information reported in the annual balance sheet. Liquidity, however, is a short-run concept—a reflection of a bank's ability to meet demands of depositors at a single moment (the date the balance sheet was prepared). Traditional measures of liquidity say little of a bank's ability to continue to operate over a sustained period of customer demand. Financial strength is a term used to describes a bank's long run ability to meet adverse economic pressures. Indicators of a bank's overall financial strength include balance-sheet analyses as well as an evaluation of managerial competence, loan policies, and overall bank philosophy.

A Practical Approach

It is likely that most potential customers are simply unwilling to go to great trouble in analyzing a bank's financial strength. For those who feel it necessary to perform at least a preliminary analysis, the following is offered as an easy and practical approach to basic bank analysis.

1. Examine reasonable and easily understood indicators of financial strength. These indicators include:

   Size of assets - a measure of the total financial clout. Generally speaking, the larger the better, although size of assets alone does not reveal the extent of a bank's true financial strength.

   Size of capital - a measure of the difference between a bank's assets and its total liabilities, often referred to as equity. Because bank equity represents the total amount of permanently invested capital and reserves, it is not subject to withdrawal by customers. Thus, when expressed as a percentage of total assets, the higher the bank equity the greater the protection from panic or *runs* on the bank.

   The total asset and capital amounts are certainly key figures in understanding a bank's financial health. As pointed out in chapter 2, however, Swiss accountants are masters of understatement. One of the more peculiar aspects of Swiss bank accounting is the deliberate understatment of both assets and reserves. Banks in Switzerland, like other Swiss companies, are allowed to accumulate vast amounts of undisclosed (or hidden) reserves to provide additional insurance against adverse economic events. Thus the "officially" reported assets and equity in Fig. 8-1 through 8-10 are conservative measurements and must be viewed as minimum rather than the actual amounts.

2. Note the date of founding for a bank being considered. Obviously, longevity does not prove financial strength. However, the fact that a bank is 150 years old does imply that the institution is not a fly-by-night operation and has adopted an apparently sound operating philosophy.

3. Ask for and read annual reports for each bank under consideration, paying particular attention to management's discussion of current economic conditions and the bank's policies in light of those conditions. Upon request, most banks will be happy to provide their latest annual report although smaller banks may not have English language editions available.

Many Americans seeking a Swiss bank account are likely to be more concerned with issues other than bank location or financial strength. The "right" bank may depend on the existence of deposit insurance, the ownership of the bank, the existence of branches or other operations inside and outside of Switzerland, and the existence of any specialized services.

DEPOSIT INSURANCE AND CANTONAL BANKS

For those depositors seeking the highest degree of safety for their deposits, it would be well to consider an account at one of Switzerland's cantonal banks. As pointed out in chapter 2, cantonal banks are similar in nature to savings banks in the United States. Because the cantonal banks are government owned, deposits at these banks have the guarantee of the cantonal governments. The special protection is not unlike deposit insurance in the United States. At no other type of bank in Switzerland are customers' deposits insured by a government or governmental agency, giving the customers of cantonal banks an exclusive safety feature.

Cantonal banks range in size from very small to extremely large. In fact, in recent years several of the larger cantonal banks have shed much of the savings bank image to rank among the largest banks in Switzerland. The largest of these are more accurately called universal banks, as their services extend to cover the broad range of services offered by the very largest Swiss banks.

Figure 8-1 lists those cantonal banks that are of a size sufficient to be able to make their services available to foreigners. Not included in the list are cantonal banks with total reported assets of less than SFr 4,000,000, most of which are extremely small local banks.

| | | | 12-31-87 | |
| | | | Total Assets | Bank Equity |
Bank	Address	Founded	(SFr 000)	(SFr 000)
Aargauische Kantonalbank	Bahnhofstrasse 58 CH-5001 Aarau	1913	5,074,184	244,920
Banque cantonale du Valais	8, rue de Cedres CH-1951 Sion	1916	4,208,583	157,479
Banque Cantonale Vaudois	14, Place St. Francois CH-1002 Lausanne	1845	10,339,006	582,500
Banque de l'Etat de Fribourg	Boulevard de Perolles 1 CH-1701 Fribourg	1892	4,539,177	122,00

Fig. 8-1. Cantonal banks.

Fig. 8-1. Continued

Bank	Address	Founded	12-31-87 Total Assets (SFr 000)	Bank Equity (Sfr 000)
Banque Hypothécaire du Canton de Genève	Place de Molard 2 CH-1211 Geneva 3	1847	4,823,107	249,00
Basellandschaftliche Kantonalbank	7 Rheinstrasse CH-4410 Liestal	1864	6,467,494	316,375
Basler Kantonalbank	Spiegelgasse 2 CH-4051 Basle	1899	5,808,557	287,150
Caisse d'Epargne de la République et Canton de Genève	4, Rue de la Corraterie CH-1211 Geneva 11	1816	4,023,498	209456
Crédit Foncier Vaudois	8, Place Chauderon CH-1000 Lausanne	1858	7,679,620	358,859
Graubünder Kantonalbank	Postrasse, PO Box 47122 CH-7002 Chur	1870	6,330,716	299,654
Hypothekarkasse des Kantons Bern	2 Schwanengasse CH-3001 Berne	1846	6,287,106	193,700
Kantonalbank Schwyz	Bahnhofstrasse 3 CH-6430 Schwyz	1890	4,082,919	144,868
Kantonalbank von Bern	Bundesgasse Postfach 2619 CH-3001 Berne	1834	11,217,254	346,000
Luzerner Kantonalbank	Pilatusstrasse 12 CH-6002 Lucerne	1850	10,310,366	511,907
St. Gallische Kantonalbank	St. Leonhardstrasse 25 CH-9001 St. Gallen	1868	9,934,896	452,168
Solothurner Kantonalbank	Amthausplatz 4 CH-4502 Solothurn	1886	4,043,420	213,060
Thurgauische Kantonalbank	Bankplatz 1 CH-8570 Weinfelden	1871	7,607,996	364,165
Zuger Kantonalbank	Bahnhofstrasse 1-5 CH-6301 Zug	1892	4,433,933	140,370
Zurcher Kantonalbank	Bahnhofstrasse 9 CH-8022 Zurich	1870	33,499,599	1,213,225

U.S.-CONTROLLED BANKS IN SWITZERLAND

Americans may want to consider whether a prospective bank is owned and controlled by American interests. A list of such banks appears in Fig. 8-2, while Fig. 8-3 lists branches of U.S. banks in Switzerland.

There exists a compelling argument for an account at a subsidiary or branch of a U.S. bank: the possibility of an indirect deposit insurance in the event that the Swiss bank should actually become insolvent. While not legally compelled to aid a failing subsidiary bank in another country, it is likely that, when faced with such a decision, most U.S. banks would not hesitate to come to the rescue. After all, there is perhaps nothing that would be more embarrassing to a U.S. bank than to admit that its own Swiss subsidiary has failed.

There is already precedent for just such an action. In late 1970, United California Bank hurriedly came to the rescue of the depositors of UCB Basle, a subsidiary bank located in Basle, Switzerland. UCB Basle found itself insolvent as the result of massive commodity trade losses incurred by an over eager bank employee with access to bank funds. It is interesting to note that United California Bank was not the sole stockholder of UCB Basle; it held merely 58% of the stock. However, in its face-saving action, the board of directors of United California Bank made the decision to guarantee the deposits of all of the bank's customers.*

Whether subsidiary or branch, every bank in Switzerland is subject to the laws of Switzerland, including the secrecy statutes. Similarly, each bank is beyond the long arm of foreign law without special intervention by the Swiss government.

			12-31-87	
			Total Assets	Bank Equity
Bank	Parent Company	Founded	(SFr 000)	(SFr 000)
American Express Bank AG Bahnhofstrasse 20 8022 Zurich	American Express Bank New York	1921	1,067,544	110,100
Bankers Trust AG Dreikoenigstrasse 6 8022 Zurich	Bankers Trust New York	1971	417,134	53,200
Chase Manhattan Bank (Suisse) SA Rue du Rhone 63 1211 Geneva 3	Chase Manhattan Bank New York	1969	479,758	60,717

Fig. 8-2. Selected U.S.-controlled banks in Switzerland.

---

*(For an interesting account of the failure of UCB Basle and its subsequent bailout, see Supermoney (Random House, 1972) by Adam Smith, himself a minority stockholder in the defunct bank.)

Fig. 8-2. Continued

Bank	Parent Company	Founded	12-31-87 Total Assets (SFr 000)	Bank Equity (SFr 000)
Chemical Bank (Suisse) SA Freigutstrasse 16 8039 Zurich	Chemical Bank New York	1984	175,793	28,243
Citicorp Investment Bank P.O. Box 244 8021 Zurich	Citicorp New York	1982	1,339,225	112,500
J.P. Morgan (Suisse) SA Places des bergues 3 1201 Geneva	Morgan Guaranty & Trust Co. New York	1980	288,874	36,400
Security Pacific Bank SA Quai de I'lle P.O. Box 241 1211 Geneva 11	Security Pacific Corp. Los Angeles	1956	230,106	47,625
State Street Bank (Switzerland) Stadelhofstrasse 22 8024 Zurich	State Street Bank & Trust Co. Boston	1971	199,583	26,420
Trade Development Bank 96-98 Rue du Rhone 1211 Geneva 11	American Express Bank New York	1960	6,384,654	558,700

At the same time, there is a potential risk of banking with the Swiss affiliate of an American bank. We observed in the celebrated Marc Rich case (chapter 4) that frustrated U.S. government officials are not above employing strong-arm tactics against U.S.-based operations to force disclosure of private records in Switzerland. It is not inconceivable that frustrated officials would attempt to use a U.S. holding company as a lever to pry open the Swiss seal of secrecy—in spite of the apparent detente that currently exists between U.S. and Swiss officials. Although a Swiss banking subsidiary would certainly prevail against such pressure, the haunting specter of such a threat may convince many that it is safer to find a less visible and potentially vulnerable depository.

OTHER FOREIGN-CONTROLLED BANKS IN SWITZERLAND

An American seeking a discreet Swiss account may want to consider other foreign-controlled banks in an effort to achieve both unguaranteed deposit insurance and freedom from American banking connections. There are approximately 100

Bank	Parent Company Location	Established in Switzerland
The Chase Manhattan Bank N.A. 63 rue de Rhone CH-1211 Geneva 3	New York	1984
Chemical Bank Freigutstrasse 16 CH-8039 Zurich also 19 rue du Rhone CH-1211 Geneva 3	New York	1971
First National Bank of Boston 7 Rue des Alpes CH-1211 Geneva 1	Boston	1986
First National Bank of Chicago 6 Places des Eaux-Vives 1211 Geneval 6	Chicago	1971
Bank of America NT & SA Bleicherweg 15 CH-8022 Zurich also 9 Rue Des Granges 1211 Geneva 3	San Francisco	1967
Citibank N.A. Seestrasse 25 CH-8022 Zurich	New York	1963
Manufacturers Hanover Trust & Co. Stockerstrasse 33 CH-8022 Zurich	New York	1974
Morgan Guaranty Trust Company Stockerstrasse 38 CH-8022 Zurich	New York	1968

Fig. 8-3. Branches of U.S. banks in Switzerland.

Bank	Parent	Founded	12-31-87 Total Assets (SFr 000)	Bank Equity (SFr 000)
Banque Nationale de Paris (Suisse) SA Aeschengraben 26 CH-4002 Basle	Banque National de Paris Paris, France	1949	2,169,718	181,600
Banque Paribas (Suisse) SA 2 Place de Hollande CH-1204 Geneva	Compagnie Financiere de Paribas Paris, France	1872	6,055,295	630,500
Banca del Gottardo Via Conova 8 CH-6900 Lugano	Sumitomo Bank Osaka, Japan	1957	4,874,759	475,250
Handelsbank N.W. Talstrasse 59 CH-8001 Zurich	National Westminister Bank London, UK	1930	3,341,583	303,000
Nordfinanz-Bank Zurich Bahnhofstrasse 1 CH-8022 Zurich	Kansallis-Osake-Pankki Helsinki, Finland	1964	3,220,349	265,500
Royal Trust Bank (Switzerland) AG Limmatquai 4 CH-8024 Zurich	Royal Trust Group Toronto, Canada	1965	3,002,316	233,000

Fig. 8-4. Selected Foreign-controlled banks in Switzerland.

foreign (non-American) controlled banks currently operating in Switzerland. Figure 8-4 provides a partial list of these banks. In addition nine foreign banks have established branches in Switzerland, which are listed in Fig. 8-5.

There exists another possible benefit to holders of accounts at foreign-controlled banks. A customer with recurring business or personal transactions at another foreign bank may find it useful to open an account in Switzerland at a subsidiary of the foreign bank. For example, an American making or receiving payments through London's National Westminster Bank will find it particularly easy to transfer funds through a personal banking relationship at National Westminster's subsidiary, Handelsbank N.W. of Zurich.

SWISS BANKS WITH OPERATIONS IN THE UNITED STATES

Eight Swiss banks have established a presence in the United States (see Fig. 8-6). The operations range from representative offices with a staff of two to branches with hundreds of employees. Although representative offices and agencies are only authorized to provide information or refer customers to their parent companies in Switzerland, the branches may accept deposits for credit to accounts in Switzerland and disburse funds from those same accounts.

A major advantage of using Swiss branches to conduct business is the relative ease of transferring funds overseas. Employees at the Swiss branches never lift an eyebrow at transfers between the U.S. and Switzerland. After all, transactions of this type constitute a large part of the bank's routine, daily business and are one of the primary reasons for the branch's existence.

Those individuals who are not customers of a U.S. branch of a Swiss bank can still use the services available to transfer amounts to and from an account located in a Swiss branch of that bank (or any other bank in Switzerland). Almost all transfers of this type are accomplished by wire.

Despite the ease associated with using a U.S. branch of a Swiss bank to conduct transactions affecting an account in Switzerland, Americans with a deep concern for confidentiality should carefully consider whether the ease of conducting business is worth the resulting loss of privacy. Just as foreign banks operating in Switzerland are subject to the Swiss strict banking regulations, foreign banks must operate their branches in the United States in accordance with U.S. laws, and are subject to the same financial reporting requirements and court orders as any other financial institution in the United States.

BANKS WITH BRANCHES OUTSIDE SWITZERLAND

For those whose personal or business affairs result in frequent travel to foreign locations, there may be advantages in selecting a Swiss bank with foreign branches. For those desiring privacy in their personal affairs, an obvious advantage is the avoidance of automatic microfilming of all U.S. banking transactions. For others, the primary advantage is to personally conduct transactions with their Swiss banks while staying in Nassau, London, or some other vacation spot. There are currently 18 Swiss banks with branches or subsidiary banks located outside both Switzerland and the United States (see Fig. 8-7).

Bank	Parent Company Location	Established in Switzerland
The British Bank of the Middle East Rue du Rhone 23 CH-1211 Geneva 11	Hong Kong	1968
Credit Lyonnais 11 Place Bel-Air CH-1204 Geneva	Paris	1876
Grindlays Bank plc 7 Quai du Mont Bianc CH-1211 Geneva	London	1969
Lloyds Bank Plc 1 Place Bel-Air CH-1211 Geneva	London	1919
Société Générale {Alsacienne de Banque} 19 rue de Candolle CH-1211 Geneva	Strasbourg	1986
Banque Indosuez 4 Avenue de la Gare CH-1002 Lausanne	Paris	1957
Bank für Aussenwirtschaft Schutengasse 1 CH-8022 Zurich	Moscow	9185
The Hong Kong and Shangai Banking Corp. Tödistrasse 44 CH-8022 Zurich	Hong Kong	1979
Société Générale Alsacienne de Banque 1 Bleicherweg CH-8022 Zurich	Strasbourg	1926

Fig. 8-5. Branches of foreign banks in Switzerland.

Estab. in U.S.	Bank	Representative Office/Agency	Branch
1980	Banca del Sempione	65 East 80th St. New York NY 10021	
1983	Banca della Svizzera Italiana		One Wall St. New York NY 10005
1940	Bank Julius Bär & Co.	Suite 1640 Four Embarcadero Center San Francisco CA	330 Madison Ave. New York NY 10017
1978	Bank Leu		Suite 310 375 Park Ave. New York NY 10152
1940	Credit Suisse	1601 First Atlanta Tower Atlanta GA 30383	100 Wall St. New York NY 10005
		200 East Randolph Dr. 65th Floor Chicago IL 60601	1200 Bricknell Ave. 16th Floor Miami FA 33131
		First Interstate Plaza Suite 3910 Houston TX 77002	800 Wilshire Blvd. Los Angeles CA 90017
		50 California St. Suite 2940 San Francisco CA 94111	
1978	Compagnie de Banque d'Investissments	Suite 1505 630 Fifth Ave. New York NY 10111	

Fig. 8-6. Swiss banks with operations in the United States.

Fig. 8-6. Continued

Estab. in U.S.	Bank	Representative Office/Agency	Branch
1939	Swiss Bank Corporation		
		285 Peachtree Ctr. Ave. NE Marquis Two Tower 23 Floor Atlanta GA 30303	4 World Trade Center New York NY 10048
		One Allen Center Suite 600 Houston TX 77002	Three First National Plaza Suite 2100 Chicago IL 60602
		500 N. Akard St. Suite 3820 Dallas TX 75201	101 California St. San Francisco CA 94111
		300 South Grand Ave. Los Angeles CA 90071	
		701 Bricknell Ave. Suite 3250 Miami FA 33131	
1974	Union Bank of Switzerland		299 Park Ave. New York NY 10171
		One Embarcadero Center Suite 3805 San Francisco CA 94111	First Interstate Plaza 1100 Louisiana Suite 4500 Houston TX 77002
			30 South Wacker Dr. Chicago IL 60606
			444 South Flower St. 46th Fl. Los Angeles CA 90071

Bank	*Foreign Branches and Subsidiaries*
Banca del Gottardo Via Canova 8 CH-6901 Lugano	Nassau, Luxembourg
Banca della Svizzera Via Magatti 2 CH-6901 Lugano	Nassau
Banco di Roma per la Svizzera Piazzetta San Carlo CH-6900 Lugano	Luxembourg
Bank Hapoalim (Schweiz) Stockerstrasse 33 CH-8039 Zurich	Luxembourg
Bank Julius Bär & Co. AG Bahnhofstrasse 36 CH-8001 Zurich	London
Bank Leu Bahnhofstrasse 32 CH-8022 Zurich	Grand Cayman, Cayman Islands
Bank Leumi le-Israel (Schweiz) Claridenstrasse 34 CH-8022 Zurich	Cayman Islands
Banque Intercommerciale de Gestion Avenue de Rumine 20 CH-1001 Lausanne	Nassau
Banque Paribas (Suisse) SA 2, Place de Hollande CH-1204 Geneva	Nassau, Guernsey
Banque Privée Edmond de Rothschild 18 Rue de Hesse CH-1204 Geneva	Luxembourg
Credit Suisse Paradeplatz 8 CH-8001 Zurich	Nassau, London, Guernesey, Singapore, Tokyo, Cairo, Bahrain, Panama Hong, Kong and Cayman Islands.

Fig. 8-7. Swiss banks with branches in foreign countries other than the United States.

Fig. 8-7. Continued

Bank	*Foreign Branches and Subsidiaries*
Discount Bank and Trust Company 3 Quai de I'lle 1211 Geneva 11	London, Amsterdam, Luxembourg, George Town (Grand Cayman) and Panama.
Habib Bank AG Zurich Bergstrasse 21 CH-8022 Zurich	Abu Dhabi, Dubai, Par Dubai, Sharjah, Muttrah, Ruwi, Salalah, Seeb, Colombo, London, Glasgow, Manchester, Port Louis, Nairobi and Mombasa.
Nordnanz-Bank Zurich 1 Bahnhofstrasse CH-8022 Zurich	Nassau
Swiss Bank Corporation Paradeplatz 6 CH-8022 Zurich	London, Cayman Islands, Bahrain Hong Kong, Tokyo and Singapore
Swiss Cantobank (International) P.O. Box 561 CH-6301 Zug	London
Swiss Volksbank Weltpoststrasse 5 CH-3015 Berne	London
Trade Development Bank 96-98 rue de Rhone CH-1204 Geneva	Nassau and London
Union Bank of Switzerland Bahnhofstrasse 45 CH-8021 Zurich	London, Hong Kong, Tokyo and Singapore
United Overseas Bank Quai de Bergues 11 CH-1121 Geneva 1	London, Luxembourg

THE BIG BANKS

As pointed out in chapter 2, the so called Big Three (Credit Suisse, Swiss Bank Corporation, and Union Bank of Switzerland) are ranked among the very largest banks in the world (Fig. 8-8). In addition, Switzerland's *other* big banks, Bank Leu and Swiss Volksbank, rank among the 100 largest banks in the world (Fig. 8-9).

	Credit Suisse	Swiss Bank Corporation	Union Bank of Switzerland
French:	Credit Suisse	Société de Banque Suisse	Union de Banques Suisses
German:	Schweizerische Kreditanstalt	Schweizerischer Bankverein	Schweizerische Bankgesellsschaft
Italian:	Credito Svizzero	Società di Banca Svizzera	Union di Banche Svizzere
Founded	1856	1872	1912
12-31-87 Assets (000SFr)	107,239,875	146,189,867	160,415,886
Equity (000SFr)	6,600,307	8,749,361	9,736,143
Head Office	Paradeplatz 8 CH-8021 Zurich	Aeschenplatz 6 CH-4002 Basle	Bahnhofstrasse 45 CH-8021 Zurich
Branches in Major Swiss Cities			
Basle	St. Alban-Graben 1-3 CH-4002 Basle	Aeschenplatz 1 CH-4002 Basle	Freie Strasse 68 CH-4002 Basle
Berne	Bundesplatz 2 CH-3001 Berne	Bärenplatz 8 CH-3001 Berne	Bubenbergplatz 3 CH-3001 Berne
Geneva	Place Bel-Air 2 CH-1211 Geneva 11	Rue de la Confédération 2 CH-1211 Geneva 11	Rue du Rhone 8 CH-1211 Geneva
Lausanne	Rue du Lion d'Or 5-7 CH-1002 Lausanne	Place St.Francois 16 CH-1002 Lausanne	Place St Francois 1 CH-1002 Lausanne
Lugano	Via Canova CH-6901 Lugano	Via Nassa 11 CH-6901 Lugano	Piazzeta della Posta CH-6901 Lugano
Zurich	Paradeplatz 8 CH-8001 Zurich	Paradeplatz 6 CH-8022 Zurich	Bahnhofstrasse 45 8021 Zurich

Fig. 8-8. The big three.

	Bank Leu	*Swiss Volksbank*
Founded	1856	1869
12-31-87		
Assets (000SFr)	14,710,515	32,195,416
Equity (000SFr)	1,090,315	1,874,515
Head Office	Bahnhofstrasse 32 CH-8022 Zurich	Weltpoststrasse 5 CH-3015 Berne

Branches in Major Swiss Cities*

Basle		Gerbergasse 30 CH-4001 Basle
Geneva		Place St. Gervais 2 CH-1211 Geneva
Lausanne		Grand-Point 6 CH-1010 Lausanne
Lugano		Via G Vegezzi 1 CH-6901 Lugano
Zurich		Bahnhofstrasse 53 CH-8021 Zurich

---

*All 15 of Bank Leu's branches are located in the Canton of Zurich.

Fig. 8-9. Other big banks.

Each of these big banks has been successful in marketing its services to foreign customers, including Americans. It seems likely that the majority of Americans who have Swiss bank accounts have seen fit to establish them at one of the five big banks.

For many Americans, the lure of an account at one of Switzerland's largest banks will be strong. The banks are well known and highly respected members of the worldwide financial community. As all are universal banks, they are capable of providing every conceivable type of banking service. Further, each maintains a network of branches in Switzerland and around the world. Since nearly every branch is capable of dealing directly with foreign customers, an American desiring to use the services of one of the big banks will be able to choose from hundreds of possible branch locations.

Because of the large securities trading departments at the big banks, they are favored by foreign investors seeking access to foreign stock and bond markets. All five of the big Swiss banks are members of the Swiss securities exchanges and own seats on several foreign exchanges as well. Each of the big banks is a major player in the gold and silver markets. Bank Leu, in addition, has achieved special renown as a dealer in gold and silver coins.

OTHER BANKS

There are hundreds of banks that, due to their size, handle only local business in their small communities and are generally unsuitable for most Americans. At the same time, a number of *other banks* are appropriate for Americans and deserve mention.

Figure 8-10 lists eight banks that are not among the previous lists but are known to willingly accept new American customers.

PRIVATE BANKS

Chapter 2 characterized private banks as unique financial institutions that provide highly personalized portfolio management services for a select group of cus-

Swiss Controlled	Address	Founded	12-31-87 Total Assets (SFr 000)	Bank Equity (SFr 000)
Cambio + Valorenbank	Postfach 535 CH-8021 Zurich	1959	98,606	30,875
Migros Bank	Seidengasse 12 CH-8023 Zurich	1957	5,112,861	277,500
Foreign Controlled				
Baninvest	Brandschenkestrasse 41	1969	510,740	68,500
Banque Ankerfina SA	Av. de la Gare	1934	81,762	17,400
[Formerly Banque Indiana (Suisse)]	1000 Lausanne			
Discount Bank & Trust Company	3 Quai de I'lle CH-1211 Geneva	1952	3,616,724	287,000
Foreign Commerce Bank [FOCO Bank]	Bellariastrasse 82 CH-8038	1958	314,679	52,120
Nederlandsche Middenstandsbank	6, Rue Petitot 1211 Geneva 11	1960	527,130	54,100
Ueberseebank	Limmatquai 2 CH-8024	1965 Zurich	275,642	41,000
United Overseas Bank	Quai des Berques 11 CH-1211 Geneva 1	1961	3,326,219	349,000

Fig. 8-10. Other banks of interest to Americans.

tomers. Not adverse to accepting new business, the banks are nevertheless extremely careful in deciding who are allowed to become customers.

In earlier years, a recommendation from an existing client was the usual ticket for admission to the inner circle of a private bank. Although a letter of recommendation from a current customer is appreciated by most private banks today, the bankers no longer expect it from each new applicant. However, a personal visit with potential customers is considered necessary to discuss the feasibility of providing services. Initial contact to arrange such a visit can be made by mail. Figure 8-11 is a complete list of Switzerland's private banks and their addresses.

Location	Bank	Founded
Basel	Baumann & Cie St. Jakobsstrasse 46 CH-4002 Basle	1920
	E. Gutzwiller & Cie 7 Kaufhausgasse CH-4051 Basle	1886
	La Roche & Co. 25 Rittergasse CH-4002 Basle	1787
	Bank Sarasin & Co 107 Freiestrasse PO Box 4055 CH-4002 Basle	1841
Geneva	Bordier & Cie 16 rue de la Hollande CH-1211 Geneva	1844
	Darier & Cie 4 Rue de Saussure CH-1211 Geneva 11	1880
	Gonet & Cie 6 Boulevard du Theatre CH-1211 Geneva 11	1845
	Hentsch & Cie 15 Rue de la Corraterie CH-1204 Geneva	1796
	Lombard, Odier & Cie 11 Corraterie CH-1211 Geneva 11	1798

Fig. 8-11. Private banks.

Fig. 8-11. Continued

Location	Bank	Founded
	Mirabaud & Cie 3 Boulevard du Theatre CH-1211 Geneva 11	1819
	Morgue d'Algue & Cie 5 Rue de la Fontaine CH-1204 Geneva	1869
	Pictet & Cie 29 blvd Georges - Favon CH-1211 Geneva 11	1805
	Tardy, Burrus & Cie Place de l'Universite 6 CH-1211 Geneva 4	1914
Lausanne	Hentsch, Chollet & Cie 11 Place St Francois CH-1002 Lausanne	1882
	Hofstetter, Landolt & Cie 6 Rue du Lion d'Or CH-1003 Lausanne	1780
Lucerne	Falck & Cie Schwanenplatz 2 CH-6002 Lucerne	1875
Neuchatel	Banhote & Cie 1 Rue Pury CH-2001 Neuchatel	1815
St. Gallen	Wegelin & Co., Inhaber Eugster & Co. Bohl 17 CH-9004 St. Gallen	1741
Yverdon	Piguet & Cie Rue de la Plaine 14 CH-1400 Yverdon	1856
Zurich	Hottinger & Cie Dreikoenigstrasse 55 CH-8027 Zurich	1968

Fig. 9-5. Fiduciary agreement.

Location	Bank	Founded
Zurich	Hugo Kahn & Co Stockerstrasse 38 5th Fl CH-8027 Zurich	1923
Zurich	Rahn & Bodmer Talstrasse 15 CH-8022 Zurich	1750

MINIMUMS

To those considering the selection of a bank, the question often arises regarding minimum balances. There is a common misconception that new account minimums must be astronomical in size: an amount that could only be raised by a third-world dictator who has just raided the local treasury.

While some banks do indeed insist on a large minimum balance, others ask for a very modest balance, perhaps no more than a customer would expect to shell out to open an account at an American bank. Balser Kantonalbank, for example, will establish savings accounts for as little as SFr 10. Also, some banks specify no minimum balance to either open an account or keep the account open.

The majority of banks, however, expect new customers to deposit somewhere between SFr 100 and SFr 1,000 (or the equivalent in another currency) to open either a current or a savings account; few banks specify a minimum balance to keep the account open.

Several banks have instituted larger minimum balances in an apparent effort to influence the type of clientele the bank wished to have as customers. For example, all accounts at Foreign Commerce Bank normally require a $10,000 minimum from American customers. Swiss Volksbank prefers a minimum deposit of SFr 200,000 from Americans to open current or savings account (SFr 100,000 for time deposits). Even larger minimums are required by most private banks to establish managed portfolio accounts.

No attempt is made here to list the minimums required by each bank as it would not be feasible to compile a reliable and current summary. Not only do minimums vary widely by type of account, Swiss bankers do not hesitate to adjust their suggested minimums to regulate the flow of new customers. Each bank publishes its current *Terms and Conditions* for the benefit of prospective customers.

LETTER OF INQUIRY

A proper letter of inquiry to a bank should indicate the desire of the writer to establish a banking relationship, request specific information about services available, and request that all necessary forms be mailed to carry out the establishment of the account. A typical letter of inquiry, addressed to a fictitious bank, is shown in Fig. 8-12.

It is not important that the letter of inquiry look exactly like Fig. 8-12. If the writer of the letter can state exactly the information needed, it would be preferable to do so. More explicit letters of inquiry are shown in Figs. 8-13 and 8-14.

An American desiring to open an account by mail should not feel uncomfortable about writing a letter of inquiry in English. Swiss bankers are neither xenophobic nor concerned that a customer cannot communicate in one of the official Swiss languages. The banking establishment in Switzerland has willingly accepted the fact that English is the worldwide language of business and commerce, and this explains, perhaps, why it is rare to find a bank or a branch of a bank in which at least one employee is not able to communicate in English.

To ensure clarity in what is being written, the letter of inquiry, like all business correspondence, should be typed. A slight problem may arise in typing foreign accent marks common in French, German or Italian names but not customarily found on American keyboards. Bank names containing a German umlaut(¨), such as Bank Julis Bär, are often anglicized by writing Bank Julius Baer (even Bank Julius Bar observes this alternative when printing its name in English). For other accent marks, there exists no alternative spellings, as in Banque de Dépôts et de Gestion, a prosperous Lausanne bank. When uncertain whether an

---

Dec. 1, 1989

Fischental Bankverein
Talstrasse 12
CH-8497 Fischental
Switzerland

Dear Sir or Madam:

I am interested in establishing a relationship with your bank. I would appreciate receiving the following:

General information about your bank.

Current terms and General Conditions for accounts available to American customers of your bank.

The necessary forms and instructions for establishing an account.

Thank you.

Very truly yours,

Billy G. Lindgren
123 Main Avenue
Anytown, USA

Fig. 8-12. Letter of inquiry No. 1.

alternative spelling exists, it is easiest to simply omit any special pronunciation marks or modify typed words with a ballpoint pen.

Notice the bank addresses in the sample letters. The second line of the bank address in Fig. 8-12 is a street address, written in the typical European fashion of street first, number second. The second line of Fig. 8-13 indicates the German equivalent of Post Office Box No. 858. In French, this would have been written B.P. 858. Figure 8-14 indicates no box number. Such an address is common in smaller towns where it would seem foolish to assign an identifying number to a well-known postal destination. The third line indicates the Swiss equivalent of a zip code. All post offices in Europe have been assigned such codes, with the first two letters identifying the country (here, Confederation Helvetica).

Dec. 1, 1989

Fischental Bankverein
Postfach 858
CH-8497 Fischental
Switzerland

Dear Sir or Madam:

I am interested in opening a current and a savings account at your bank. I would appreciate receiving the following:

Current terms and General Conditions for current and savings accounts.

The necessary forms and instructions for opening the accounts.

Enclosed is Cashier's Check No. 420-533 drawn on First Bank of Anytown in the amount of $10,000. Please deposit $5,000 of the amount in the current account. I wish to have the remainder converted to Swiss francs at the current rate of exchange and deposited in the savings account.

Thank you for your prompt and discreet response to this request.

Very truly yours,

Robert Randal Sebring
1000 First Street
Anytown, USA

Fig. 8-13. Letter of inquiry No. 2.

Dec. 1, 1989

Fischental Bankverein
Postfach
CH-8497 Fischental
Switzerland

Dear Sir or Madam:

I am interested in establishing a relationship with Fischental Bankverein. In particular, I desire to invest in fiduciary time deposits through your bank. I would appreciate receiving the following:

General information about your bank.

Information about investments in fiduciary time deposits available through your bank.

The necessary forms for establishing an account that will permit the investment in fiduciary time deposits.

Thank you for your prompt and discreet response to this request.

Very truly yours,

O.B. Hoban
P.O. Box 1969
Anytown, USA

Fig. 8-14. Letter of inquiry No. 3.

BANK RESPONSES

Responses to letters of inquiry will take from one to two weeks. The responses themselves might vary from small, slim envelopes to oversized ones bulging with information. Some banks have prepared beautifully colored brochures describing the bank's history, portraying polished walnut and marble offices together with highly sophisticated electronic trading operations, and, of course, advertising the services available to customers. Some information is prepared especially for Americans. Other information, judging from the multilingual nature of the material, is obviously prepared for most anyone who might inquire.

The current terms for each of the types of accounts available might also be described in colorful pamphlets or on businesslike rate sheets. The degree to which the various accounts are described in the bank literature varies among the institutions. Some banks obviously expect that the customer is already familiar with the accounts and services that are offered by a Swiss bank. For those who are not, chapter 7 provides guidance for most of the normal types of accounts.

MAKING THE SELECTION

As can be seen, there is a variety of considerations in choosing a Swiss bank. A new customer should give greatest consideration to those factors that are most relevant in the decision to have a Swiss account. Before making a choice, however, it would be wise to contact at least two or three banks to compare the services and rates available. Having narrowed the list of candidates to a single bank, the process of opening the new account must be undertaken. That process is explained fully in the next chapter.

9

Opening an Account

THE OPENING OF AN ACCOUNT AT A BANK IN SWITZERLAND IS VERY MUCH LIKE THE process at an American bank: a new customer fills out a few forms and delivers the paperwork, together with an initial deposit, to the bank. Upon accepting the completed forms and deposit, the bank issues a deposit receipt and supplies the customer with an account number to be used in future transactions. If desired, a checkbook is also issued at this time.

Despite the similarities, persons opening an account in Switzerland for the first time will encounter a few different practices and documents to be completed. This chapter covers all the steps required to open demand and savings-type accounts (with more specialized accounts described in chapters 12 and 13).

IN PERSON OR BY MAIL?

Although the opening process is very much like that at an American bank, a new American customer of a Swiss bank has the option of opening the account in person or through the mail. Some customers will no doubt prefer to be present to open their accounts. The thought of entrusting personal money to the care of unknown persons in a foreign country might seem to be too much of a risk, even for those who are comfortable with earning their wealth through risk-taking ventures. Potential customers can elect to do it during a vacation to Switzerland, while traveling through Europe, or during a special trip to accomplish the task.

The choice as to whether a customer should appear personally is not always available. Some Swiss banks require that *all* new customers be present in order to open an account. This requirement is especially true for most small banks and virtually all private banks.

For the smaller banks, the requirement is understandable due to the unusual nature of the request. Small banks are usually found in small communities, and the request to open an account by a foreign customer might come as a surprise to the local banker. The local banker would likely be agreeable to opening an account but would want to meet the customer. After all, the banker knows all the bank's other customers.

For private banks, a request for personal appearance is also understandable. As mentioned earlier, private bankers specialize primarily in investment and portfolio management services. Because of the nature of the service, the banker would require the type of clear understanding that only a personal encounter may produce.

During the initial meeting, a new customer will be asked to present a passport as proof of identity. The fact is that all Swiss banks (like American banks) are required to establish the identity of new customers. Passports are considered sufficient for this purpose.

Some bankers also like to see a letter of reference from the American customer's bank. It is a good idea for persons traveling to Switzerland for opening an account to take along such a letter. Normal banking references include such information as length of relationship and whether the person has been shown to be a responsible customer during that period. In order to preserve the discreet nature of the opening process, the letter may be addressed to "to whom it may concern" without letting the American banker being any the wiser about the purpose of the letter.

BANK FORMS

Whether an account is opened in person or by mail, the customer will have to complete a number of official forms. As in the United States, a bureaucracy of forms (in duplicate or triplicate) is commonplace when dealing with financial institutions.

Application for Opening an Account

The primary form to be completed in opening an account is the application. For some banks, this form is all that is required to initiate the opening process; other forms are mailed only after a completed application is received. As shown in Fig. 9-1, the application form can be quite simple indeed, generally requesting more in the way of instructions to the bank than information about the new customer. Note the section on the application regarding account holders. As with American banks, accounts may be held individually or in the name of two or more parties (called joint and several accounts). A distinguishing feature of joint and several accounts is that any of the holders, individually and independently of the others, is entitled to withdraw the entire balance of the account. Joint depositors must determine among themselves their respective rights and obligations, and these are

Fischental Bankverein
QQQQQQQQQQQQQQQQQQ

Application for the Opening of an Account

I wish to open an account with your bank.

Surname	First Name(s)	Date of Birth

Residence Address/Postal Code/Country

Nationality	Passport No.	Date of Birth	Profession

Type of Account

☐ Current Account in SFr
☐ Current Account in U.S.$
☐ Current Account in _____
☐ Deposit Account in SFr

☐ Savings Account in SFr
☐ Investment Savings Account in SFr
☐ Senior Citizen Savings Account in SFr
☐ Youth Savings Account in SFr

Account Holders

☐ The account is to be solely in the applicant's name
☐ The account is to be held jointly in the name(s) of
_____ and/or
_____

Correspondence   (Language _____)

☐ To be sent to the following address
_____
_____

☐ To be retained by the bank and forwarded to account holder only upon special request.

This request is to be accompanied by an initial deposit of at least SFr 1,000.

Date _____   Signature(s)_____
                                                           _____

Fig. 9-1. Application for opening a Swiss bank account.

considered to be of no concern to the bank. Swiss banking law views joint and several accounts as owned by individuals with identical claims to the account balances.

Declaration on Opening an Account

The Declaration on Opening an Account (Fig. 9-2) will be unfamiliar to Americans as there exists no similar form in American banks. Known as Form A, the declaration serves to clarify two significant features of the account.

Ultimate ownership of bank funds   It was once possible for an individual to open an account in Switzerland on behalf of another, unspecified individual (called the beneficial owner). However, Swiss bankers became increasingly sensitive to worldwide charges that, by not demanding to know who the owners really were, the banks were contributing to organized criminal activities by allowing foreign criminals to use the accounts to launder their *dirty money.*

In 1977 the Swiss Bankers' Association, in what many observers considered a significant concession to international pressure, agreed to observe greater care in opening accounts and accepting deposits. By signing an agreement with the Swiss National Bank known as the *Convention de diligence,* the banking establishment agreed to ascertain the true identity of all new account holders as well as the beneficial owners (if different). The banks further agreed to refuse acceptance of any funds believed to have arisen from unlawful transactions. Upon adoption of the convention, Form A became a routine part of an account opening process. (Note: See chapter 4 for a discussion of exceptions to the convention and Form B accounts).

Limitation of bank secrecy   If the first purpose of Form A is to provide clarification of funds ownership to the bank, a second purpose is to provide a clear message to the customer: secrecy privileges allowed to Swiss bank accounts under law are limited. Furthermore, the limitations to secrecy are expressly extended to include any so-called *numbered accounts.*

Power of Attorney

Figure 9-3 illustrates a typical Power of Attorney. Serving the same purpose as an American power of attorney, the instrument is designed to convey to a third party (or parties) the right to represent the account holder in banking transactions. Because of the broad nature of Swiss banking activities, those who grant powers of attorney should be aware that the powers may extend beyond typical American banking activities and include control over fiduciary investments, securities and metals transactions, and other routine transactions.

It is important to understand that Swiss powers of attorney convey a special privilege that is unknown in America. Under Swiss law a power of attorney remains in force in the event of death or incapacity on the part of the grantor. Revocation of the instrument must be made in writing by the holder. Similar to American law, however, is another Swiss provision that forbids deferring the validity of the instrument until the death of the account holder.

A   Account No.: _____   Holder: _____

_____

Declaration on opening an account or securities account

(Form A as per Art. 3 and 4 CDB)

The undersigned hereby declares:
(mark with a cross where applicable)

☐ **as holder of the account,**

   ☐ that he is the beneficial owner of the assets to be deposited with the bank,

   ☐ that the beneficial owner of the assets to be deposited with the bank is:

     Full name (or firm)   Address/Domicile/Country
                                      (or location of head office)

_____

☐ **as representative of the account holder,**

that the following person(s) is/are the beneficial owner(s) of the assets to be deposited with the bank:

     Full name (or firm)   Address/Domicile/Country
                                      (or location of head office)

_____

The undersigned takes due note that:

– the banking secrecy privilege protected by Art. 47 of the Federal Law on Banks and Savings Banks of November 8, 1934/March 11, 1971 is not unrestricted. The officers, employees and mandataries of the bank are liable to provide evidence and information vis-à-vis the authorities when required to do so under federal or cantonal laws (such as during a criminal proceeding). Such an obligation also exists vis-à-vis foreign authorities, insofar as the Swiss Confederation grants judicial assistance to the country concerned;

– the system of numbered or coded accounts and deposits is a purely internal measure of the bank and in no way affects the obligation to provide evidence or to testify to the authorities.

_____

Full name, or firm, if applicable

_____

Exact address

_____

Place and date   Signature

Fig. 9-2a. Declaration on opening an account.

Declaration on opening an account or deposit

(Form A according to Art. 4 and 5 ACB)

The undersigned hereby declares:

☐ that he is acting for his own account,

☐ that he is acting for the account of the following person(s):

Name/Company   Domicile, Country

_____

☐ that the domiciliary company he is representing is controlled by the following individual(s):

Name(s)   Christian name(s)   Place of residence, Country

_____

(cross where applicable)

The undersigned is aware of the fact that banking secrecy, protected in accordance with Art. 47 of the Federal Law on Banks and Savings Banks of 8th November, 1934/11th March, 1971, is not unrestricted: The organs, employees and mandataries of the bank are liable to give evidence and information vis-à-vis the authorities where federal and cantonal stipulations require their so doing (e.g. in criminal proceedings). This obligation also exists vis-à-vis foreign authorities insofar as the Swiss Confederation grants judicial assistance to the country in question.
The undersigned is also aware of the fact that the establishment of accounts and deposits maintained under numbers or passwords is a purely internal measure of the bank affecting in no way its obligation vis-à-vis the authorities to testify or to furnish information.

_____

Name   Christian name

_____

Address of residence

_____

Place, date   Signature

Fig. 9-2b.

Fischental Bankverein

POWER OF ATTORNEY

I/we the undersigned

_____

_____

hereby bestow/s **FULL POWER OF ATTORNEY to**

_____

_____

to be my/our representative under the law in any way whatsoever in dealings with Fischental Bankverein. The Attorney(s) is/are empowered to represent me/us in every respect including the right to purchase, sell, pledge, and withdraw securities or other items of value.

It is expressly laid down that this power of attorney does not terminate with the loss of capacity to act or with the death of the principal, but shall remain in force.

Any dispute arising from this agreement shall be decided according to Swiss law The place of performance, the place for prosecution of customers domiciled abroad, as well as the exclusive jurisdiction of lawsuits and any other kinds of legal proceedings, shall be Zurich, except that Fischental Bankverein may sue the customer in any competent court at the domicile of the customer or in any other court having jurisdiction.

Place and Date   Signature(s) of the Principals

_____   _____

                                        _____

Signature(s) of the Attorney(s)

_____

_____

Fig. 9-3. Power of attorney.

Signature Card

Those customers who do not appear in person to open an account will be asked to provide a specimen signature, which is certified (or guaranteed) by a well-known bank or an office of a Swiss diplomatic representative. If the account is a joint account, each of the joint owners must supply a certified signature. Although a few banks will accept notarized signatures, this is not generally the case.

A certified signature card (see Fig. 9-4) serves two distinct functions. Aside from providing the bank with an identifying signature to validate future instructions, the document allows the bank to show that it has proven the identity of the new customer (as required under the *Convention de diligence*). Under Article 3 of the convention, a bank-certified signature will serve to establish the identity of a customer if the certifying bank is listed in a recognized publication of banks, such as Banker's Almanac and Yearbook, The Banker's World Directory, and Polk's World Bank Directory.

It is interesting to note that on most signature cards the bank's name is not evident. A generic signature card is a typically Swiss courtesy that provides discretion when signatures are certified by other bank personnel. In actuality, however, the specimen signature cards are not necessary. Banks will generally permit the specimen signature to be made on a blank sheet of paper. If a blank sheet of paper is used, it must contain the same information as the specimen signature card, as well as the seal of the bank certifying the signature.

The undersigned herewith confirms the authenticity of the specimen signature appearing below:

Surname: _____   Christian Name: _____

Nationality: _____   Date of Birth: _____

Specimen:

Place and Date: _____   Seal and Authorized Signature: _____

Fig. 9-4. Specimen signature card.

Fiduciary Agreement

Fiduciary time deposits were described in chapter 7 as money market investments made in the name of a bank on behalf of one of its customers. Account balances are invested in money market instruments issued outside Switzerland, resulting in low-risk, anonymous investments free of Swiss income taxes.

In order for the bank to execute fiduciary transactions, there must exist a bank account (usually a current or deposit account) from which the investment costs can be paid and to which the investment proceeds can be credited. Furthermore, the bank will require that an agreement be signed that outlines the rights and obligations of both the customer and the bank. A typical agreement is shown in Fig. 9-5.

An astute observer may have noticed that remarkably absent from all forms is a request for the customer's social security number. The truth is that Swiss bankers are entirely uninterested in any American's social security number. Although the lack of interest may not be surprising, it may nonetheless be refreshing to many Americans.

GENERAL CONDITIONS

In response to their letters of inquiry, potential customers of Swiss banks will not only receive information and forms necessary to establish a bank account but also a copy of the bank's General Conditions (Allgemeine Geschäftsbedingungen). The General Conditions are intended to clearly outline the regulations that govern the relationship between the bank and its clients. Although certain client rights are covered in the regulations, the primary intent of the document is to provide the bank with an airtight set of rules protecting it against losses arising from client actions and external conditions.

A few banks regard the General Conditions as a contract requiring customer signature. Generally, however, this is not the case, although a sentence may be appended to an account application form (signature card) stating that the customer has read the General Conditions and agrees to be bound by them.

A copy of the General Conditions for Fischental Bankverein, our fictitious bank, is shown in Fig. 9-6. The form is intended as a representative example of the General Conditions for most Swiss banks.

COMPLETING THE PROCESS

It is not unknown for a bank to respond to a letter of inquiry by requesting that an initial deposit be made prior to mailing that customer any forms necessary to open an account. In such cases, the deposit serves as a kind of "earnest money," proving the intentions of the person expressing a desire to open an account. While there is no reason to fear the loss of the earnest money deposit, it is understandable that many Americans would be put off by such a seemingly backward process. At most banks, however, whether an account is opened by mail or in person, an initial deposit is expected at the time the completed forms are submitted. In this regard the banks are no different from American banks.

Fischental Bankverein
ꟼꟼꟼꟼꟼꟼꟼꟼꟼꟼꟼꟼꟼ

Fiduciary Agreement

between_____ (hereinafter referred to as the "Client")

and **Fischental Bankverein** hereinafter referred to as **FB**)

the following provisions are agreed:

1. The customer hereby instructs FB to effect capital investments in the form of time deposits with foreign banks or foreign companies in FB's own name, but for the account and at the risk of the Client. FB acts at its own discretion and as Agent within the meaning of Article 394ff. of the Swiss Federal Code of Obligations. However, the Client is expressly authorized under this Agreement to issue specific written instructions to the Bank for the operation of such time deposits.

2. The amount, the debtor, and the conditions of the investments involved shall be designated at the discretion of the FB or by the Client in the specific written instructions. Specific instructions in writing concerning the renewal of time deposits which are due for repayment must reach FB at the latest one week prior to the due date, otherwise FB decides at its option on the renewal, if any, and the conditions of the investment.

3. Time deposits are effected within the limits of the Client's existing credit balances. It is deemed agreed that in the case of investments which FB places at its own discretion, it may not utilize any of the credit facilities granted to the Client.

4. FB has the sole obligation of paying to the Client such amounts as have been credited to FB, at its free disposal, in the form of repayment of the principal and of interest, at its domicile specified in paragraph 7.

5. If the debtor does not fulfill its commitments or fulfills them only partially, or if it cannot meet its obligations due to transfer restrictions and foreign exchange controls imposed in its own country of domicile or in the country of the denominating currency, FB is obligated solely to assign the Client the claim held on his behalf. FB is under no obligation to perform any other services.
   The Client undertakes to pay an order commission of 1/2% per annum in advance to FB, calculated on the amount(s) invested with the debtor(s) from time to time, but to pay in any case the minimum order commission of SFr. 50 or equivalent stipulated by the bank.

6. All legal aspects of the relationship between the Client and FB shall be governed by Swiss law. The place of performance, exclusive place of jurisdiction for lawsuits and other kinds of legal proceedings as well as place of foreclosure, but the latter only for clients with domicile outside of Switzerland, shall be Fischental, except only that FB may also sue the Client in any competent court at his domicile or any other court having jurisdiction.

Place and Date: Signature (Client)

Fig. 9-5. Fiduciary agreement.

Fischental Bankverein

GENERAL CONDITIONS

The following conditions shall govern the relationship between the Bank and the customer.

1. Due Care and Secrecy
a) The Bank undertakes to conduct all business transactions with due care and attention.
b) In all matters between the Bank and customer, bank officials and employees will observe strictest secrecy in accordance with Swiss Banking law.

2. Power of Disposition The signatures of persons authorized to sign for the customer, which has been filed with Bank, shall be binding until revoked in writing by the customer.

3. Communications of the Bank Communications of the Bank shall be deemed to have been properly made if they have been dispatched to the last address given to it by the customer. The date of dispatch is deemed to be the date appearing on the copy or dispatch lists in possession of the Bank. Mail to be held by the bank shall be regarded as delivered on the date indicated thereon.

4. Errors in Transmission Damages resulting from the use of mails, telegraph, telephone, telex or other forms of transmission or transport enterprises due to loss, delay, misunderstandings, duplicates, or to any other reason shall be borne by the customer unless attributable to gross fault on the part of the Bank.

5. Errors in Executing Transactions If a loss occurs from the nonexecution or erroneous execution of orders, the Bank is liable only for the loss of interest, unless it has been warned of imminent risk of a more extensive loss.

6. Incapacity to Act The customer bears any damages caused by his/her own or third party's incapacity to act unless such incapacity has been published in a Swiss official gazette or communicated to the Bank in writing in case of a third party.

7. Verification of Signatures & Identity The customer bears all damage resulting from the nondiscovery of forgeries or faulty identification unless the Bank is guilty of gross negligence.

8. Lien and Right of Set-off
a) In all cases where the customer has debt obligations toward the Bank, the latter has a lien on all assets which it holds in custody for the account of the client at any of its branches or elsewhere. This also applies to specifically secured or completely unsecured credits and loans.
b) Nonbearer securities are hereby pledged to the Bank to secure its claims.
c) The Bank has a right of set-off with respect to any claims against it, without regard to the due date or currency of its own claims.
d) If the client is in arrears, the Bank may, at its choice, dispose of the assets on which it has a lien either by way of legal enforcement or by free sale.

9. Drafts, Cheques, and Other Instruments If drafts, cheques, or other instruments already discounted or credited remain unpaid, the Bank reserves the right to redebit them. Up to the settlement of a possible debit balance, the Bank reserves the right to claim from each obligee of the instrument the full amount of the drafts, cheques, and other instruments with secondary claims. Insofar as it is called upon the Bank's services for foreign bills of exchange and cheques within the period of limitation prevailing abroad, the owner of the account will be responsible for all consequences.

10. Holidays In transactions with the Bank, Saturdays are treated the same as officially recognized public holidays.

11. Termination The Bank has the right to terminate existing business relations at any time

Fig. 9-6. General conditions—Fischental Bankverein.

Fig. 9-6. Continued

with immediate effect. In particular, the Bank may cancel promised or used credits, and call in its credit balances which thereby become immediately due for repayment.

12. Amendments to General Conditions   The Bank reserves the right to amend the General Conditions at any time. Customer will be notified of amendments by circular letter or other appropriate means and will be considered as having been accepted if no objections are raised within one month.

13. Applicable Law and Jurisdiction   All legal relations with the Bank are subject to Swiss law. Place of performance and of exclusive jurisdiction for all proceedings is Fischental. The Bank, however, has the unilateral right to sue the customer at the competent court of his/her residence or at any other competent court.

Date

_____

Signature

_____

The minimum amount required to open an account will be clearly noted in the bank's correspondence sent with the account forms. The minimum initial deposit is just that and does not imply required amounts for future deposits.

Also included with the forms will be instructions for the remittance of the initial deposit. There are a variety of ways in which the funds may be transmitted to Switzerland. Normally, a bank will request that the transfer be made by cashier's check, bank draft, or wire transfer. Subsequent deposits, however, can be effected through a variety of other means. Chapter 10 will discuss all the major mechanisms available to transfer funds both to and from a Swiss bank.

Good business sense dictates that copies of all documents be retained for future reference. This applies also to copies of financial instruments, including checks, drafts, and receipts for wire transfers.

Assuming that the customer has elected to receive correspondence from the bank, a slight time delay of one to two weeks should be expected before receiving a written confirmation from the bank that the funds have been received and the account is opened. For those not wishing to receive regular correspondence from their bank, it is recommended that the bank be instructed to send only an acknowledgement of the opening of the account and a receipt for the initial deposit.

Some banks will send a deposit receipt prior to other official notification that an account has been established. This is especially true if the funds were transferred separately from the forms establishing the account (e.g., wire transfer). Within a short time, however, the official confirmation of the account opening should arrive. In addition, some banks will send to new customers identification cards, deposit transmittal slips, and various other forms for conducting future transactions.

Those looking to a Swiss bank account as a means of achieving confidentiality in personal financial affairs will be comforted to know that the celebrated secrecy laws of Switzerland cover all banking activities. Thus, the contents of the letter of inquiry, as well as any data on completed forms, are guarded by the same secrecy statutes that guard all banking records.

CONCLUDING REMARKS

This chapter has described the general procedures and forms used by most banks in opening a new account. Obviously, there will be some variation in the procedures among the 622 banks in Switzerland. Most often the variation will be in the documents to be completed by the prospective customers. It is not uncommon to find dual purpose forms (e.g., power of attorney on one side, signature specimen on the reverse) or multilanguage forms, with as many as four languages used on a single form.

Americans will find a number of similarities between their Swiss banks and their local American banks. A possible disappointment is that no toasters, teddy bears, or other gifts are awarded to those who open accounts in Switzerland. Most would agree, however, that the other benefits of Swiss accounts sufficiently compensate for the lack of token gifts.

10

Account Maintenance

Once an American has opened a bank account in Switzerland, the new customer needs to understand the various ways in which routine transactions may be carried out. But first, the customer should be congizant of the various legal aspects relating to deposit and withdrawal transactions.

THE LEGALITIES

Transaction Reporting

With the passage of the Bank Secrecy Act of 1970, the U.S. government imposed reporting requirements on all large transfers of cash crossing U.S. borders. Under current statutes, anyone transporting, mailing, shipping, or receiving amounts of $10,000 or more on any one occasion is required to communicate that fact on Customs Form 4790 (see Fig. 4-2).

Form 4790, together with instructions for completion, is available from all U.S. Customs Service offices. Persons shipping or mailing reportable amounts must file the report on or before the date of the shipment. Travelers carrying reportable amounts with them must file the form at the time of departure or entry into the United States, and persons receiving reportable funds have 30 days in which to make the report. Penalties for failure to file the report may include fines, imprisonment, and seizure and forfeiture of the funds.

Customs reporting is not limited to cash movements only. The reports are mandatory for transfers of all *monetary instruments*, regardless of type. Monetary instruments include currencies (U.S. and foreign) and all financial instruments that are in bearer form.

Bearer instruments are characterized by their free negotiability (cash-like transferability). Generally, the words "pay to the bearer" signal the identity of a bearer instrument while "pay to the order of" identifies a nonbearer instrument. However, bearer instruments also include checks made payable to cash and other drafts drawn without specifying the name of a payee.

It is important to understand that a *non*monetary instrument (not reportable) can become a monetary instrument (reportable) if it has been endorsed in blank. A blank endorsement is one that specifies no particular endorsee and usually consists only of the payee's signature or name stamp. *Restrictive* endorsements, on the other hand, containing words such as "For Deposit only at Fischental Bank," preclude negotiability by any bearer and are considered nonbearer instruments.

Thus, customs reporting requirements extend to such instruments as money orders, personal checks, and bank (cashiers) checks, but only if they are made payable to cash or if they do not specify the name of a payee. Travelers checks that have been countersigned but do not name a payee are also included in this category. In addition, the broad definition of monetary instruments encompasses all investment securities payable *to bearer* or in any form that permits title to pass upon delivery.

Excluded from the reporting requirements are those instruments payable to specific individuals or companies. Travelers' checks, money orders, and bank checks that specify the name of a payee are considered nonmonetary instruments and, as such, are excluded from customs reporting. Also excluded are any securities registered in the owner's name.

The intent of the reporting law is not difficult to comprehend. Bearer instruments, including currencies, leave no trail because they are freely negotiable and previous owners normally cannot be identified. By imposing the reporting law, the federal government has ensured that a trail will be created whenever a material amount of cash and cash-like instruments leaves or enters the United States. Nonmonetary instruments, by their nature, provide a record of the holders of the instruments, and no further trail is considered necessary by regulatory and enforcement agencies.

Transfers of money through banking channels (such as wire transfers) are also excluded from customs reporting. Not all go unreported, however. As pointed out in chapter 4, transfers of $10,000 or more are automatically reported to the IRS by the banks involved.

Account Reporting

In addition to reporting transactional information, U.S. statutes require owners of foreign accounts to annually report their accounts to the federal government. More specifically, every U.S. citizen, resident, partnership, corporation, estate, or trust that has signature authority (or any other control) over an account in a foreign country must report that fact to the U.S. Department of the Treasury. The report is to be made on Treasury Department form TD F 90-22.1 (see Fig. 10-1) and filed by June 30 of the year following any year in which such an account existed.

The annual report is waived for depositors whose aggregate account balances do not exceed $10,000 (or the equivalent) at any time during the year. However, in determining whether the aggregate amount exceeds $10,000, all accounts must be included. Thus, an individual owning two accounts, each with a balance of $9,000, is required to file the report, as the total aggregate value ($18,000) exceeds the $10,000 amount.

For purposes of determining the aggregate value of the account(s), foreign currencies are valued using end-of-year exchange rates. Securities values are determined based on end-of-year market values or, if the securities were withdrawn from the account during the year, the value at the date of withdrawal.

Again, the intent of the law is clear. As the bottom of the form indicates, the information is wanted because of its "high degree of usefulness in criminal, tax, or regulatory investigations or proceedings." At one time the information now included on form TD F 90-22.1 was disclosed on a separate schedule in the account owner's federal income tax return. Because of the relative difficulty for other governmental agencies to gain access to IRS files, the information is now filed with the Department of the Treasury, making legal access easier for other investigators. Although the schedule is no longer a part of the income tax return, individual taxpayers must still alert the IRS of the existence of foreign accounts. This is done in the completion of Schedule B of Form 1040 (see Fig. 10-2). Again, taxpayers must only inform the IRS if the aggregate balances of all foreign accounts exceeds $10,000.

Freedom of Capital Movement

Americans can take some comfort from the fact that, at present, the U.S. government does not restrict the *amount* of money that one of its citizens may take out of or bring into the United States. In this respect, the United States differs from the majority of the world's countries. The federal government has not always permitted such a freeflowing policy to its citizens, and no one can predict with any degree of certainty how far into the future the current policy may extend.

As we have seen, freedom of money movement does *not* extend to dirty money or other booty hidden for the purpose of evading income taxes. The United States has assembled and deployed defensive weapons to combat these illegal flows. One of the first deterrents against illegal flows was the imposition of record-keeping and reporting requirements by the Bank Secrecy Act. The provisions of the law were clearly aimed at disrupting money laundering schemes of tax evaders, drug traffickers, and other criminals by causing a trail to be created whenever the money moves through the U.S. banking system. A useful adjunct to the Secrecy Act was the enactment of the Money Laundering Control Act of 1986. This legislation made it a criminal act to structure transactions in such a manner as to avoid reporting under the Secrecy Act.

Department of the Treasury **TD F 90-22.1** (9-83) SUPERSEDES ALL PREVIOUS EDITIONS	**REPORT OF FOREIGN BANK AND FINANCIAL ACCOUNTS** For the calendar year 19 **Do not file this form with your Federal Tax Return**	**Form Approved: OMB No. 1505-0021**

This form should be used to report financial interest in or signature authority or other authority over one or more bank accounts, securities accounts, or other financial accounts in foreign countries as required by Department of the Treasury Regulations (31 CFR 103). You are not required to file a report if the aggregate value of the accounts did not exceed $5,000. Check all appropriate boxes. SEE INSTRUCTIONS ON BACK FOR DEFINITIONS. File this form with Dept. of the Treasury, P.O. Box 1918 Memphis, TN 38101

1. Name (Last, First, Middle) 4. Address (Street, City, State, Country, ZIP)	2. Social security number or employer identification number if other than individual	3. Name in item 1 refers to ☐ Individual ☐ Partnership ☐ Corporation ☐ Fiduciary

5. ☐ I had signature authority or other authority over one or more foreign accounts, but I had no "financial interest" in such accounts (see instruction J). Indicate for these accounts:

(a)   Name and social security number or taxpayer identification number of each owner _____

(b)   Address of each owner _____

(Do not complete item 9 for these accounts)

6. ☐ I had a "financial interest" in one or more foreign accounts owned by a domestic corporation, partnership or trust which is required to file TD F 90-22.1. (See instruction L). Indicate for these accounts

(a)   Name and taxpayer identification number of each such corporation, partnership or trust _____

(b)   Address of each such corporation, partnership or trust _____

(Do not complete item 9 for these accounts)

7. ☐ I had a "financial interest" in one or more foreign accounts, but the total maximum value of these accounts (see instruction I) did not exceed $10,000 at any time during the year. (If you checked this box, do not complete item 9).

8. ☐ I had a "financial interest" in 25 or more foreign accounts. (If you checked this box, do not complete item 9.)

9. If you had a "financial interest" in one or more but fewer than 25 foreign accounts which are required to be reported, and the total maximum value of the accounts exceeded $10,000 during the year (see instruction I), write the total number of those accounts in the box below:
Complete items (a) through (f) below for one of the accounts and attach a separate TD F 90-22.1 for each of the others.
Items 1, 2, 3, 9, and 10 must be completed for each account.

Check here if this is an attachment. ☐

(a) Name in which account is maintained	(b) Name of bank or other person with whom account is maintained
(c) Number and other account designation, if any	(d) Address of office or branch where account is maintained

(e) Type of account. (If not certain of English name for the type of account, give the foreign language name and describe the nature of the account. Attach additional sheets if necessary.)

☐ Bank Account   ☐ Securities Account   ☐ Other (specify)

(f) Maximum value of account (see instruction I) ☐ Under $10,000	☐ $10,000 to $50,000	☐ $50,000 to $100,000	☐ Over $100,000

10. Signature	11. Title (Not necessary if reporting personal account)	12. Date

PRIVACY ACT NOTIFICATION

Pursuant to the requirements of Public Law 93-579, (Privacy Act of 1974), notice is hereby given that the authority to collect information on TD F 90-22.1 in accordance with 5 U.S.C. 552(e)(3) is Public Law 91-508; 31 U.S.C. 1121; 5 U.S.C. 301, 31 CFR Part 103.

The principal purpose for collecting the information is to assure maintenance of reports or records where such reports or records have a high degree of usefulness in criminal, tax, or regulatory investigations or proceedings. The information collected may be provided to those officers and employees of any constituent unit of the Department of the Treasury who have a need for the records in the performance of their duties. The records may be referred to any other department or agency of the Federal Government upon the request of the head of such department or agency for use in a criminal, tax, or regulatory investigation or proceeding

Disclosure of this information is mandatory. Civil and criminal penalties, including under certain circumstances a fine of not more than $500,000 and imprisonment of not more than five years, are provided for failure to file a report, supply information, and for filing a false or fraudulent report.

Disclosure of the social security number is mandatory. The authority to collect this number is 31 CFR 103. The social security number will be used as a means to identify the individual who files the report.

Fig. 10-1. Form TD F 90-22.1—Report of foreign bank and financial accounts.

Fig. 10-1. Continued

INSTRUCTIONS

A. Who Must File a Report—Each United States person who has a financial interest in or signature authority or other authority over bank, securities, or other financial accounts in a foreign country. which exceeds $5,000 in aggregate value at any time during the calendar year, must report that relationship each calendar year by filing TD F 90-22.1 with the Department of the Treasury on or before June 30, of the succeeding year.

An officer or employee of a commercial bank which is subject to the supervision of the Comptroller of the Currency, the Board of Governors of the Federal Reserve System or the Federal Deposit Insurance Corpora tion need not report that he has signature or other authority over a foreign bank. securi ties or other financial account maintained by the bank unless he has a personal finan cial interest in the account

In addition, an officer or employee of a domestic corporation whose securities are listed upon national securities exchanges or which has assets exceeding $1 million and 500 or more shareholders of record need not file such a report concerning his signature authority over a foreign financial account of the corporation, if he has no personal finan cial interest in the account and has been ad vised in writing by the chief financial officer of the corporation that the corporation has filed a current report which includes that account

B. United States Person—The term "United States person" means (1) a citizen or resident of the United States. (2) a domestic partnership, (3) a domestic corpo ration, or (4) a domestic estate or trust.

C. When and where to File—This report shall be filed on or before June 30 each cal endar year with the Department of the Treasury. Post Office Box 1918. Memphis. TN. 38101. or it may be hand carried to any local office of the Internal Revenue Service for forwarding to the Department of the Treasury. Memphis. TN

D. Account in a Foreign Country—A "foreign country" includes all geographical areas located outside the United States. Guam. Puerto Rico, and the Virgin Islands

Report any account maintained with a bank (except a military banking facility as defined in instruction E) or broker or dealer in securities that is located in a foreign country, even if it is a part of a United States bank or other institution. Do not report any account maintained with a branch. agency or other office of a foreign bank of other in stitution that is located in the United States. Guam. Puerto Rico. and the Virgin Islands

E. Military Banking Facility—Do not con sider as an account in a foreign country, an account in an institution known as a "United States military banking facility" (or "United States military finance facility") operated by a United States financial institution designated by the United States Govern ment to serve U.S. Government installations abroad, even if the United States military banking facility is located in a foreign country.

F. Bank, Financial Account—The term "bank account" means a savings. demand. checking. deposit. loan or any other account maintained with a financial institution or other person engaged in the business of banking. It includes certificates of deposit.

The term "securities account" means an account maintained with a financial institu tion or other person who buys. sells. holds. or trades stock or other securities for the benefit of another.

The term "other financial account" means any other account maintained with a finan cial institution or other person who accepts deposits, exchanges or transmits funds. or acts as a broker or dealer for future trans actions in any commodity on (or subject to the rules of) a commodity exchange or association.

G. Financial Interest—A financial interest in a bank, securities, or other financial ac count in a foreign country means an interest described in either of the following two paragraphs:

(1) A United States person has a financial interest in each account for which such per son is the owner of records or has legal title. whether the account is maintained for his or her own benefit or for the benefit of others including non-United States persons. If an account is maintained in the name of two persons jointly. or if several persons each own a partial interest in an account, each of those United States persons has a financial interest in that account.

(2) A United States person has a financial interest in each bank. securities. or other financial account in a foreign country for which the owner of record or holder of legal title is: (a) a person acting as an agent. nominee, attorney, or in some other capacity on behalf of the U.S. person; (b) a corpora tion in which the United States person owns directly or indirectly more than 50 percent of the total value of shares of stock; (c) a part nership in which the United States person owns an interest in more than 50 percent of the profits (distributive share of income), or (d) a trust in which the United States person either has a present beneficial interest in more than 50 percent of the assets or from which such person receives more than 50 percent of the current income.

H. Signature or Other Authority Over an Account—

Signature Authority—A person has signature authority over an account if such person can control the disposition of money or other property in it by delivery of a docu ment containing his or here signature (or his or her signature and that of one or more other persons) to the bank or other person with whom the account is maintained.

Other authority exists in a person who can exercise comparable power over an ac count by direct communication to the bank or other person with whom the account is maintained. either orally or by some other means.

I. Account Valuation—For items 7, 9. and Instruction A. the maximum value of an ac count is the largest amount of currency and non-monetary assets that appear on any quarterly or more frequent account state ment issued for the applicable year. If periodic account statements are not so issued, the maximum account asset value is the largest amount of currency and non monetary assets in the account at any time during the year. Convert foreign currency by using the official exchange rate at the end of the year. In valuing currency of a country that uses multiple exchange rates. use the rate which would apply if the currency in the account were converted into United States dollars at the close of the calendar year.

The value of stock, other securities or other non-monetary assets in an account reported on TD F 90-22.1 is the fair market value at the end of the calendar year, or if withdrawn from the account, at the time of the withdrawal.

For purposes of items 7, 9, and Instruction A, if you had a financial interest in more than one account, each account is to be valued separately in accordance with the foregoing two paragraphs.

If you had a financial interest in one or more but fewer than 25 accounts, and you are unable to determine whether the max imum value of these accounts exceeded $10,000 at any time during the year, check item 9 (do not check item 7) and complete item 9 for each of these accounts.

J. United States Persons with Authority Over but No Interest in an Account—Except as provided in Instruction A and the follow ing paragraph, you must state the name. ad dress, and identifying number of each owner of an account over which you had authority, but if you check item 5 for more than one ac count of the same owner, you need identify the owner only once.

If you check item 5 for one or more ac counts in which no United States person had a financial interest, you may state on the first line of this item, in lieu of supplying information about the owner. "No U.S. per son had any financial interest in the foreign accounts." This statement must be based upon the actual belief of the person filing this form after he or she has taken reasonable measures to endure its correct ness.

If you check item 5 for accounts owned by a domestic corporation and its domestic and/or foreign subsidiaries. you may treat them as one owner and write in the space provided. the name of the parent corpora tion, followed by "and related entities." and the identifying number and address of the parent corporation.

K. Consolidated Reporting—A corpora tion which owns directly or indirectly more than 50 percent interest in one or more other entities will be permitted to file a con solidated report on TD F 90-22.1. on behalf of itself and such other entities provided that a listing of them is made part of the con solidated report. Such reports should be signed by an authorized official of the parent corporation.

If the group of entities covered by a con solidated report has a financial interest in 25 or more foreign financial accounts. the reporting corporation need only note that fact on the form, it will, however. be required to provide detailed information concerning each account when so requested by the Secretary or his delegate.

L. Avoiding Duplicate Reporting—If you had financial interest (as defined in instruc tion G(2)(b). (c) or (d) in one or more accounts which are owned by a domestic corporation. partnership or trust which is required to file TD F 90-22.1 with respect to these accounts in lieu of completing item 9 for each account you may check item 6 and provide the re quired information.

M. Providing Additional Information—Any person who does not complete item 9, shall when requested by the Department of the Treasury provide the information called for in item 9.

N. Signature (Item 10)—*This report must be signed* by the person named in Item 1. If the report is being filed on behalf of a part nership, corporation, or fiduciary. it must be signed by an authorized individual.

O. Penalties—For criminal penalties for failure to file a report. supply information, and for filing a false or fraudulent report see 31 U.S.C. 5322(a), 31 U.S.C. 5322(b). and 1R U.S.C. 1001.

Schedules A&B (Form 1040) 1988

OMB No. 1545-0074   Page **2**

Name(s) as shown on Form 1040. (Do not ente   ne and social security number if shown on other side.)

Your social security number

Schedule B—Interest and Dividend Income

Attachment
Sequence No. **08**

**Part I
Interest
Income**

(See
Instructions on
pages 10 and 26.)

If you received more than $400 in taxable interest income, you must complete Part I and Part III and list ALL interest received. You must report all interest on Form 1040, even if you are not required to complete Part I and Part III. If you received, as a nominee, interest that actually belongs to another person, or you received or paid accrued interest on securities transferred between interest payment dates, see page 27.

Interest Income		Amount	
1 Interest income from seller-financed mortgages. (See Instructions and list name of payer.) ▶	1		
2 Other interest income (list name of payer) ▶			
	2		
3 Add the amounts on lines 1 and 2. Enter the total here and on Form 1040, line 8a. ▶	3		

Note: If you received a Form 1099–INT or Form 1099–OID from a brokerage firm, list the firm's name as the payer and enter the total interest shown on that form.

**Part II
Dividend
Income**

(See
Instructions on
pages 11 and
27.)

If you received more than $400 in gross dividends and/or other distributions on stock, complete Part II and Part III. You must report all taxable dividends on Form 1040, even if you are not required to complete Part II and Part III. If you received, as a nominee, dividends that actually belong to another person, see page 27.

Dividend Income		Amount	
4 Dividend income (list name of payer—include on this line capital gain distributions, nontaxable distributions, etc.) ▶			
	4		

Note: If you received a Form 1099-DIV from a brokerage firm, list the firm's name as the payer and enter the total dividends shown on that form.

5 Add the amounts on line 4. Enter the total here	5		
6 Capital gain distributions. Enter here and on line 13, Schedule D.*	6		
7 Nontaxable distributions. (See Schedule D Instructions for adjustment to basis.)	7		
8 Add the amounts on lines 6 and 7. Enter the total here	8		
9 Subtract line 8 from line 5. Enter the result here and on Form 1040, line 9 . . . ▶	9		

If you received capital gain distributions but do not need Schedule D to report any other gains or losses, enter your capital gain distributions on Form 1040, line 14.

**Part III
Foreign
Accounts
and
Foreign
Trusts**

(See
Instructions
on page 27.)

If you received more than $400 of interest or dividends, OR if you had a foreign account or were a grantor of, or a transferor to, a foreign trust, you must answer both questions in Part III.

	Yes	No
10 At any time during the tax year, did you have an interest in or a signature or other authority over a financial account in a foreign country (such as a bank account, securities account, or other financial account)? (See page 27 of the Instructions for exceptions and filing requirements for Form TD F 90-22.1.)		
If "Yes," enter the name of the foreign country ▶		
11 Were you the grantor of, or transferor to, a foreign trust which existed during the current tax year, whether or not you have any beneficial interest in it? If "Yes," you may have to file Form 3520, 3520-A, or 926 . . .		

For Paperwork Reduction Act Notice, see Form 1040 Instructions.

Schedule B (Form 1040) 1988

Fig. 10-2. IRS Form 1040, Schedule B.

Given the resolve of Congress and those charged with the responsibility of enforcing the federal statutes, money launderers have already learned that their game is dangerous, their foes are formidable, and the sympathy and cooperation among international law enforcement officials is ever growing.

No doubt the majority of international currency transactions are perfectly legal, and it is toward these money movements that the remainder of this chapter is directed. Yet, remaining on the side of the law does not preclude taking advantage of the veil of secrecy that Swiss bank accounts are able to provide. Because secrecy is one of the fundamental reasons many Americans open accounts in Switzerland, it is necessary to comment on the way in which various transactions with a Swiss bank may be legally executed to minimize public notice and assure genuine confidentiality.

DEPOSITS

General Mechanics

Americans are accustomed to filling out deposit (or credit) slips whenever deposits are made at a bank. American banks typically provide different types of deposit slips for different types of bank accounts. Swiss banks also make deposit slips available but generally restrict their use to transactions carried out in the banks' lobbies. Although a few banks will make a supply of deposit slips available to foreign customers, this is not a widespread practice. Instead, a written set of instructions accompanying a deposit is considered appropriate.

In all correspondence relating to deposits, it is necessary to include the account number(s) involved and the customer's full name. Reference to an account number only may not be accepted unless previously agreed to by both parties (i.e., the customer and the bank) or unless the customer has already established a special *numbered account*.

Deposit receipts are handed to customers who make their deposits at a bank's premises. Similarly, deposits made by mail or bank transfers are acknowledged by a mailed deposit receipt unless, of course, the customer has previously requested that the bank hold all correspondence.

Cash   Cash deposits may be made either through the mail or by delivering the cash in person. Even though a surprising number of Americans continue to send cash to their local banks through the mail system, the mailing of cash can only be considered a foolhardy practice. While the risk of a letter being lost may not be great, the chances of recovering lost cash are almost nil.

There may be advantages in personally delivering cash to a bank for deposit. With a personal delivery, the depositor knows with certainty the moment the money has arrived at the bank. Also, because the funds do not have to be collected through an interbank clearing process, the depositor is assured that the deposit is earning interest immediately. Furthermore, delivering cash allows the customer the opportunity to become personally acquainted with the bank's staff.

Regardless of the benefits, a wise customer should consider carefully the negative aspects associated with carrying cash to the bank. The risk of loss is unquestionably highest when a customer carries cash, and lost cash is neither traceable nor replaceable. Further, cash is bulky and not easily concealed. But even if these matters are of little concern to the bank customer, matters of economics preclude most people from personally transporting their cash deposits. It is simply too expensive for most Americans to routinely travel to Switzerland to conduct their personal banking affairs.

Those who prefer to personally push their cash across the teller's counter may want to consider making their deposits at an American branch of their Swiss bank.* The American branch will handle the details of transferring the money to the proper branch location in Switzerland. Because the actual transfer of the cash is made by the bank, the customer is under no obligation to report the transaction to customs officials.

There are certain differences between making cash deposits at a bank in Switzerland and at an American branch of a Swiss bank. Cash deposits at banks in Switzerland can be made in any widely circulated currency; foreign branches, however, are unlikely to accept any currency other than local currencies. More importantly, American customers should be aware that transactions made at American branches of Swiss banks are under the jurisdiction of U.S. laws, and therefore the branches can offer no greater security in terms of confidentiality than any other bank on American soil.

Travelers' Checks   Traveler's checks are an acceptable form of money for the American customer traveling to a bank in Switzerland. In fact, given the fast replacement of lost or stolen travelers checks, they are perhaps the safest form of money to carry abroad.

If secrecy is the customer's goal, however, travelers checks make little sense. Although travelers' checks that have been cashed are not filed by the purchaser's names, records of purchasers do exist, and investigators (particularly from the IRS) have been known to search the records of old travelers' checks to trace the fiscal trail of suspected wrongdoers.

Personal checks   It is always possible for an American to transmit funds to a Swiss account by sending a personal check drawn on an American checking account. Checks may be drawn in favor of the bank or the account owner. If the check is made payable to the account owner, the instrument should contain a restrictive endorsement, such as:

> Pay to the order of (name of Swiss bank) for
> deposit to my (our) account.
>
> Signature(s)_____

Checks are perhaps the most common form of deposits in U.S. banks. In spite of the familiarity and ease associated with writing and depositing personal checks,

---

*(Business may be transacted at branches only. Representative offices of Swiss banks in the United States are not allowed to handle ordinary transactions. See chapter 8 for a complete list of Swiss banks with branches in the United States.)

there are reasons why this is not a preferred method to transmit funds to Switzerland. Most important among these reasons is that deposits received in the form of checks can only be credited to the account after the funds are collected. Collection refers to the process of a bank actually receiving (collecting) funds that have been charged to the account of the checkwriter. Thus, collection ensures that the check will not be returned to the bank for lack of sufficient funds. The collection process for a personal check may involve considerable delay, sometimes as long as three to four weeks. During this period, the depositor can neither withdraw the funds nor enjoy the earning of interest on the funds. Further, the bank will charge a collection fee and possibly other handling fees for performing the collection service.

If lost interest, miscellaneous fees, and lack of availability of funds are not sufficient to discourage sending deposits by personal check, it is important to remember that customers lose all confidentiality of financial affairs by writing checks. As previously noted, each check written on an American bank account is microfilmed and stored for possible future inspection.

Some customers of foreign banks seek to improve their chances of confidentiality by only depositing checks made payable to them by third parties. Although these checks also leave a microfilmed trail, the information may be difficult to locate as all evidence is filed in someone else's account records. Still, the problems associated with a long collection period remain.

Bank (Wire) Transfers   The fastest way to transmit funds between banks is via bank wire. In most cases, a transfer of funds from a bank account in the United States to an account in Switzerland can be accomplished within 24 hours. Funds received by bank wire are always considered collected and the amount begins earning interest immediately.

Swiss bankers recommend wire transfers as a preferred method of transmitting money. No doubt American enforcement agencies also prefer wire transfers due to the easy availability of all banking records. To wire money abroad, American banks require the name of the sender as well as the recipient's name, bank, and branch name, and account number.

Most large U.S. banks are capable of wiring a deposit to Switzerland in either U.S. dollars or Swiss francs. Sending banks charge a flat fee of $20 to $25 for all wire transfers to Europe. Receiving banks never charge a fee for processing incoming transfers. Considering the modest cost and complete avoidance of chance of loss, wire transfers should be considered by all customers sending deposits to their Swiss accounts.

Bank Drafts   Bank drafts are checks drawn by one bank on its own funds on deposit in a foreign (correspondent) bank. Drafts are normally used by persons wishing to send funds denominated in a foreign currency. Because most large banks maintain accounts at foreign banks in major cities, it is possible for bank drafts to be made out in most freely convertible foreign currencies. The drafts can be purchased by individuals in any amount and made payable to whomever the customer designates.

There are certain advantages in using bank drafts to transmit funds to foreign accounts. Because the U.S. dollars can be converted into a foreign currency at the time the draft is purchased, the purchaser knows in advance the exact amount that will be credited to the account. Another advantage is the very short collection period associated with bank drafts. The reason for the short period is that nearly every large American bank has a correspondent bank in Switzerland on which the draft may be written.

Fees for bank drafts are based on the amount of the draft. Typical fees are 1/8 of 1% of the amount of the draft, with a minimum of $15. Someone wishing to purchase a bank draft from a U.S. bank will normally be expected to pay for the draft with cash or, if the purchaser is a customer of the bank selling the draft, with a check representing collected funds on deposit in the customer's account.

Obviously, for those unconcerned with confidentiality, it is often cheaper and easier to simply wire funds to foreign destinations. However, those concerned with leaving a trail of their fiscal activities will find an advantage in purchasing and using bank drafts. The reason is that purchasers of the draft are able to attain some degree of anonymity. Although purchasers are asked to give their names and addresses and sign a receipt for the draft, banks do not file copies of purchased drafts by purchasers' names. Further, it is unlikely that a bank would ask for proof of a purchaser's identity when that consumer is paying cash. Tellers in most banks are only instructed to ask for proof of identification when the amount is unusually large or the purchaser appears to be acting in a suspicious manner. Because many small banks in the United States do not issue foreign drafts, those who sell foreign drafts at larger banks are quite accustomed to selling drafts to noncustomers.

An even higher level of confidentiality can be achieved by only depositing foreign drafts received from third parties. An owner of a Swiss account can request that amounts owed be remitted only in foreign funds drawn on a bank in Switzerland and payable to the account owner's Swiss bank. Although a dauntless investigator could conceivably uncover such a maneuver, there nevertheless remains an additional layer of secrecy from prying eyes.

Cashier's Check   A cashier's check is a bank's own check drawn upon itself and signed by the bank's cashier or some other authorized officer. A direct obligation of the bank, the instrument is normally used to pay obligations of the bank or to disburse loan proceeds. The instruments are frequently sold to customers when a personal check is not acceptable or when the customer does not maintain a checking account.

Fees for cashier's checks are quite inexpensive, ranging from three to five dollars (often depending on whether the purchaser is a bank customer). Because cashier's checks are available in dollars only, Swiss bank customers will need to await their credit advices to learn of the actual deposited amount when their accounts are denominated in currencies other than the dollar. Because the check is drawn on a U.S. bank, the customer will also have to wait for the check to be processed through normal collection procedures.

Secrecy considerations are the same for cashier's checks as for bank drafts. The degree of confidentiality that might be achieved depends on where it is purchased, how it is paid for, and to whom the check is made payable. Individuals purchasing cashier's checks from a bank where they are unknown will be asked to pay cash and, possibily, to explain why they are not purchasing the check from their own bank. Simple responses, such as "My credit union doesn't issue cashier's checks," are usually sufficient to satisfy a teller's curiosity.

Money Orders   People who do not maintain a checking account but who wish to send money to a distant party frequently make use of money orders to accomplish the task. Although money orders may be purchased from a variety of vendors, including banks, the post office, drug stores, and even gas stations, they are all very similar in nature. Money orders come in three parts. The vendor, after imprinting the amount on the face of the money order, keeps one copy (containing only the imprinted amount and the serial number) and hands over the actual money order and a copy to the purchaser. The purchaser is obligated to complete the instrument by filling in the name of the payee and the date and providing the purchaser's signature and address.

The only major difference among the money orders offered for sale by the various vendors is the maximum amount of the instruments. Banks usually limit the size of their money orders to $1,000 (recommending cashier's checks for larger amounts). The U.S. Post Office, on the other hand, places the limit at $700. Other limits placed on sellers of money orders may be considered a real bargain. Prices range from $.50 to $2.50, depending on where purchased. Postal money orders are $.75 for amounts up to $35 and $1 up to the $700 limit.

Like checks, money orders are paid through the Federal Reserve clearing system. Once endorsed, they may be deposited directly into a bank account.

Money orders provide an excellent mechanism to maintain privacy in transferring money abroad. The only evidence of the purchaser's identity is the signature and address at the bottom of the money order. Further, when one considers the illegible handwriting produced by so many individuals, there is reason to believe that the information entered on the money order by the purchaser would often prove to be useless information.

It is interesting to note that postal regulations are designed to make it difficult for anyone using postal money orders for transferring large amounts of money. Current regulations forbid a post office to sell more than $10,000 in money orders to any single customer per day. Postal employees are advised to be on the alert for customers who appear to be visiting various postal facilities or structuring money order purchases in any way to exceed the $10,000 per day limit and report the information to postal inspectors.

Those with foreign bank accounts should avoid using International Postal Money Orders to send deposits abroad. The International Postal Money Orders are designed to allow customers to send funds denominated in foreign currencies. The post office handles all conversions through its central money order facility in St. Louis and delivers the amount to the proper addressee. Customers lose all confidentiality in such transactions (by completion of Postal Form 6701) and can expect as long as four to six weeks before delivery actually takes place.

TRANSFERS AND WITHDRAWALS

As with deposits, there are a number of mechanisms available to transfer or withdraw money on deposit in a Swiss bank. There are two basic rules that need to be obeyed in order for an American to transfer or repatriate funds on deposit in Switzerland.

The first rule relates to the form of the request. Just like their American counterparts, Swiss bankers demand that all withdrawal requests be made in writing. Even withdrawals made in person in the bank's lobby require a signed withdrawal slip. Orders received by telex, telegram, or telephone cannot be accepted unless previous arrangement has been made between customer and banker. Even if a prior arrangement has been made, the banker will customarily request a written confirmation to follow.

The second rule is to observe any withdrawal restrictions on account balances. As pointed out in chapter 7, withdrawal restrictions vary based on type of account, the amount of the transaction, and the length of advance notice. For current accounts, withdrawals and transfers may be made for up to the entire balance in the account without prior notice to the bank. For other types of accounts, however, regulations regarding amounts and prior notice should be strictly observed.

Except for withdrawals effected through personal check, an advice of charge (or debit memorandum) will be sent for each withdrawal transaction.

Transfer orders   Transfer orders are merely instructions advising the bank to move funds from one account to another. Assuming all withdraw provisions are met, the transfer is easily accomplished with instructions to the bank. Figure 10-3 illustrates a simple transfer request.

Notice that the letter, although brief, is very explicit regarding the date of the transfer, amount, the currency, all accounts involved, and account numbers. Each of these items is absolutely necessary to ensure that the bank's actions comply with the depositor's intentions. In addition, the request for transfer must include the account owner's signature.

Figure 10-4 illustrates a notification of the *intention* to transfer funds between accounts. A request such as this is necessary when withdrawal or transfer privileges are limited by regulations governing the account.

Cash Withdrawals   Americans traveling to Switzerland might wish to withdraw all or a portion of their account balance in person at their Swiss bank. Assuming that any withdrawal restrictions are met, the process is identical to that in the United States. Customers need merely fill out a withdrawal slip to receive the funds.

Customers withdrawing funds from a branch other than the one where the account is domiciled will have to establish their identity to the branch. A valid passport is usually all that is necessary to prove the identity of the customer. If the amount of the transaction is unusually large, however, the customer may be asked to wait as long as one day while identity and signature are verified. To avoid such a delay, the customer might want to go directly to the branch where the account is located.

December 1, 1989

Fischental Bankverein
Talstrasse 12
CH-8497 Fischental
Switzerland

Dear Sir or Madam:

Please make the following transfer from my Savings Account to my Current Account on the date indicated:

Date	From Savings Account Number 4G-345.282	To Current Account Number 4G-728.197
January 15, 1990	SFr 20,000	SFr 20,000

Also, please advise me when the transfer has been effected.

Thank you.

Very truly yours,

James Edward McCoy
123 Main Avenue
Anytown, USA

Fig. 10-3. Transfer request.

Customers of Swiss banks with branches in the United States might want to withdraw cash balances at the counters of U.S. branches. Again, it is necessary to prove the identity of the account owner. When in doubt, the American branch might require a few days to establish proof of identity by communication with the branch in Switzerland holding the depositor's signature record. As more and more foreign banks adopt the practice of verifying remote signatures through electronic facsimile machines, the delays for purposes of comparing signature records are likely to become nonexistent.

December 1, 1989

Fischental Bankverein
Postfach 858
CH-8497 Fischental
Switzerland

Dear Sirs:

Please be advised that on June 15 of next year, I intend to make the
following transfer:

From Investment Savings Account No. 63-063-11	To Deposit Account No. 63-072-81	To Current Account No. 63-551-08
SFr 250,000	SFr 200,000	SFr 50,000

The purpose of this letter is to comply with the notification
requirements for withdrawals governing my Investment Savings Account.

Thank you.

Very truly yours,

Michelle Dawn Sebring
321 Sandra Street
Anytown, USA

Fig. 10-4. Notice of intention to transfer funds.

Checks   Checkbooks are normally only available to customers with balances
in current or deposit accounts. The checks are very much like American checks,
although the checkwriter must often specify the type of currency as well as the
amount.

Americans wishing to write checks on balances in their Swiss accounts must
realize that very few individuals or businesses in the United States are likely to
accept the checks. Anyone accepting a foreign check will most likely also receive
an education in the collection process for foreign instruments and, after experi-
encing the resultant delay, will not be so likely to accept such a check again. That
is, of course, unless that person deposits the check in his or her own Swiss bank
account, in which case the collection process is less drawn out.

Because of the inconveniences associated with using checks, there are few instances when the instruments are useful. Their usefulness is restricted primarily to facilitating transfers between banks by simply depositing a check. A check will substitute for other, more formally written instructions. A bank transfer accomplished via check should only be used when a long collection period is of little or no consequence.

Wire Transfers   For transfers of funds between banks, a wire transfer remains the quickest and most efficient method possible. A wire transfer between the United States and Switzerland not only avoids a lengthy collection period, it obviates the bother of disclosing the transfer to U.S. Customs officials.

December 1, 1989

Fischental Bankverein
Postfach
CH-8497 Fischental
Switzerland

Dear Sirs:

From my Private Account (Number AN 67.441.741), please transfer immediately by means of bank wire the sum of U.S. $25,000 to

First National Bank
Downtown Branch
Anytown, USA

to be credited to the account of

Ms. Jennifer Jones
3925 Rusty Drive
Anytown, USA

Account Number 103-618665-1

Thank you.

Very truly yours,

Katie E. Jones
1812 Bonaparte Avenue
Anytown, USA

Fig. 10-5. Request for wire transfer.

Whether the funds are to be transferred to the American account of the Swiss bank customer or to the credit of a third party, the instructions to the Swiss bank should be complete and precise. At a minimum, the instructions should include the name and address of the beneficiary of the transfer and the beneficiary's bank, bank address, and bank account number. An example of a request for wire transfer is shown in Fig. 10-5.

Bank Drafts　A final means of withdrawing funds from a Swiss Account is to request the bank to mail a bank draft for the amount desired. The draft (frequently in the form of a cashier's check) can be made payable to the account holder or to another party.

The Swiss bank will customarily draw the instrument on a U.S. branch or, if the bank has no branches in the United States, on its account at an American correspondent bank. Thus, the funds will be in dollars and the collection process should be the same as for any check written on an American bank. As with all fund transfers other than wire transfers, amounts exceeding $10,000 require customs reporting.

11

Investment Services Securities

SWITZERLAND IS BY FAR THE LARGEST PER CAPITA SHARE-TRADING COUNTRY ON THE globe. Its position is due, in no small part, to the fact that the country is home to many of the largest investors in the world (Swiss banks). Union Bank of Switzerland occupies the premier position as the world's single largest investor, with discretionary control of assests totaling more than $150 billion. No American institution, including huge insurance companies and pension funds, comes close to this level of managed assets. Even Credit Suisse (Switzerland's third largest investment manager behind Swiss Bank Corporation) controls assets greater than such American giants as Metropolitan Life Insurance, Merrill Lynch Asset Management, Bankers Trust, TIAA/CREF, Wells Fargo Investment, and Dreyfus Corporation.

Not only do Swiss bankers manage security portfolios, but, as we have seen, they provide brokerage services as well. Thus, aside from overseeing the investments of private and institutional funds, the banks are available to execute trading orders for individual bank customers. Bank involvement in securities transactions is natural in the Swiss financial center, where banks are at the center of all financial activity.

Although brokerage firms also thrive in Switzerland, banks handle the majority of the brokerage business. Many of the transactions are carried out on one of the country's eight stock exchanges. But the banks can execute, purchase, and sell orders on any of the world's major stock exchanges as well. Many banks have acquired their own trading seats on stock exchanges in places such as New York, London, Paris, Amsterdam, and Tokyo.

But stocks are just one type of security of the many investments available. Bank customers have the ability to purchase nearly any type of financial instrument, including bonds, options, warrants, futures, and mutual funds.

SECURITIES TRADING ACCOUNTS

To take advantage of a bank's expertise and trading facilities, customers need to open the appropriate securities accounts at their bank. The two types of accounts necessary to enable a customer to begin securities trading are a *cash account* and a *safe custody account*.

Cash Account

A cash account is used by the bank to carry out various investment transactions requested by a customer. Account balances are used to purchase new investments and to pay brokerage fees. In addition, the proceeds from the sale of investments are returned to the account. The customer can make deposits to the account at any time; however, withdrawals must be made in accordance with the regulations governing type of cash account used.

Some customers prefer their cash accounts to be *current* accounts. Banks make current accounts available in a variety of currencies and allow deposits and withdrawals to be made in whatever currency the customer desires. A current account balance earns no interest; however, the entire balance is available for withdrawal or payment orders without restriction.

As an alternative, a customer may choose to maintain a cash account in the form of a *deposit* account. The purpose of the account is the same: to permit settlement of buy and sell orders. A major difference, however, is in the size and timing of withdrawals from the account. While the entire balance of a deposit account is always available for the purchase of securities, an advance notice is required for withdrawals or payment orders that exceed the bank's free limit. Depending on the bank, deposit accounts, might or might not be available in foreign currencies. All deposit accounts, however, pay interest.

For a more complete discussion of the characteristics of both current and deposit accounts, refer to chapter 7.

Safe Custody Accounts

Securities purchased through a bank and not physically delivered to the customer are placed in a safe custody account. Similar in many ways to a securities account at a brokerage firm, a safe custody account allows the owner to avoid the risks and responsibilities associated with taking possession of securities.

Instead of the securities, customers are given receipts for the items placed in custody. The receipts are nontransferable and may not be pledged or assigned in any manner. Because they do not constitute title to the instruments, the receipts serve merely as credit memoranda.

As long as the securities remain on deposit, the bank undertakes all the usual tasks of ownership. Dividend and interest payments are collected by the bank, which automatically transfers the amounts to the cash account. The bank also monitors notices of redemption, handles conversions, and exercises or sells any rights or options in accordance with the depositor's wishes.

Two types of safe custody accounts are available. Most customers keep their securities in *Collective Safe Custody*, an arrangement whereby securities belonging to customers are kept together with those belonging to the bank in a collective safe or central depository. While in collective custody, the actual securities owned by an individual customer cannot be identified by serial number. All securities remain registered in the name of the bank and the customer posesses a legal right of co-ownership in the holdings of the bank. Foreign securities are also registered in the bank's name but are usually stored in safekeeping at a correspondent bank in the country of origin.

Securities registered in the name of the bank customer, together with any securities that the owner wishes to have stored separately, are said to be held in *Separate Custody*. A separate custody arrangement makes it possible for the bank to inform the customer of the actual securities' numbers. Those who desire separate custody must grant to the bank the right to store the securities externally and must pay a premium for the service.

The basic annual fee for collective safe custody of valuables is set by the Swiss Bankers Association. Currently, the fee structure is:

Ordinary accounts	.15% of market value per annum
Numbered accounts	.18% of market value per annum

Thus, securities with a value of $20,000 require an annual safekeeping fee of $30. Minimum fees are SFr 10 per annum for each lot of securities with a minimum SFr 30 per annum per deposit. In addition to these fees, any fees charged by a bank's correspondents for storage of foreign securities (generally 1% of the market price) may be added to the annual fee.

Most banks will allow a reduction or waiver of safekeeping charges for securities of the bank. The reduced fees vary widely by bank but generally cover bank stock, participation certificates, cash bonds, and other deposit certificates.

Forms

Forms for opening both a current and deposit account were illustrated in chapter 9. The same forms would be used for establishing an account to allow securities trading. A few banks require an additional form: the Safe Custody Regulations (Fig. 11-1). Although many banks do not require the customer to sign a copy of the regulations, others feel it wise for the customer to indicate acknowledgement of the regulations by returning a signed copy of the form.

Fischental Bankverein

SAFE CUSTODY REGULATIONS

Fischental Bankverein accepts for safekeeping securities and other valuables in a safe custody account in accordance with the following regulations:

General Regulations

The Bank accepts for safekeeping:
a) on **open deposit**, securities of any kind as well as precious metals;
b) on **sealed deposit**, documents, valuables, and other similar items. The Bank shall have the right at any time to refuse a deposit or to terminate existing deposits without giving any reason for doing so.

1. Safekeeping The Bank undertakes to keep all items entrusted to it in a safe place and to exercise the same due care as for its own valuables.

2. Lien In the event that the customer becomes a debtor of the Bank, the valuables on deposit shall become collateral to the extent the Bank shall deem necessary to guarantee the debt.

3. Statements At the close of each year the Bank shall send a deposit statement, with request to check same and to confirm agreement with contents. Statements shall be deemed correct within one month from mailing unless the Bank receives a notice in writing contesting the statement.

4. Fees The Bank shall charge an annual fee to be computed on the basis of the tariff schedule currently in force and be charged to the depositor at the end of December each year. No charge is made for the safekeeping and administration of shares, participation certificates, and savings books issued by Fischental Bankverein.

5. Duration of Deposit Deposits are accepted for an indefinite period. The customer is entitled to request return of the items at any time during normal banking hours.

Open Deposits – Special Provisions

6. Safekeeping The customer agrees that the Bank is entitled to place the items deposited, or any part thereof, in collective custody, either within the Bank itself or in a central depository. The customer shall enjoy a right of co-ownership in such collective deposit proportionate to the number of items deposited by him. For securities held in collective custody or in deposit with correspondents abroad, if the customer requests a listing of identifying numbers, the customer shall become liable for all the expenses involved in a separate safekeeping.

7. Deposits Abroad Securities held abroad shall be placed by the Bank with one of its correspondents, in the name of the Bank but for the account of and at the risk of the customer.

8. Secrecy The Bank's management and staff are bound by the terms of Swiss Banking Law to observe the strictest secrecy regarding all dealings between Bank and the customer.

9. Management In absence of specific instructions from the customer, the Bank undertakes to
a) collect all dividends, interest, and securities called for redemption;
b) monitor investments for drawings, notices of redemption, conversions, and options on the basis of lists at its disposal without assuming any responsibility in this connection;
c) to exchange provisional securities for permanent certificates and to renew coupon sheets;
The Bank also undertakes upon written instructions received in good time from the customer to provide for
d) conversions;
e) making payments on securities not fully paid up;
f) collecting principal and interest on mortgages;
g) exercising or selling option rights.

10. Transit Insurance Unless otherwise instructed, the Bank shall arrange for insurance to cover the transport of valuables deposited, where such insurance

Fig. 11-1. Safe custody regulations.

Fig. 11-1. Continued

is customary and can be covered under a policy with an insurance company. The cost of the insurance is to be borne by the customer.

Sealed Deposits – Special Provisions

11. Form Deposits must be sealed with wax or lead in such a manner as to make it impossible to open the cover without damaging the seal. Deposits must bear on the cover the customer's exact name and address and a statement of the value.

12. Contents Under no circumstances shall sealed deposits contain any objects that are inflammable or in any manner dangerous, or unsuitable for bank deposit. Customer shall be liable for any damage that might occur as a result of failure to observe this requirement. The bank shall be entitled to ask customer for such proof as considered necessary with the respect to any objects deposited.

13. Liability The Bank's liability shall be limited to the declared value of the valuables on deposit. Any damage must be proved by the customer. On withdrawal, the customer must make sure that the seals are intact, and sign a receipt that releases the Bank from any further liability.

_____

The above is a translation of the Bank's Safe Custody Regulations. In the event of any discrepancy, the French original shall prevail.

Date

_____

Signature

_____

COMMISSIONS

For many years, Switzerland had a reputation as an expensive place to buy and sell securities. Fixed commissions, set by the Association of Swiss Stock Exchanges, together with high transfer taxes levied by federal and cantonal governments, convinced investors not interested in Swiss privacy to shop elsewhere for brokerage services. A revised commission schedule for securities transactions, effective in 1986, brought an influx of new securities business. The revised rates provided a sliding scale of charges based on transaction size with freely negotiable commissions on very large transactions (see Fig. 11-2). The new rate structure has been viewed as a first step toward completely negotiable commissions in the future. Until then, those banks and brokerage houses executing trades on one of the Swiss stock exchanges are expected to conform to the present schedule of charges without deviation.

Not all security trading takes place on Switzerland's eight exchanges. Switzerland has no compulsory exchange trading rules. Thus, traders are free to trade *off the floor* of the exchanges if a deal can be made. Off-the-floor trades can result in more favorable commission rates, although federal and cantonal taxes must still be paid.

While the securities industry of Switzerland has made an effort to improve the competitive position of its trading floors, the federal government in Berne has remained firmly attached to a relatively high stamp tax (or turnover tax), which is levied on buyers and sellers in each securities transaction (see Table 11-1). As can be seen, the federal tax makes up the lion's share of the total tax for security trades.

Arguing that the tax drives business away, bankers have sought for years to have the tax reduced. But federal officials, particularly the country's finance min-

		Taxes &
Stocks & Bonds	Commission	Duties

Swiss Stock

up to SFr 50,000	0.8%	+ 0.09%
for the next SFr 50,000	0.7%	+ 0.09%
for the next SFr 50,000	0.6%	+ 0.09%
for the next SFr 150,000	0.5%	+ 0.09%
for the next SFr 300,000	0.4%	+ 0.09%
for the next SFr 400,000	0.3%	+ 0.09%
for the next SFr 1 million	0.2%	+ 0.09%
amounts exceeding SFr 2 million	Negotiable	+ 0.09%

Foreign Stock

up to SFr 50,000	1.0%	+ 0.165%
for the next SFr 50,000	0.9%	+ 0.165%
for the next SFr 50,000	0.7%	+ 0.165%
for the next SFr 150,000	0.5%	+ 0.165%
for the next SFr 300,000	0.4%	+ 0.165%
for the next SFr 400,000	0.3%	+ 0.165%
for the next SFr 1 million	0.2%	+ 0.165%
amounts exceeding SFr 2 million	Negotiable	+ 0.165%

Swiss Franc Bonds

up to SFr 50,000	0.6%	+ 0.09%
for the next SFr 50,000	0.4%	+ 0.09%
for the next SFr 200,000	0.3%	+ 0.09%
for the next SFr 700,000	0.2%	+ 0.09%
for the next SFr 1 million	0.1%	+ 0.09%
amounts exceeding SFr 2million	Negotiable	+ 0.09%

Foreign Currency Bonds

up to SFr 50,000	0.6%	+ 0.165%
for the next SFr 50,000	0.5%	+ 0.165%
for the next SFr 50,000	0.4%	+ 0.165%
for the next SFr 150,000	0.3%	+ 0.165%
for the next SFr 700,000	0.2%	+ 0.165%
amounts exceeding SFr 1 million	Negotiable	+ 0.165%

Fig. 11-2. Current commissions and taxes on stock and bond investments.

**Table 11-1. Swiss Stamp Tax
———— on Securities Trading.————**

	Swiss Securities	Foreign Securities
Federal stamp tax	.075%	.150%
		(3% on new issues)
Cantonal tax	.010%	.010%
Stock exchange fees	.005%	.005%
Total	.090%	.165%

ister, have been unable to find a new source of revenue to replace the SFr 2 billion or so that the tax generates each year. Nonetheless, there are efforts in both chambers of the Swiss Parliament to reduce the stamp tax.

In the meantime, the sheer size of the tax revenues indicates that many investors are willing to accept the current commission and tax rate structure. With the 1986 revision of rates, the country is now in line with (or below) most other European exchanges. In fact, given the reduced rate available for Swiss stocks and Swiss franc obligations, the country remains the least expensive place to buy these securities.

COMMON STOCK INVESTMENTS—Non-Swiss

As mentioned earlier, banks in Switzerland have the capability of buying and selling shares of stock on exchanges throughout the world. But many foreign companies have their stocks listed on Swiss stock exchanges, enabling members of the Swiss exchanges to trade much more quickly and, in many cases, at a lesser cost. The number of foreign securities traded at the Zurich Stock Exchange, Switzerland's largest, has grown steadily in recent years (see Table 11-2).

**Table 11-2. Foreign Securities
—on the Zurich Stock Exchange.——**

	Foreign Bonds	Foreign Stocks	Total
1950	95	38	133
1960	137	60	197
1970	253	91	344
1980	397	166	563
1987	866	217	1,083
1988	880*	226**	1,106

* 149 are U.S. issues

** 110 are U.S. issues

Abbott Laboratories
Aetna Life and Casualty
Allied-Signal
ALCOA
Amax Inc.
American Brands
American Cyanamid
American Express
American General
American Information Technologies
American Medical International
A T & T
Amoco
AMR Corporation
Anheuser-Busch
Archer-Daniels-Midland
Atlantic Richfield
Baker Hughes Inc.
Battle Mountain Gold Company
Baxter Travenol Laboratories
Bell Atlantic
BellSouth
Black and Decker
Boeing
Borden
Bowater Incorporated
Campbell Soup Company
Caterpillar
Chevron
Chrysler
Citicorp
Coca Cola
Colgate-Palmolive
Communications Satellite Corporation
Consolidated Natural Gas
Control Data
Corning Glass Works
CPC International
CSX Corporation
Digital Equipment Corporation
Disney Company
Dow Chemical Company
E.I. DuPont de Nemours & Co.
Dun & Bradstreet
Eastman Kodak
Englehard Corporation
Exxon

Fluor Corporation
Ford Motor Company
General Electric
General Motors
Gillette
Goodyear Tire & Rubber
W.R. Grace & Company
GTE Corporation
Gulf & Western
Halliburton
Hercules
Homestake Mining
Honeywell
IBM
Intel
International Paper
ITT
Kraft
Eli Lilly
Litton
Lockheed
Louisiana Land & Exploration
Maxus Energy
Minnesota Mining & Manufacturing
Mobil
Monsanto
J.P. Morgan & Co.
National Distillers and Chemical
NCR Corporation
NYNEX Corporation
Occidental Petroleum
Pacific Gas & Electric
Pacific Telesis Group
Pennzoil
PepsiCo
Pfizer
Phillip Morris
Phillips Petroleum
Primerica
Procter & Gamble
Quantum Chemical
RJR Nabisco
Rockwell International
Sears, Roebuck & Co.
SmithKline Beckman
Southwestern Bell
Squibb

Fig. 11-3. U.S. stocks traded on the Zurich stock exchange.

Fig. 11-3. Continued

Sun Company	USF & G Corporation
Tenneco	USX Corporation
Texaco	Wang Laboratories
Texas Instruments	Warner-Lambert
Transamerica	Waste Management
Union Carbide	F.W. Woolworth
Unisys	Xerox
United Technologies	Zenith Electronics
US West	

Although the 149 American bonds traded on the exchange represents less than 20 percent of the total foreign bonds traded, American stocks comprise nearly one half of the foreign stocks. As can be seen in Fig. 11-3, many of the listed American stocks represent large, blue-chip companies.

Other foreign securities traded are for companies spread across six continents. The 731 non-American bonds represent governmental and corporate issues from 40 countries. Foreign stocks are from 17 different countries, with the majority coming from West Germany, The Netherlands, South Africa, and Japan. A partial list of foreign stocks is shown in Fig. 11-4.

Although the Zurich stock exchange is the largest in Switzerland, it is not the only center for dealing in international stocks and bonds. The Basle and Geneva exchanges rival the Zurich exchange in the number of international securities traded. Many of the same international securities are traded on all three of the major exchanges. Lesser numbers of foreign securities are traded on the smaller exchanges.

West Germany

Daimler-Benz
Nixdorf Computer
Volkswagen

The Netherlands

Elsevier
ROBECO
Philips
Royal Dutch Petroleum
Unilever

Great Britain

Bowater Industries
British Petroleum
Consolidated Gold Fields

South Africa

Barlow Rand Ltd.

Japan

Honda Motor Company
NEC Corporation
Sanyo Electric
Sharp Corporation
Sony Corporation
Toshiba Corporation

DeBeers Consolidated Mines
General Mining Union Corp.
Gold Fields of South Africa Ltd.

Fig. 11-4. Selected foreign stocks traded on the Zurich stock exchange.

Because of the international character of the securities markets in Switzerland, the newsstands in Switzerland make available a great number of worldwide financial publications. It is little wonder that the *Wall Street Journal*, when looking for a new location to print its European edition, selected Lucerne, Switzerland, as an ideal location.

COMMON STOCK INVESTMENTS—Swiss

Investors establishing securities trading accounts through their Swiss banks may wish to take advantage of investments available in Swiss stocks. Selected Swiss companies traded on the major Swiss stock exchanges appear in Fig. 11-5.

Although many of the companies are well known, the types of stock issued by the companies might appear unusual to many Americans. Corporations in Switzerland can issue common stock in three different varieties: registered stock, bearer shares, and certificates of participation. Most large corporations have all three types outstanding.

Bank Leu
Ciba-Geigy
Credit Suisse
Elektrowatt AG
Hoffman-LaRoche
Lindt & Sprungli Chocolate
Nestle
Oerlikon-Buehrle
Sandoz
Swissair
Swiss Bank Corporation
Swiss Reinsurance
Union Bank of Switzerland
Winterthur Insurance
Zurich Insurance

Fig. 11-5. Selected Swiss blue chip stocks.

Registered Stock

In many ways, registered stock of Swiss companies is much like common stock in American companies. Shares with a par value are issued to investors whose names are printed on the face of the stock certificates and recorded in the list of the company's shareholders. Because the shareholders are known to the company, they are able to receive dividend payments through the mail.

Unlike American companies, Swiss corporations have the ability to restrict the ownership of their registered stock. Ownership of these shares is almost always limited to citizens or residents of Switzerland. In addition, the company is allowed to decide how many shares any individual investor may hold. Unqualified investors find it impossible to acquire the stock as all new shareholders must have the approval of the board of directors before shares can be registered in a new

Table 11-3. Selected Swiss Stock Prices ($), December 31, 1988.

Company	Bearer Shares	Registered Shares	Certificates of Participation
Ciba-Geigy	1,764	1,414	1,400
Credit Suisse	1,801	350	N/A
Nestle	4,829	4,462	874
Sandoz	6,387	5,003	1,057
Swiss Bank Corporation	226	200	195
Union Bank of Switzerland	2,134	414	76
Vontobel Holding	6,370	N/A	N/A

N/A = Stock not issued or not publicly available

owner's name. As might be expected, bankers in Switzerland are ever careful to avoid accepting buy orders from customers who are unqualified to own registered shares.

Registered shares typically trade at a large discount from the price of other shares issued by the same company (see Table 11-3). The discount results from the decreased liquidity of the shares due to a relatively restricted market. Nonetheless, the shares enjoy full voting privileges and share equal dividends with other classes of stock. A reduced price and an equal dividend adds up to a higher rate of return for Swiss investors vis-à-vis foreigners who must purchase other, more expensive shares.

Bearer Stock

Identical to registered stock in terms of voting and dividend privileges, bearer shares possess characteristics similar to corporate bearer bonds. Owner's names are unknown to the company, and each stock certificate proclaims that the bearer of the certificate is the owner of the stock. Because of the bearer status, the shares are freely transferable. Owners of bearer stock must detach and present coupons for dividend payments. Old certificates must be surrendered for new certificates when all dividend coupons have been paid.

Certificates of Participation

Non-Swiss investors may be able to increase their investment yields by buying nonvoting bearer stock in the form of certificates of participation. The increased yield results from the fact that the certificates of participation generally trade at a discount from bearer share prices (see Table 11-3) but earn equal dividends. Because all other rights are the same, the amount of the discount can be said to reflect what investors believe the value of voting rights to be.

Certificates of participation offer an advantage to the issuing company in being able to attract amounts of capital without giving up control of the company to outsiders.

Changes in Ownership Eligibility

Because the legal right to determine who can purchase registered shares resides with the issuing company, that company can also revise ownership qualifications. Several years ago some companies began doing just that, including Landis & Gyr, the renowned Swiss maker of precision measuring instruments. The company, by a vote of its board of directors, removed Swiss citizenship as a prerequisite to owning registered stock. Nestle, Switzerland's largest industrial company, announced a similar change in November 1988. Nestle justified the relaxation of rules based on a need to raise large amounts of additional capital, capital that only foreign investors desiring the less expensive registered shares could be expected to provide. A unique twist in Nestle's new ownership rules is the limitation on voting rights that may be acquired. The company's board of directors, in allowing foreigners to purchase unlimited amounts of registered shares, set a maximum of 3% voting rights for any stockholder, regardless of the amount of shares held.

Foreign governments are urging officials in Berne to persuade more Swiss companies to drop the Swiss nationality requirement for owning registered stock. Their complaints arise from a Swiss company's ability to launch large corporate takeovers of foreign firms without allowing themselves to be similarly acquired. Whether other Swiss companies will join the ranks of Nestle and Landis & Gyr remains to be seen.

DEBT INVESTMENTS

Because Swiss banks have access to all of the world's securities markets, almost any financial instrument is available to bank customers. Swiss bankers are familiar with the world's debt markets and act as advisors and underwriters for companies and governments seeking to raise capital.* As brokers, they are competent to execute orders for almost any kind of bond, including government, corporate, convertible, domestic, Eurobond, zero coupon, perpetual, commodity-backed, warrants-attached or stripped; whether the debt is denominated in dollars, francs, pesos, cruzeiros, marks, yen, or drachmas.

Volumes have been written on the multitude of debt instruments available to investors in today's markets. No attempt will be made to discuss the instruments here. It is necessary, however, to mention a unique type of debt certificate issued only by Swiss banks and generally unfamiliar to Americans: the Cash Bond.

Cash Bond

Sometimes called term savings notes, cash bonds represent medium-term (three to eight-year) obligations of Swiss banks. The instruments provide investors with a higher interest yield than deposit or savings accounts but with the same debtor risk. As of January 1988, the terms related to cash bonds at most Swiss banks are shown in Table 11-4.

---

*As an example, in January 1988, the Soviet Union went to the international bond market to borrow money for the first time since the Czar had sought to finance his wars. To assist the country in placing its debt, the Soviets relied on the guiding hand of knowledgeable Swiss bankers. Zurich's Bank fur Kredit und Aussenhandel headed the syndicate of 17 banks that floated Sfr 100 million ($73 million) bond issue.

_____ **Table 11-4. Cash Bond Terms.** _____

	Term	Interest
	3-6 years	$4^1/2\%$
	7-8 years	$4^3/4\%$
Denominations	SFr 1,000	
	SFr 5,000	
	SFr 10,000	
Issue Price	100% + .15% stamp duty at time of purchase	
Income Tax Withholding	35%, partially refundable for Americans	

A secondary market for cash bonds does not formally exist, and investors should plan to hold the instruments until maturity. Should the holder need the funds prior to maturity, a banker will either arrange a loan secured by the debt or attempt to sell the instrument at its current value.

OTHER INVESTMENTS

Naturally, all forms of hybrid investments (e.g., options, warrants, and financial futures) are available through Swiss banker/brokers. The Swiss have become innovators in this area and have gone to great effort to develop markets for these securities.

A recent example is the 1988 opening of SOFFEX (Swiss Options and Financial Futures Exchange), the world's first fully computerized options and futures exchange. Swiss banks have been major players in the options and futures markets for years, but the new exchange is intended to bring much of the action to Swiss turf. Initial announcement of the creation of the exchange sent American and European brokerage firms scrambling to obtain one of the few memberships open to foreigners. Most members of the exchange are Swiss banks, and every corner of the country is represented. After years of development, the exchange began trading in puts and calls of major Swiss stocks. Current plans are to expand trading to include options of other firms, interest rate futures, stock index futures, and a new financial instrument: options on a Swiss stock index.

Another innovation in financial instruments has been the creation of trading in warrants of registered stock of Swiss companies. As we have seen, ownership of these shares is generally reserved for citizens or residents of Switzerland. The warrants, which are actually options to purchase the registered shares, can be purchased by anyone, although non-Swiss investors may be prohibited from taking possession of the underlying shares by exercising the options. Instead, the Swiss banks that create the instruments guarantee to buy them back from investors at market prices. In this manner, investors unable to exercise the warrants can nonetheless participate in the profits that result from increases in the stock prices. Initially offered to investors in late 1986, the warrants (which are now available for most local blue chip stocks) have become extremely popular and widely held. All of Switzerland's major banks participate in the market.

MUTUAL FUNDS AND UNIT INVESTMENT TRUSTS

Owing to their presence in foreign financial markets, Swiss bankers have the ability to obtain foreign shares in mutual funds and unit trust investments. But investments of these types have proliferated in Switzerland for decades, and an astonishing variety of Swiss funds also is available. As investors have come to recognize the benefits associated with specialized funds, a number of investment companies and banks (including large private banking houses) have developed funds to meet investors' objectives. A seemingly endless variety of funds exist, including: bond funds, stock funds, and Real Estate Investment Trusts.

Bond Funds

Bond funds are specialized portfolios constructed on the basis of currency type, country of origin, special bond features (e.g., convertibles or warrants attached), type of industry, etc.

Stock Funds

Based on country of origin, capital growth, dividend payout, industry, and combinations of these and other features, there is a seemingly endless variety of stock and balanced (stock and bond) funds available.

Real Estate Investment Trusts

With emphasis on Swiss properties, portfolios are designed to meet objectives of capital growth, income, or a combination. Given the relatively closed market for foreigners seeking real estate in Switzerland, Real Estate Investment Trust (REIT) shares represent one of the few ways Americans can profit from Swiss real estate.

Most funds are of the open-end mutual fund variety, which provide for an unlimited purchase of new shares by investors and an easy redemption of shares. Unlike mutual funds, unit trusts have a limited number of shares outstanding. Purchasers of the interest in the funds receive securities known as Investment Trust Certificates, which are actively traded in Switzerland's over-the-counter securities market. Some Swiss investment trusts are of such a large size that their certificates are traded on the stock exchange. Figure 11-6 lists those investment trusts traded on the Zurich stock exchange.

Both mutual funds and investment trusts are subject to the Federal Law on Investment Funds and are under the supervision of the Swiss Banking Commission. Because Swiss mutual funds and investment trusts refuse to go through the expensive process of registration with the SEC in order for the securities to be advertised and offered for sale in the United States, most of these investments are unknown to the average American investor. However, it is perfectly legal for any American to purchase these and any other Swiss security through a Swiss bank.

Investment Trust	Investment Activity
AMCA	American and Canadian securities
Anfos	Swiss real estate
BOND-INVEST	International bond investments
CONVERT-INVEST	International convertible bonds
EURIT	European stocks
FONSA	Swiss stocks
GLOBINVEST	International investments
HELVETINVEST	Swiss bonds
IMMOFONDS	Swiss real estate
IMMOVIT	Swiss real estate
INTERSWISS	Swiss real estate
PACIFIC-INVEST	Investments in the Pacific area
SAFIT	South Africa Trust Fund
SAMURAI PORTFOLIO	Japanese securities
< <Schweizeraktien> >	Swiss securities
SIAT	Swiss real estate
SIMA	Swiss real estate
SWISSBAR	Swiss stocks
Swissimmobil	Swiss real estate
Swissreal	Swiss real estate

Fig. 11-6. Investment trust certificates
traded on the Zurich stock exchange.

INVESTMENT COUNSELING

Aside from the execution of buy and sell orders on behalf of their customers, Swiss bankers stand ready to provide the other functions customarily expected by Americans of a full-service broker. Perhaps the most significant of these services is in the area of investment counseling. Banks employ financial planners who are expert not only in worldwide securities, but also in areas of taxation, estate settlement, and trust management. For their customers, the bankers are willing to aid in the formulation of investment philosophy and strategy, portfolio design, and selection of appropriate individual securities.

In providing investment counseling services, the banks almost always require that the customer appear in person at the bank offices. With the exception of safe deposit box services, investment counseling is the only service provided by Swiss banks that normally requires the personal presence of the customer.

PORTFOLIO MANAGEMENT

Swiss banks are truly giants in the arena of portfolio management. As indicated at the beginning of this chapter, Swiss banks are among the largest investors in the world when measured by the level of funds under full discretionary control. In years past, the money managed by bankers in Switzerland normally belonged to well-to-do individuals. In the modern world of pension funds, employee welfare programs, and corporate trusts, institutions have become the largest source of money seeking professional management. Given their long tradition of providing sound portfolio management, it is little wonder that Swiss banks have attracted so much of the business.

But the banks are not turning away individuals with portfolio management needs. They continue to provide the same personal services as their ancestors did 200 years ago. Although the minimums are at times quite large, Americans are believed to be increasingly abandoning their long time stateside money managers in favor of those in Geneva and Zurich. Published government statistics indicate that, following the October 19, 1987, stock market crash (Black Monday), there was a tremendous surge in foreign money into professionally managed portfolios of Swiss banks. The influx is not surprising; frightened money at home often finds its way into the protective security of Swiss vaults.

To better understand the portfolio management services that Swiss bankers offer, it is necessary to first understand the difference between nondiscretionary and discretionary portfolio management. Nondiscretionary management describes an arrangement whereby the actual owner of the funds makes the decision regarding selection and timing of investment transactions. Although the owner might seek advice from the banker, the actual responsibility for the investment decisions remains with the owner. Technically, nondiscretionary portfolio management is not portfolio management at all from a banker's point of view. Aside from being available for consultation with a client, the banker's responsibility extends only to brokerage and safe custody services.

For an investor who does not have the time, interest, or expertise in investment matters, bankers will assume full responsibility for managing that customer's investments. This arrangement, called a discretionary (or fully discretionary) account, places responsibility for investment decisions directly on an individual banker (or, frequently, a team of investment managers). The customer's obligation in this arrangement is to articulate general guidelines for the portfolio, including investment goals and the amount of risk that is acceptable in achieving the goals. The bank's job is to diversify the customer's assets in a manner consistent with the customer's wishes. In essence, a discretionary portfolio is custom-tailored to the needs and objectives of an individual investor. Portfolios are systematically reviewed and changes in holdings, if deemed necessary by the manager, are made without consultation with the investor. Investors become silent owners in custom-managed portfolios. In fact, once a discretionary account has been established for a customer, no special investment instructions can be accepted by the bank. A Portfolio Management Agreement (see example in Fig. 11-7) will outline the fundamental responsibilities of both parties.

The minimum portfolio size that Swiss banks are willing to accept for a discretionary account varies considerably from bank to bank. Complicating matters is a tendency on the part of banks to speak in terms of *preferred* balances, as opposed to absolute minimums. All of the larger banks request an initial portfolio size of at least $250,000 in a discretionary account. Smaller, nonprivate banks refuse to advertise minimums. When pressed for information about minimums on discretionary accounts, most suggest an opening balance of at least $100,000. Nearly every bank requires that additional deposits and all withdrawals be at some minimum amount. Customary minimums are $10,000 to $25,000.

Fischental Bankverein

PORTFOLIO MANAGEMENT AGREEMENT

Description of the account:

I/We, as Principals, hereby authorize Fischental Bankverein to manage and administer on my/our behalf the said account hereinabove mentioned.

The Bank will act in its sole discretion for the account of and at the risk of the Principal(s). The Bank is, in particular, authorized to buy or sell assets and precious metals on a covered and secured basis; to purchase or sell foreign exchange; to invest in the money market, including fiduciary instruments; to make conversions, to exercise or sell option rights as well as to conclude arbitrage and option transactions insofar as these appear reasonable in respect to the Principal(s)' situation.

The present authority will not lapse by death, incapacity to act, declaration of absence, or bankruptcy of the Principal(s).

The Principal(s) may at any time withdraw the present authority in writing.

The Bank is authorized to charge an annual fee based on a percentage of the total amount of the Principal(s) assets. The fee will be calculated according to rates in use by the Bank. In case of withdrawal of the present authority, the fee shall be calculated on pro rata temporis.

All provisions contained in Fischental Bankverein's General Conditions and Safe Custody Regulations, specifically concerning the Court of Jurisdiction and applicable law, shall equally apply to this document.

Date _____ Signature(s) _____

Fig. 11-7. Portfolio management agreement.

In order to make bank-managed portfolios available to smaller investors, a number of banks have created portfolio *models*, which allow clients to have their funds invested in a professionally managed pool of money. Investors can choose a predesigned model, which is consistent with the investor's objectives. In a sense, the portfolio models resemble mutual funds, although shares are not issued. Ueberseebank, for example, offers four portfolio models, each designed to meet some particular investor objective or combination of objectives. Ueberseebank has set minimums for model portfolios, ranging from $50,000 to $125,000.

Fees for bank-managed portfolios tend to favor the larger portfolios, with sliding scales in effect at many banks. Customary rates begin at one percent per

annum on smaller portfolios ($100,000-$250,000) with rates dropping to as low as
.125 percent for portfolios in excess of a million dollars. Charges are made at year
end or on a quarterly basis in accordance with individual bank practice. In addition to the management fee, safekeeping charges (as described above) apply to
professionally managed accounts.

All customers setting up discretionary portfolios are required to specify a *reference currency* in which accounts are to be valued and statements are to be prepared. Although it is normal to specify a reference currency for the country in
which the majority of investments are to be made, certain portfolios may not
favor any particular country's securities, and the choice of reference currency is
left to the customer. Statements can be prepared quarterly or annually depending,
again, on customer preference.

12

Investment Services Precious Metals

As NOTED IN PREVIOUS CHAPTERS, SWISS BANKS OFFER A MULTITUDE OF SERVICES TO customers seeking to build their investment portfolios from debt and equity securities. But many investors also desire to augment their security investment portfolios with positions in gold, silver, and other precious metals. Some even construct an investment portfolio entirely of precious metals, preferring the tangible assets to the less certain value of paper claims. Thus, it is perfectly natural that Swiss bankers have become experts in precious metal investments.

The Swiss have had a long love affair with gold. For centuries they have acted as gold brokers for the world, buying and selling for private individuals, governments, kings, and czars. Much of the country's own national wealth has been stored in the form of gold bars, filling the Swiss National Bank's huge subterranean vault. That vault holds more gold per capita (approximately 13 ounces for every Swiss citizen) than any other country's national treasury. But the amount of gold held by the Swiss National Bank is miniscule compared to the vast amounts held in bank vaults for private individuals.

Since 1968, Zurich has been recognized as the world center for gold trading. It was in that year that Switzerland's Big Three (Credit Suisse, Swiss Bank Corporation, and Union Bank of Switzerland) formed the Zurich Gold Pool and successfully wrested from London its monopoly on newly mined South African gold. Today approximately one half of the world's physical gold trading takes place in Zurich. Each of the Big Three banks has its own refinery and produces shiny gold bars bearing bank markings and serial numbers. Investors worldwide can purchase the bars from any Swiss bank and ask that they be stored on the bank's premises.

Banks in Switzerland do not deal exclusively in gold. Most provide investors with other metal investments as well, including silver, platinum, and palladium.

SAFE CUSTODY ACCOUNT

While it is possible for bank customers to take delivery of precious metals, most prefer to have banks store the metals in their secure, underground vaults. In most cases, customers elect to have their purchases held in collective safe custody, whereby a customer owns the right to claim metals stored in a common vault containing unsegregated metals belonging to many customers. The arrangement may sound similar in nature to safe custody accounts used for securities, as described in the previous chapter. In fact, it is the same account, and an account statement may well show balances comprised of both securities and gold. Also similar to securities trading is the requirement that a customer maintain a cash account (either a current account or a deposit account) in a freely convertible currency to facilitate transaction settlements and payments of the yearly custody fee.

Banks are able to determine their own schedule of charges for precious metals held in collective custody. Normal annual fees are shown in Fig. 12-1. A customer can liquidate a claim at any time by simply instructing the bank to do so. The metal is liquidated at the prevailing market rate and the amount, less any storage charges that might have accrued, is returned to the customer's cash account.

Those customers wishing to have their precious metals stored in individual (rather than collective) safe custody can request so. Because of the special handling costs, bank fees for individual safe custody are subject to a surcharge of around 50 percent of the standard fee. Individual safe custody is required in the case of precious metals in nonstandard form and rare coins.

As in the United States, precious metals can also be stored in bank vaults in safe deposit boxes rented by customers. Safe deposit storage cannot be arranged by correspondence, however, and all deposits and withdrawals must be made in person by the bank customer.

Metal	Safe Custody Account Fees
Silver	1/4 of one percent (.25%) of average value on deposit
Gold, Platinum and Palladium	1/5 of one percent (.20%) of average value on deposit
Minimum annual charges	SFr 30

Fig. 12-1. Safe custody account fees.

DELIVERY

A customer whose precious metal investment is stored in a safe deposit box can personally withdraw the metal by appearing at the bank and removing the contents of the safe deposit box. Those with precious metal investments held in either collective or individual safe custody can also take delivery of metals corresponding to the balances held in the safe custody account. Small amounts can even be withdrawn upon demand. All banks, however, require a 2- to-3- day notice for large deliveries.

For collective safe custody balances, bullion is delivered in large bars satisfying normal standards for fineness and weight, unless otherwise agreed. Customers desiring smaller bars might be required to pay an additional small bar fabrication premium (discussed in the following section).

Most deliveries are made at the branch where the account is held. It is possible to make arrangements to have the balance delivered to another location, either in Switzerland or abroad. The bank will ship coins or bullion, fully insured, to the customer's designated destination. The customer, of course, bears all costs of special delivery instructions.

In addition to a bank's General Conditions and Safe Custody Regulations, a special set of regulations exist regarding precious metals in a safe custody account and delivery thereof. A sample of such regulations is shown in Fig. 12-2.

GOLD

On December 31, 1974, after a 41-year ban on private ownership, American citizens were granted the right to own, buy, and sell gold bullion. A new industry, gold trading, sprang up immediately on the American financial scene. Although many Americans began speculating in the new gold market, others turned to the more established markets in Europe, particularly in London and in Switzerland.

In search of a new revenue source, Swiss government officials in 1980 instituted a 6.2 percent turnover tax (Warenusatzsteuer) on gold transactions. In spite of the dreaded tax, many foreigners continued to conduct gold trading transactions through their Swiss banks. The Swiss government in 1986 abolished the turnover tax in favor of a more competitive gold market. Today, Switzerland's gold trading center is free of all government restrictions and taxes.

Investors considering investment in gold need to determine the type of gold holdings that best serve their purposes. Gold can be purchased in the form of bars or coins. In addition, investors might wish to consider investments in gold securities, including mining stocks, futures, and gold options.

Gold Bars

While most Americans traditionally think of gold values in terms of price per (troy) ounce, Swiss bankers follow the practice observed in metric countries of valuing gold in terms of price per gram. In fact, even though Americans can see daily quotations of the price per ounce of gold, the published prices are actually based on transactions involving 12.5 kilogram (401.875 troy ounce) bars. The 12.5-kilogram bars, with a fineness of 995/1000 are often referred to. as *good delivery bars* and are considered standard units for most commercial transactions.

Investors are not restricted to purchases and sales of 12.5-kilogram bars only. A large range of smaller bars (with a fineness of 999.9) are available to choose

Fischental Bankverein
0000000000000000000

REGULATIONS GOVERNING METAL ACCOUNTS

These regulations are supplementary to the Bank's General Conditions and Safe Custody Regulations.

1. The Bank holds at the customer's disposal in its own name, lodged with the bank or with third parties either in Switzerland or abroad, a quantity equivalent in the minimum, to the total of precious metal deposits.

   Each customer has a right of co-ownership over the bank's metal holdings and the share of each customer is determined by the proportion of his/her participation in the total of the collective deposit.

2. The Bank manages the joint deposit and protects the customer's rights toward the other co-owners and vis-à-vis third persons.

3. A customer must maintain minimum metal balances. These minimum amounts are fixed from time to time by the Bank in kilograms, grams, ounces, or by number of coins.

4. The customer is entitled to a delivery of a quantity of precious metal corresponding to the balance of his/her account. Delivery is to be made at the counter of the Bank. Upon special request, the Bank shall deliver the precious metal to a different location, provided the delivery is practical and legal in the place of delivery. The customer bears all costs and risk of such a delivery.

5. In the event of exceptional situations, such as war, transfer restrictions, etc., the Bank has the right to deliver the precious metal, at the cost and risk of the customer, to the place and in the manner it deems to be most suitable under the circumstances.

6. The Bank may demand two (2) business days' notice for large deliveries in order to make all necessary preparations.

7. Unless deposits are expressed in specific weight units, the Bank shall be entitled to deliver bars of any weight, provided the metal titrates at 995/1000 fineness for gold and 999/1000 fineness for other metals.

8. A customer holding gold or silver coins in an account is entitled to delivery of standard commercial quality coins corresponding to his/her balance. The customer has no right to request delivery of coins of a particular year or a specific minting.

9. Precious metal balances earn no interest.

10. The Bank charges accounts holding precious metals with a custody fee according to a separate list.

11. Any taxes, fees, charges, etc., existing at the time of the signature of the present regulations or introduced afterwards shall be borne by the depositor.

Fig. 12-2. Regulations governing metal accounts.

from. Smaller bars, however, are subject to a surcharge (fabrication premium). Various bar sizes and normal surcharges are listed in Table 12-1.

Every bank specifies minimum amounts for gold purchases. The minimum at many banks is 1 kilogram (or 32.15 ounces), but banks are free to establish any minimum they wish. Some banks prefer to specify minimums in terms of money, and $10,000 or SFr 25,000 minimums are also common.

___ Table 12-1. Gold Bar Sizes Available.___

Bar Size (grams)	Bar Size (troy ounces)	Small Bar Surcharge
12,500	401.875	None*
1,000	32.150	SFr 65.00
500	16.075	SFr 37.50
250	8.037	SFr 25.00
100	3.215	SFr 20.00
50	1.607	SFr 15.00
_____	1.000	SFr 10.00

*good delivery bars

It is important to understand that investors purchasing, say, $10,000 worth of gold to be held in collective safe custody may end up owning fractional bar units in their accounts. As collective safe custody involves bookkeeping entries rather than physical movement of the metal, fractional bars present no problem for the bank. Anyone wishing physical delivery of the bars, however, will likely be required to accept small bars (paying the appropriate surcharge) and make a cash settlement for odd fractions owned.

No commissions are charged on purchases and sales of gold bars. The bars are traded at current bid and ask prices, and the difference in the prices, or *spread*, is the profit earned by the banks. A few banks with relatively small minimum sizes for transactions might charge small commissions of 1/2 percent on purchases and sales of smaller-than-average amounts.

It is possible to give banks either *market orders* (for the current market price of gold) or *limit orders* (stating a minimum or maximum price at which the bank can execute a transaction). Market orders are executed immediately, while limit orders can only be executed if the price of the gold reaches the indicated limit. Depending on the bank, limit orders are valid for anywhere from 30 days to six months. "Good till canceled orders" are not normally accepted, nor are limit orders that deviate significantly (20-25 percent) from current market prices.

Gold Coins

As alternative to gold-bar investments, many banks are also dealers in gold coins. Despite the great variety available, all gold coins may be divided into two types: numismatic and bullion (or current) coins. Numismatic coins are those minted before 1810, or, roughly, before the Napoleonic era. Normally, the values of numismatic coins far exceed the gold content of the coins. While values may vary somewhat along with the overall price of gold, each coin trades at an individual price based on the date of minting, mint markings, and general condition of the coin.

Coins struck after 1810 are generally considered to be bullion coins. These coins are purchased by investors primarily for their gold content, and have little or no value as collectors' items. Consequently, the value of bullion coins tends to fluctuate directly with the value of gold bars. An example is the South African Krugerrand, an extremely well-known coin that makes up three-fourths of the total market for bullion coins. Each Krugerrand, which contains one troy ounce of gold that is 916.66/1000 fine, sells for a slight premium over the market price of gold. The premium results from the coins being legal tender. Also legal tender is the Canadian Maple Leaf, which, unlike the Krugerrand, contains pure gold and trades at a slightly higher premium.

Because of the nature of bullion coins, it is possible for investors to purchase them through a Swiss bank and have them held in collective safe custody in a manner similar to gold bars. As with gold bars, coins in collective safe custody are identified only by bookkeeping entries indicating quantity owned by each investor. It is not possible for investors to request special markings or special mint dates. Also, banks will not sort bullion coins by date or mint if delivery is taken. The bank only warrants the coins to be of standard commercial quality (good condition with normal traces of circulation).

An individual safe custody account or safe deposit box is necessary for customers wishing to invest and own specially designated bullion coins and all numismatic coins.

Minimum balances for gold coin transactions are expressed in terms of number of coins or dollar amount and vary widely by bank. Examples of minimum purchases for coins to be held in safe custody at Union Bank of Switzerland are shown in Table 12-2.

___ Table 12-2. Gold Coins—Minimum Quantity Purchases.___

Type of Coin	Minimum-Quantity Purchase
Krugerrand	30 coins
Maple Leaf	30 coins
Mexican 50 peso	30 coins
Elizabeth II (after 1973)	50 coins
Swiss Vreneli (SFr 20)	50 coins

SILVER

In many respects, trading in silver through Swiss banks is the same as trading in gold. The most significant difference is in the forms of the metal made available. While a few Swiss banks make silver coins available to investors, the majority that offer silver deal exclusively in silver bars.

Silver Bars

As with the gold markets, silver is customarily traded in bars of standard size and fineness. A number of different *standards* are available, however. While all silver bars contain 999/1000 pure silver, the bars may be measured in metric sizes (35 kilogram and 1 kilogram bars) or in ounces (with 1,000-ounce bars most common). Bars of all the common sizes may be credited to a safe custody account.

A single safe custody account can contain metals and securities claims. Annual statements list all quantities of securities and metals on deposit with a current valuation of each. The annual safe custody fee for silver is based on the average value of the account and is customarily around 0.3 percent of the value on deposit.

As with gold purchases, there are no commissions on purchases and sales of silver. Instead, prices are based on current bid-and-ask spreads. Also like gold, minimum silver purchases vary widely among banks, and may be specified by weight or price. Bank Leu requires a minimum initial purchase of 10 kilograms (321.5 ounces) for silver to be held in safe custody.

Silver Coins

As mentioned, only a few banks deal in silver coins. Those that do specialize primarily in numismatic coins. Foreign Commerce bank makes available bags of U.S. silver coins containing $1,000 of 1964 or earlier quarters and dimes. Each bag contains 720 troy ounces of pure silver. Storage and insurance is provided through brokers in New York at an annual rate of $30 per bag.

OTHER PRECIOUS METALS

For those seeking a bit of the exotic in their precious metal portfolios, it is possible to make investments in both platinum and palladium bars and in platinum coins. Purchases, sales and safe custody accounts of the *P-metals* are handled exactly the same as for gold and silver. The only differences are in the areas of bar size and storage costs.

Prices for platinum and palladium are based on the international metal market transactions (in London, New York, and Zurich) for standard 3-kilogram bars of 999.5/1000 pure metal. Bars offered for sale at Swiss banks are listed in Table 12-3.

Small-bar premiums may be charged for delivery taken in small bars or for individual safe custody purchases of other than 3-kilogram bars. Bank Leu's transaction minimums of 1 kilogram for platinum and 3 kilograms for palladium are normal for those banks who deal in these metals. Safe custody fees for both metals are around 0.15 percent of value per annum.

___Table 12-3. Platinum and Palladium Bar Sizes.___

Platinum Bars	Palladium Bars
3,000 grams (3 kg.)	3,000 grams
1,000 grams	1 ounce
100 grams	
10 grams	
5 grams	
1 ounce	

Only a few mints have struck coins from platinum. All are considered to be bullion coins and sell at 5% to 10% above the bullion price. The most known platinum coin is the *One Noble* from the PABJOY Mint on the Isle of Man. The coin is made of one ounce of 999.5% fine platinum and was first introduced in 1983. Switzerland also has introduced a platinum coin known as the *Shooting Thaler.* A 100-franc coin, it has the distinction of being legal tender only one week of each year (during the week of national of shooting competition). The coin is one ounce of 99.9% pure platinum.

PRECIOUS METAL FUTURES AND OPTIONS

Investors wishing to take speculative or hedging positions in the futures and options markets will find their Swiss banks willing and able to provide the proper investment vehicles. Trading volume in precious metal futures and options has grown rapidly in recent years, and well-developed markets for these instruments currently exist.

Future Contracts

Standard futures contracts are available for gold, silver, platinum, and palladium. Reflecting the influence of London and New York on futures markets, the standard contracts are stated in ounces rather than grams. Contracts may currently be negotiated in the sizes noted in Table 12-5.

Maturities are available for investment periods ranging from 1 to 12 months. An initial margin of at least 35% must be on deposit and remains in a blocked, noninterest-bearing account until the contract is liquidated. Customers are expected to maintain their banks' maintenance margin requirements and banks reserve the right to liquidate any position if the difference between market value and the bank advance is reduced to 15% of the contract price. Excessive margin can be released if the cover amounts to 50% depending on individual bank policy. Place of delivery for most contracts is Zurich, and deliveries are subject to the same conditions as those for metal accounts.

___Table 12-4. Contract Sizes of Precious Metal Futures.___

Precious Metal	Standard Contract
Gold	100 ounces
Silver	5,000 ounces
Platinum	100 ounces
Palladium	500 ounces

Gold and Silver Options

Standardized option contracts are available for gold and silver only. Investors may purchase either call or put options through their banks and may also write them if sufficient corresponding cover is on deposit. Standard contract sizes and maturities for metal options are listed in Table 12-5.

Options are traded in the nearest three of the four expiration months. As a convenience to Americans, striking prices and premiums are usually quoted in U.S. dollars. Commissions are normally $35 per contract.

Profits also can be realized by selling (or buying) options back from the bank or by exercising the options. The options can be exercised at any time during the life of the contract up to two bank working days before the end of the month of maturity. Exercising an option at the respective striking price usually involves charging or crediting the investor's metal account for the number of ounces covered by the contracts.

___Table 12-5. Precious Metal Options.___

Metal	Standard Option Size	Standard Maturities			
Gold	100 ounces	Feb	May	Aug	Nov
Silver	5,000 ounces	Jan	Apr	July	Oct

METAL ACCUMULATION PLANS

A number of banks have begun offering plans enabling investors to acquire precious metals through monthly purchases. After an initial investment of around $5,000, customers can make future purchases for as little as $100 per month. All monthly purchases are charged to the customer's cash account and credited to a metal account at the current metal price.

All accumulation plans are based on a dollar-cost averaging approach, where fixed purchase amounts result in less metal being purchased when prices are expensive and more being acquired when prices are cheaper.

Because the monthly amount is fixed, purchases are recorded in terms of an odd number of grams. The plans, however, are designed to allow customers to eventually accumulate large bars.

Ueberseebank and Foreign Commerce Bank have offered gold accumulation plans for many years. Larger banks have recently begun to show an interest in developing broader plans. Credit Suisse, for example, began offering metal accumulation plans for all precious metals in March 1986.

13

Tax Matters

A BOOK ABOUT SWISS BANK ACCOUNTS FOR AMERICANS WOULD BE INCOMPLETE WITHOUT a general discussion of taxes, both Swiss and American, which affect customers of the banks. In several previous chapters, the subject of taxes has been mentioned. The purpose of the current chapter is to present, in one place, a summary of both Swiss and American tax rules and procedures that affect American deposits in Swiss banks.

The chapter is intended to provide only a selective review of general rules. Because of the extremely complex nature of federal, state, and local income tax laws in the United States and the uniqueness of each individual's financial position, the reader is advised to obtain competent personal advice before making significant investment decisions.

SWISS TAXES

A discussion of Swiss taxes affecting American citizens must necessarily center around income taxes on earnings. Swiss laws completely ignore capital gains that accrue to holders of investments, and there exists no Swiss equivalent of the U.S. capital gains tax. Thus, although taxable in the United States, profits on trading securities (except for interest and dividends) and profits from precious metal transactions are not taxable in Switzerland.

Similar to American tax laws, the federal government in Switzerland levies an income tax on dividends and interest. Unlike American laws, the Swiss income tax is not based on a tangled assortment of exclusions and deductions, minimums and maximums, exemptions and tax tables. Instead, dividends and interest are subject to a flat 35% tax, which applies equally to all categories of taxpayers, whether individual or corporate, domestic or foreign, rich or poor.

The 35% tax (called an anticipatory tax) is withheld prior to payment of the earnings into accounts. Banks pay the entire amount of their withholdings to the federal government in a single lump sum. Because of the simplicity and effectiveness of the law, it is impossible for account holders to avoid paying taxes on their earnings and foreign account holders are relieved from the necessity of filing income tax returns in Switzerland. The system ensures that all customers' identities are protected, for it is unnecessary for Swiss tax authorities to identify which customer paid how much in taxes.

Refunds to Americans

Payment of Swiss income taxes on earnings in Switzerland does not relieve Americans of the need to report the same earnings on their U.S. tax returns. American tax laws apply to all income, wherever it may have been earned. Thus, it is possible for taxes on foreign earnings to be paid twice: once to foreign tax authorities and once again to the IRS.

The U.S. government, in an effort to provide some relief to those paying double taxes on foreign earnings, has entered into tax treaties with a number of foreign governments. Typical of most treaties, the treaty with Switzerland (dated May 24, 1951) allows both Swiss and American taxpayers to receive a partial refund of taxes paid to the other country's government. Thus, Americans can apply to the Swiss government for a rebate of amounts withheld from their Swiss bank accounts. Application for a refund of Swiss taxes, however, requires that the identity of the account owner be made known to both Swiss and American tax authorities.

Essentially, the refund process involves proving that a Swiss bank account owner is an American citizen and that the owner has paid taxes on earnings in the account. To apply for the refund, the account owner must file Form 82 with the Swiss Federal Tax Administration. Although Form 82 is a Swiss tax form, it can be obtained in the United States by requesting it from the IRS. It can also be obtained from the Swiss Federal Tax Administration, Schweizerische Steuerverwaltung, Eigerstrasse 65, CH-3003, Berne, Switzerland.

Form 82 is a four-copy document that requires information about the claimant, Swiss securities and accounts owned, the name of the bank(s) where the securities and accounts are located, and the amount of taxes paid on earnings during the year. Three copies of the form, duly notarized, must be sent to the Swiss Federal Tax Administration no later than December 31 of the third year following the year in which the income was earned. Included with the form must be documentary evidence of withheld taxes (bank statements, certificates of deduction, signed bank vouchers, credit slips, etc.).

The tax authorities in Berne do three things after receiving a claim. First, they verify the amounts reported with the appropriate bank or banks. Second, depending on instructions filled in on Form 82, a refund is sent directly to the claimant or deposited into an account in Switzerland. Third, in conformity with the treaty provisions, one copy of the form is forwarded to the IRS for its own records.

As stated above, the refund is only for a portion of the taxes withheld. The amount refunded depends on whether the income is interest or dividends. The U.S./Swiss tax treaty allows for the refunds listed in Table 13-1.

_____Table 13-1. Tax Treaty Refunds._____

	% Withheld	% Refunded	% Net Paid
Interest	35	30	5
Dividends	35	20	15

For example, a depositor with SFr 100,000 on deposit in a savings account earning 3.00-percent interest would pay the net taxes shown in Table 13-2.

____ Table 13-2. Example of Refund.____

	Refund Rate	Tax Rate (%)
Interest for the year	SFr 3,000	
Taxes withheld	SFr 1,050	35
Interest deposited	SFr 1,950	65
Taxes withheld	SFr 1,050	35
Refund	SFr 900	30
Net Taxes paid	SFr 150	5

Thus, Americans receive a refund of 6/7 of the amount of taxes withheld from interest on account balances. Similarly, a 4/7 refund is available on earnings in the form of dividends from Swiss stocks. Not all tax treaties between Switzerland and other countries result in the same net taxes. Comparative refund rates and net taxes for selected countries are shown in Table 13-3.

It should be remembered that certain income credited to bank accounts is not subject to Swiss income taxes and thus is not subject to the 35 percent withholding rules. In general, any earnings on foreign (non-Swiss) investments that are held in Swiss accounts is free from the income tax. Nontaxable investments, therefore, include any fiduciary time deposits (Euromarket and U.S. money market deposits—see chapter 7) and investments in foreign securities (both stocks and bonds—see chapter 11). Further, the income from certain Swiss investment trusts is free from withholding taxes if the owner of the trust shares resides outside of

Table 13-3. Refund Rates for Selected Countries
___Having Double Taxation Treaties with Switzerland.___

	Dividends		Interest	
	Relief	Net Tax	Relief	Net Tax
Australia	20	15	25	10
Austria	30	5	30	5
Belgium	20	15	25	10
Canada	20	15	20	15
Denmark	35	0	35	0
Finland	25	10	35	0
France	30	5	25	10
Germany	20	15	35	0
Great Britain	20	15	35	0
Ireland	20	15	35	0
Italy	20	15	22.5	12.5
Japan	20	15	25	10
Netherlands	20	15	30	5
Norway	30	5	30	5
South Africa	27.5	7.5	0	35
Spain	20	15	25	10
Sweden	30	5	30	5
United States	20	15	30	5

Switzerland and the shares are on deposit at a Swiss bank. Because of the special restrictive provisions placed on the unit trusts, investors must inquire about the taxability of earnings for any specific trusts.

U.S. TAXES ON FOREIGN INCOME

As discussed in chapter 10, all Americans are required to annually disclose the existence of foreign bank accounts with balances exceeding $10,000 to the IRS. The information is no doubt useful in aiding revenue agents to ensure that all sources of income are reported. Under U.S. tax laws, the worldwide income of Americans is taxable, regardless of where it is earned, the currency in which it is earned, and the tax laws of other countries that apply to the income.

Foreign earnings must be reported on Form 1040 along with all domestic income. All amounts must be expressed in U.S. dollars. For those customers of Swiss banks who choose to have their balances denominated in dollars, no translation is necessary. Earnings in other currencies require the taxpayer to translate the amounts at the rates in effect when the earnings are credited to the account. As most interest on savings account balances is paid at December 31, the amount of the entire year's interest can be translated using a single, end-of-year rate. For accounts receiving interest and dividends at various times during the year, multiple exchange rates must be used.

As noted, the effect of U.S. tax law can be that taxes are paid twice on the same income, once to a foreign government and once again to the U.S. government. A partial refund of taxes might be available from a foreign government if a bilateral tax treaty exists. It is interesting to note that tax treaties are not subordinate to tax laws specified in the Internal Revenue Code. (Actually, the provisions of tax treaties take precedence over any conflicting provisions in U.S. tax laws [Code Sec. 7852(d)].)

An additional form of relief is possible, whereby an American taxpayer can elect to claim a tax credit for foreign taxes paid during the tax year. A one-dollar tax credit represents a one-dollar reduction in the amount of U.S. income taxes paid. Thus, after receiving a partial refund of Swiss taxes, an American taxpayer can also use the net amount of taxes paid to the Swiss government as an offset against the U.S. tax liability.

A limitation exists, however, on the amount of foreign tax credit (FTC) allowable in a given year. Under current law, the allowable amount is the smaller of:

1. The amount of net foreign taxes paid or accrued

or

2. The FTC limitation amount

An example of the determination of allowable FTC is shown in Fig. 13-1.

Taxpayers will generally be able to use the entire amount of foreign taxes paid as a tax credit. The limitation is only reached in the event that taxes on foreign income are at high rates or the proportion of foreign income earned is quite small. The taxpayer always has the option of using foreign taxes paid as an itemized deduction and *not* take a tax credit. Even if the limitation is reached, however, it is generally more profitable to take advantage of the tax credit than to use foreign taxes paid as a deduction. To be certain of the correct election, the taxpayer should compute the tax liability both ways and select the most favorable outcome.

Again, Americans are urged to consult with their accountants or tax attorneys when uncertain as to the appropriate elections concerning tax issues relating to foreign income. In addition, the IRS makes available a free brochure outlining the provisions of the foreign tax credit (IRS Publication 514).

INHERITANCE TAXES

In Switzerland, no inheritance taxes are levied on the estates of nonresidents. Following the death of an owner of an account, any joint owner may freely withdraw money, securities, or precious metals without administrative delays in probate. The freedom of an American to withdraw balances, however, does not remove the legal requirement to report such funds in U.S. probate proceedings.

Assume Mr. Alvin Frank, an American taxpayer, has a U.S. tax liability of $8,700 based on worldwide income as follows:

	Income
Swiss bank account (dividends and interest)	$30,000
Other foreign income	$10,000
Foreign Income	$40,000
U.S. Income	$5,000
Total Income	$85,000

Step 1   Determine amount of foreign taxes paid

	Taxes Paid
Swiss bank account (dividends and interest)	$3,700
Other foreign income	$4,600
Total	$8,300

Step 2   Determine FTC limitation

The limitation is computed on IRS Form 1116 according to the formula:

$$\text{U.S. tax} \times \frac{\text{taxable income from foreign sources}}{\text{taxable income from all sources}}$$

Thus, the FTC limitations amounts to

$$\$8,700 \times \frac{\$40,000}{\$45,000} = \$7,733$$

Step 3   Determine the allowable FTC

Frank is limited to the smaller amount of foreign taxes paid ($8,300) or the FTC limitation ($7,733). Thus, he can use a maximum of $7,733 as a credit against his current tax liability.

Fig. 13-1. Determination of allowable foreign tax credit.

14

Other Considerations

CHAPTERS 7 THROUGH 13 DISCUSSED DEMAND ACCOUNTS, SAVINGS ACCOUNTS, securities accounts, precious metal accounts, and various services that Swiss banks provide to owners of these accounts. To be sure, the primary service of banks, aside from lending activities, is providing various types of accounts for customers to preserve their wealth. But other services are also available and Swiss banks, like those in the United States, continually seek to provide new banking services for their customers. While some services roughly parallel those offered by U.S. banks, others are of a type that only Swiss banks could offer.

BANK CARDS

In the 1950s and early 1960s, Europeans showed a general reluctance to adopt the use of credit cards for conducting their personal transactions. While businesses throughout Europe slowly began accepting credit cards as a means of payment, usage was largely from American travelers, and the cards accepted for payment were most frequently those issued by American institutions, such as BankAmericard (later VISA), Diners Club, and American Express. European credit cards became available from larger banks, but the cards remained generally unknown or unrecognized. In the mid 1960s, Europeans suddenly discovered the convenience of plastic money, and the late 1960s witnessed a surge in credit card applications by bank customers throughout Europe. Recognizing the potential profits that widespread use of credit cards would entail, the remaining large banks and many smaller banks rushed to join in the credit card boom.

While American credit cards are still widely accepted in Europe, Eurocard has become the most recognized and most widely accepted of the European cards. A Eurocard issued in one country can be used in virtually every western European country. For this reason, the card has become extremely popular among Europeans who travel frequently. In addition, Eurocard is a Mastercard in the United States and an Access card in the United Kingdom, which extends its possible use to hundreds of thousands of locations around the globe.

Most Swiss banks now make Eurocard available. Customers holding Swiss Eurocards, however, enjoy an advantage not available to holders of Eurocards issued by other European banks: the guarded confidentiality of all customer transactions. Because of the existing bank secrecy laws in Switzerland, transaction records of card customers receive the same degree of protection as any other bank information. Thus, Swiss Eurocards offer a level of discretion not available through bank cards of other banks. It is important to remember, however, that the use of a Swiss Eurocard outside of Switzerland (and particularly in the United States) can generate a financial trail easily opened for inspection.

Aside from matters of privacy, Eurocards issued by Swiss banks offer another service that American customers may find desirable: the automatic payment of card balances by direct charges against bank account balances. Swiss banks do not send monthly statements of card account balances. Instead, notification of card charges against a bank account are included in the periodic account statement (assuming, of course, the customer elects to receive the statement).

Eurocard charges made in the United States are ultimately settled in this fashion. Each day Mastercard notifies Eurocard headquarters in Brussels of charges made on Eurocards in the United States. The Brussels headquarters relays the information to the proper Eurocard operations in the various European countries, including Eurocard Switzerland in Zurich. Eurocard Switzerland in turn communicates the information to the appropriate banks, which make the deductions from customers' accounts.

Because of the payment procedure, customers are normally required to maintain an account with a credit balance sufficient to handle most purchases. Balances in the form of metals and securities can be liquidated if an insufficient cash balance is available to cover current charges. The bank will notify a customer, however, before any liquidations of investments occur, giving the customer an option to assume a loan for the balance of the unpaid charges. Unlike American credit card balances, with interest accruing at 18% to 21%, the loans from Swiss banks reflect Swiss rates of interest, ranging from 6% on Swiss franc balances to about 9% on U.S. dollar balances.

In addition to Eurocard, many banks have begun selling Eurocheque, the European answer to American traveler's checks. Like other travelers check's, Eurocheques are available in a variety of currencies and are widely recognized throughout the world.

SAFEKEEPING SERVICES

In the United States, safekeeping services are provided by making safe deposit boxes available to customers. Swiss banks also provide safe deposit boxes, and the rules of strict access are similar to American bank rules. The boxes are stored in a bank vault but under control of the customer, who maintains custody of the key. A personal visit is always necessary to make a deposit or withdraw the contents of a box.

Americans able to travel to Switzerland might wish to store their valuables in Swiss safe deposit boxes, although no real advantage exists over the same services offered by U.S. banks. Still, Swiss vaults are widely used by many foreigners to cache their valuables. At some banks, safe deposit vaults have been expanded by excavating beneath existing vaults. Layered, underground safe deposit chambers (as many as five layers deep) exist along Geneva's rue de la Corraterie and Zurich's Bahnhofstrasse.

Safe deposit boxes, however, are a relatively modern service. For as long as there have been banks in Switzerland, customers have been depositing treasured objects other than money, securities, and precious metals. Instead of using private boxes, the objects are sometimes placed under the control of bank personnel in the bank's own vault. In modern times, most deposits of this type are important documents. Whatever the items, banks usually require that they be securely packed in a closed container or envelope which can be sealed with wax or lead. Because of the elaborate procedure, deposits of this type are customarily referred to as *sealed deposits*.

Each sealed deposit must be tagged with the depositor's address, signature, and declaration of value. The stated value serves two purposes: it provides the basis for the safe custody charges and establishes the maximum liability of the bank for any losses that might occur. For items with a stated value, the normal annual charges are 0.15 percent of the stated value, with a minimum charge of SFr 10 per annum per sealed unit. Items without a stated value are customarily charged the minimum amount. It is not unusual for banks to charge reduced (one half) rates for deposits of securities issued by the bank (e.g., stock, CDs or cash bonds).

It is not unknown for a customer to deposit personal items in a safe deposit box and subsequently deposit the safe deposit key in a safekeeping envelope at the same or another bank. All banks reserve the right to request that the nature of the contents be disclosed to them and regulations forbid the deposit of any items considered flammable, dangerous, or in any way unsuitable for storage in a bank vault.

INNOVATIONS

Swiss banks are not being left behind in the search for new services. As with other modern, successful companies, they continue to search for innovative products to complement their time honored services. For example, Royal Trust Bank (formerly Dow Banking Corporation) announced in 1985 the availability of two unique services. Royal Trust Bank's Discretionary Foreign Exchange Account (minimum balance SFr 200,000) offers to customers a money market account in which deposits are invested in foreign currencies expected to strengthen in the foreign exchange markets. A speculative type of investment, the fee structure gives the depositor a unique assurance that the bank will attempt to maximize profits. The half-yearly fee is 20 percent of all foreign exchange gains; there is no fee if a loss occurs during the six-month period.

For any customers who are concerned that another European war would put deposits in Switzerland at risk, Royal Trust Bank has also developed a managed portfolio account, which, combined with a sealed deposit, will go a long way in calming the investors' fears of loss. As long as peacetime conditions exist in Europe, the portfolio account is managed by portfolio managers in Switzerland. In the event of a European war, Royal Trust Bank would immediately transfer a customer's financial assets to the United States, to be deposited in a large, reputable bank until the end of the hostilities. The assets would be registered in the name of Royal Trust Bank, but for the benefit of undisclosed customers. The management of the assets would continue through a subsidiary of Royal Trust Bank located in the Cayman Islands. Also on deposit in the Cayman Islands would be a sealed deposit with sufficient documentary evidence to permit the customer to claim the assets. Presumably, all assets remaining on deposit at the end of the wartime period would be returned to Switzerland.

THE ONLY ULTRASECRET (AND LEGAL) ACCOUNT

In spite of all the services, Swiss bankers are fully aware that foreign customers are as much attracted by secrecy provisions as any other single service the banks have to offer. As explained at length in chapters 4, 5, and 10, secrecy limitations do exist and Americans contemplating the use of a Swiss bank account to take advantage of the secrecy laws should be fully aware of the limitations.

We have seen that financial secrecy for Americans is often diminished by laws requiring the reporting of foreign bank accounts and international transfers of monetary items. Still, it is possible to legally establish and possess an account in Switzerland which is entirely shielded from the view of inquisitive government officials and snoopy private individuals.

Americans can ignore the statutory reporting requirements of accounts and transactions affecting those accounts if they remain mindful of threshold reporting requirements. Foreign bank accounts need not be reported to the IRS or the Treasury Department as long as the aggregate balances of all such accounts do not exceed $10,000 during a given year. Similarly, the transportation of monetary items across the U.S. borders need not be disclosed as long as the amount of the transfers do not exceed $10,000. Thus, the only ultrasecret (and legal) account that an American can own in Switzerland is one that, because of the size of its balance, does not require reporting by its owner. According to a number of Swiss bankers, this is exactly the type of account many Americans have established in recent years.

What purpose would such an account serve? Why have Americans found such accounts desirable?

No doubt many Americans are attracted to Swiss banks for the simple benefit of having assets spread among different locations. Foreign bank accounts offer a simple vehicle to diversify holdings of wealth, and Swiss banks are considered as solid as any banks on earth. A compelling reason for a *secret* account is the fear of possible probes if the account were disclosed. Although the IRS will not say whether the disclosure of a foreign account will increase the chances of a tax audit, it nonetheless insists that any foreign accounts (with total balances in excess of $10,000) be disclosed on taxpayers' annual tax returns.

For others, the fear of a tax audit is of less concern than the fears of living in a world with an unstable economic climate. A fear of a collapse of the American banking system and the inability of the U.S. government to prop up a collapsing banking system has prompted some to establish a safe, offshore account. In the event of an economic catastrophe, it is quite possible that the U.S. government would reinstate controls to discourage or forbid the export of savings to other countries. A previously established bank account in Switzerland would provide a mechanism to allow immediate transfer of savings before a currency control apparatus could be implemented. The depositors would only need to deal with reporting requirements after the money is safely out of the country.

Whatever the reason for establishing a Swiss bank account, that is invisible to government officials, a drawback for many is the low threshold level for reporting the account. Many would like to see this reporting level raised. The level has been increased in past years and will likely be increased in the future.

As for *illegal* foreign accounts owned by Americans, there simply aren't any. At present, ownership of foreign funds is perfectly legal for Americans, regardless of the size of the holdings. The owner of a foreign account only violates the law when reportable foreign balances are not reported to U.S. authorities. No doubt, many sizeable, unreported foreign accounts exist, and the reasons for the nondisclosure may vary from ignorance of the law to outright disregard for it. Given the growing spirit of cooperation between Swiss and American officials, ownership of unreported funds could prove to be a dangerous position for American citizens.

While some individuals only want to hide their foreign holdings from government regulators, others are concerned with an entirely different kind of menace: an invasion of privacy by other private individuals. Whether fear of disclosure is due to a general desire for privacy or concern about specific individuals gaining knowledge of the account, an invisible account in Switzerland provides a significant measure of security. The account holder has complete control over whether anyone else learns of the account.

WHEN AN ACCOUNT HOLDER DIES

A natural question asked by people considering opening an account in Switzerland is, "What happens to my account when I die?" If the account has not been kept a secret from others but merely used as an investment vehicle for the deceased, there are no unusual problems faced by the heirs or executors that are not also faced in the United States. Swiss banks will surrender account assets to a legally appointed executor provided that appropriate court documents, including the death certificate, are certified by a Swiss consulate and delivered to the bank.

Problems may arise in situations where the account owner has successfully hidden a bank account's existence from those who would be most interested in the account. An account that is never disclosed by the owner to another party, and for which all correspondence is being held by the bank, could possibly remain secret forever if the owner were to die. The Swiss bank may have no reason to suspect that a dormant account is owned by a deceased individual. It is possible that many account balances are currently sitting in Swiss vaults and continuing to earn interest that will never be claimed. On the other hand, funds untouched for many years are occasionally claimed by depositors who have been relying on the bank's silence through the years while waiting for the proper time to claim the funds.

Most banks have no policy regarding dormant accounts other than to continue abiding by the owners' instructions. One large Swiss bank claims that it will initiate an investigation into the ownership of dormant accounts but points out that there is no legal requirement that it do so. Further, the bank has no formal policy regarding the length of time an account must be dormant until an investigative action is undertaken. Obviously, a bank must be extremely careful in such an investigation for a careless question could lead to exactly the kind of disclosure that the customer is relying on the bank to avoid.

Because of the uncertainties involved with secret accounts, all owners need to plan for the identification of beneficiaries and the orderly disposition of account balances in the event of death.

The most common solution is to make each account a joint account (often called a *joint and several account*). The account is opened in the name of two or more parties who may or may not be related. Joint owners are considered by the bank to have equal rights with respect to the disposition of account balances and regulations governing joint accounts are independent of any agreements between the joint owners. Thus, in the event of death of one of the owners, bank regulations allow the surviving joint owner(s) to dispose of the assets. Obviously, a joint account arrangement to avoid *lost assets* places a large amount of reliance on a surviving owner to divulge the account's existence to the estate of the deceased. Although a joint owner may legally dispose of assets, the fact does not imply a lack of legal obligation among joint owners to the rightful heirs.

Another common solution to the lost-account problem is the granting of a power of attorney to a third party. The power of attorney remains in force after the death of the account owner and makes it possible for the authorized party to operate the account without interruption. In addition, the authorized party can dispose of the account assets while avoiding the lengthy and complicated legal formalities of succession. Powers of attorney were discussed, and a specimen exhibited, in chapter 9.

Both joint accounts and powers of attorney involve multiple signature powers over an account. A depositor who is concerned with the possibility of abuse of signature power may wish to take another precautionary step. The owner can arrange with an attorney to deliver a letter upon the owner's death advising an executor or heir of a previously secret bank account's existence. The recipient of the letter may either request the account assets directly from a party holding signature power or seek the assets through normal probate procedures. Under Swiss law, banks are required to provide information to a duly identified executor or testamentary heir of a deceased account owner. The bank will provide information on the contents of the account on the day of death and the names of any joint account holders or agents to whom powers of attorney have been conferred.

Depositors are strongly discouraged from preparing a second or *hidden* will, which is intended to dispose of only assets on deposit in Switzerland. A second will may be interpreted as revocation of a previous will, causing only confusion in probate courts. Depositors should also be warned that under Swiss law, banks cannot accept instructions that become valid only after the death of the account holder.

Nonresidents of Switzerland pay no estate taxes or death duties. Hence, joint owners, attorneys for the deceased, and heirs may dispose of all the assets on deposit held by a Swiss bank without the interference of any Swiss fiscal authorities. If an account holder is a resident of Switzerland at the time of death, the estate tax laws of the appropriate canton will apply.

A FINAL WORD

Much of this book, in both Parts I and II, has been devoted to a discussion of the comparative advantages available to American customers of Swiss banks. The author believes that Switzerland's banks will be advantageous for Americans as long as three conditions remain:

1. U.S. bank and thrift institutions continue to fail at record rates as the industry attempts to attract new customers through the promotion of deposit insurance rather than proof of sound management decisions
2. Swiss banks maintain their commitment to incorporate advances in technology while maintaining traditional values in providing customer service
3. Switzerland's secrecy statutes provide superior protection for depositors.

Bankers are in the business of taking risks. In this sense, Swiss bankers are no different than those in other countries. What distinguishes Swiss banks from banks elsewhere is a low tolerance for risk coupled with high regard for safety for customer deposits. The famed caution of Swiss banks is evident in their published financial statements, which show that Swiss banks maintain equity at a higher proportion of total assets than banks of any other country (at a level widely believed understated by one half its true amount).

A climate of risk-adverse banking, blended with effective federal regulation and centuries of tradition, provides an environment for savings and investment that is readily available to Americans and exists nowhere else in the world.

Appendix A
Crimes for Which
Secrecy May Be Breached

THE FOLLOWING LIST OF OFFENSES IS EXTRACTED FROM THE TREATY BETWEEN THE United States of America and the Swiss Confederation on Mutual Assistance in Criminal Matters, May 25, 1973, 27 U.S.T. 2019, T.I.A.S. No. 8302 (1977).

1. Murder.
2. Voluntary manslaughter.
3. Involuntary manslaughter.
4. Malicious wounding; inflicting grievous bodily harm intentionally or through gross negligence.
5. Threat to commit murder; threat to inflict grievous bodily harm.
6. Unlawful throwing or application of any corrosive or injurious substances upon the person of another.
7. Kidnapping; false imprisonment or other unlawful deprivation of the freedom of an individual.
8. Willful nonsupport or willful abandonment of a minor or other dependent person when the life of that minor or other dependent person is or is likely to be injured or endangered.
9. Rape; indecent assault.
10. Unlawful sexual acts with or upon children under the age of sixteen years.

11. Illegal abortion.

12. Traffic in women and children.

13. Bigamy.

14. Robbery.

15. Larceny; burglary; house-breaking or shop-breaking.

16. Embezzlement; misapplication or misuse of funds.

17. Extortion; blackmail.

18. Receiving or transporting money, securities, or other property, knowing the same to have been embezzled, stolen, or fraudulently obtained.

19. Fraud, including:
    a. obtaining property, services, money, or securities by false pretenses or by defrauding by means of deceit, falsehood, or any fraudulent means;
    b. fraud against the requesting State, its states or cantons or municipalities thereof;
    c. fraud or breach of trust committed by any person;
    d. use of the mails or other means of communication with intent to defraud or deceive, as punishable under the laws of the requesting State.

20. Fraudulent bankruptcy.

21. False business declarations regarding companies and cooperative associations, including speculation, unfaithful management, suppression of documents.

22. Bribery, including soliciting, offering, and accepting.

23. Forgery and counterfeiting, including:
    a. the counterfeiting or forgery of public or private securities, obligations, instructions to make payment, invoices, instruments of credit or other instruments.
    b. the counterfeiting or alteration of coin or money.
    c. the counterfeiting or forgery of public seals, stamps or marks;
    d. the fraudulent use of the foregoing counterfeited or forged articles;
    e. knowingly and without lawful authority, making or having in possession any instrument, instrumentality, tool or machine adapted or intended for the counterfeiting of money, whether coin or paper.

24. Knowingly and willfully making, directly or through another, a false, fictitious or fraudulent statement or representation in a matter within the jurisdiction of any department or agency in the requesting State, and relating to an offense mentioned in this Schedule or otherwise falling under this Treaty.

25. Perjury, subornation of perjury and other false statements under oath.

26. Offenses against the laws relating to bookmaking, lotteries and gambling when conducted as a business.

27. Arson.

28. Willful and unlawful destruction or obstruction of a railroad, aircraft, vessel or other means of transportation or any malicious act done with intent to endanger the safety of any person travelling upon a railroad, or in any aircraft, vessel or other means of transportation.

29. Piracy; mutiny or revolt on board an aircraft or vessel against the authority of the captain or commander of such aircraft or vessel; any seizure of exercise of control, by force or violence, of an aircraft or vessel.

30. Offenses against laws (whether in the form of tax laws or other laws) prohibiting, restricting or controlling the traffic in, importation or exportation, possession, concealment, manufacture, production or use of:
    a. narcotic drugs, cannabis sativa-L, psychotropic drugs, cocaine and its derivatives;
    b. poisonous chemicals and substances injurious to health;
    c. firearms, other weapons, explosive and incendiary devices; when violation of such laws causes the violator to be liable to criminal prosecution and imprisonment.

31. Unlawful obstruction of court proceedings or proceedings before governmental bodies or interference with an investigation of a violation of a criminal statute by the influencing, bribing, impeding, threatening, or injuring of any officer of the court, juror, witness, or duly authorized criminal investigator.

32. Unlawful abuse of official authority which results in deprivation of the life, liberty or property of any person.

33. Unlawful injury, intimidation or interference with voting or candidacy for public office, jury service, government employment, or the receipt or the enjoyment of benefits provided by government agencies.

34. Attempts to commit, conspiracy to commit, or participation in, any of the offenses enumerated in the preceding paragraphs of the Schedule; accessory after the fact to the commission of any of the offenses enumerated in this Schedule.

35. Any offense of which one of the above listed offenses is a substantial element, even if, for purposes of jurisdiction of the United States Government, elements such as transporting, transportation, the use of the mails or interstate facilities are also included.

Appendix B
Swiss Insider Trading Statutes

Exploitation of the Knowledge of Confidential Facts*

1. Whoever as a member of a board of directors, of a management, of an auditing body, or as an agent of a stock corporation or of a corporation controlling such stock corporation or depending from it,

    as a member of a public authority or as a public officer,

    or as the auxiliary of the above named persons,

    obtains a pecuniary advantage for himself or a third person by exploiting the knowledge of a confidential fact, which, when becoming known, will in a foreseeable way have a considerable influence on the market price of shares, other securities, or corresponding ledger securities of the corporation or of options traded in Switzerland on a Stock Exchange or on a pre-Stock Exchange market, or who reveals such fact to a third person,

    shall be punished with imprisonment or with a fine.

2. Whoever becomes informed directly or indirectly of such a fact by one of the persons referred to in paragraph 1 and who obtains a pecuniary advantage for himself or a third person by exploiting this information,

    shall be punished with imprisonment of up to one year or with a fine.

---

*Swiss Criminal Code § 161

3. To be considered as facts in the meaning of paragraphs 2 and 3 are a forthcoming issue of new equity participations, a consolidation of companies, or a similar fact of comparable bearing.

4. If the consolidation of two stock corporations is planned, then paragraphs 1 to 3 apply to both corporations.

5. Paragraphs 1 to 4 apply by analogy if the exploitation of the knowledge of a confidential fact relates to shares, other securities, ledger securities, or corresponding options of a cooperative association or of a foreign company.

Index

Other Bestsellers of Related Interest

TAX-CUTTING TACTICS FOR INVESTORS: Legal Loopholes For The 1990s—Denise Lamaute

Denise Lamaute describes in layman's terms how to use your home and other securities, avoid the alternative minimum tax, minimize taxable gain and maximize capital losses, and capitalize on tax-free exchange of assets. Other key topics include: retirement, viable tax shelters, tax-smart recordkeeping, deductible borrowing, deductions and credits, and more. 208 pages. Book No. 30048, $14.95 paperback, $29.95 hardcover

AVOIDING PROBATE: Tamper-Proof Estate Planning—Cliff Roberson

Discover how to hand down everything you own to anyone you choose without interference from courts, creditors, relatives, or the IRS. In this easy-to-read planning guide, attorney Cliff Roberson shows how you can avoid the horrors of probate court. Sample wills and trust agreements and checklists in every chapter make planning each step easy. *Avoiding Probate* covers: living trusts, life insurance, specific property, wills, family businesses, valuing your estate, estate taxes, and more. 236 pages. Book No. 30074, $14.95 paperback, $29.95 hardcover

INSTANT LEGAL FORMS: Ready-to-Use Documents for Almost Any Occasion—Ralph E. Troisi

By following the clear instructions provided in this book, you can write your own will, lend or borrow money or personal property, buy or sell a car, rent out a house or appartment, check your credit, hire contractors, and grant power of attorney—all without the expense or complication of a lawyer. Author-attorney Ralph E. Troisi supplies ready-to-use forms and step-by-step guidance in filling them out and modifying them to meet your specific needs. 224 pages, Illustrated. Book No. 30028, $16.95 paperback only

HOW TO WRITE YOUR OWN WILL—2nd Edition—John C. Howell

"*...a clearly written, helpful book.*"—The Newspaper, Brookline, Mass.

A surprising number of people do not prepare a will, mistakenly believing this vital document is too expensive or too complicated to deal with. This book explains how anyone can prepare a legal will without a lawyer, without intimidation, at little expense. All legal terms are defined and sample forms are included. 208 pages. Book No. 30037, $12.95 paperback only

THE ENTREPRENEUR'S GUIDE TO STARTING A SUCCESSFUL BUSINESS—James W. Halloran

Here's a realistic approach to what it takes to start a small business. You'll learn step-by-step every phase of business start-up from initial idea to realizing a profit. Included is advice on: designing a store layout, pricing formulas and strategies, advertising and promotion, small business organization charts, an analysis of future small business opportunities. 256 pages, 97 illustrations. Book No. 30049, $15.95 paperback only

LENDING OPPORTUNITIES IN REAL ESTATE, A High-Profit Strategy for Every Investor—James C. Allen

Earn high yields at low risk by making short-term secured loans! This book offers specific advice and procedures for investing in short-term loans secured by real estate. Samples of actual forms involved are included. Topics addressed cover: preparing a personal financial statement, sources of free advice, borrowing investment capital, setting rates and terms in any market, advantages of smaller notes, avoiding foreclosure, and "prospecting" made easy. 192 pages, 42 illustrations. Book No. 30019, $24.95 hardcover only

Other Bestsellers of Related Interest

FIGHT THE IRS AND WIN! A Self-Defense Guide for Taxpayers—Cliff Roberson

With this practical guide you can obtain the best results possible—protect your individual and property rights—in any dispute with the IRS. The outstanding feature of this book is that it takes complicated IRS operations and provides the average taxpayer with advice on how to protect himself in IRS controversies. It is the taxpayer's self-defense book. 224 pages. Book No. 30021, $12.95 paperback

MONEY MINDER: Simplify, Organize, and Manage Your Personal Financial Records—Michael E. Feder

"I like (the book's) flexibility. The forms encourage you to think creatively and profitably about how you are spending and investing your money."—Jean Ross Peterson Author of Organize Your Personal Finances

Offers an excellent, streamlined method for straightening out your finances. This book offers step-by-step guidance and ready-to-use forms that will enable you to consolidate important financial facts and figures in one place. 128 pages, 88 illustrations. Book No. 30039, $12.95 paperback only

---

Look for These and Other TAB Books at Your Local Bookstore

To Order Call Toll Free 1-800-822-8158
(in PA and AK call 717-794-2191)

or write to TAB BOOKS Inc., Blue Ridge Summit, PA 17294-0840.

Title		Product No.	Quantity	Price

☐ Check or money order made payable to TAB BOOKS Inc.

Charge my ☐ VISA ☐ MasterCard ☐ American Express

Acct. No. _____ Exp. _____

Signature: _____

Name: _____

City: _____

State: _____ Zip: _____

Subtotal $ _____

Postage and Handling
($3.00 in U.S., $5.00 outside U.S.) $ _____

In PA, NY, & ME add
applicable sales tax $ _____

TOTAL $ _____

TAB BOOKS catalog free with purchase; otherwise send $1.00 in check or money order and receive $1.00 credit on your next purchase.

Orders outside U.S. must pay with international money order in U.S. dollars.

TAB Guarantee: If for any reason you are not satisfied with the book(s) you order, simply return it (them) within 15 days and receive a full refund.   **BC**